Empi.
A Study of the Revolution

Richard Greenhorn

Super flumina Babylonis, illic sedimus et flevimus
cum recordaremur Sion.

ii

Empire of Hatred: A Study of the Revolution

Contents

Introduction

It is difficult for a man to be able to justify his thoughts and deeds on a day-to-day basis. When a man finishes a book that holds within it the statements and ideas spanning five years, he must be all the more forgiven for trying to justify himself. When looking back through the book, there are sections that could only have been written in 2018, when the first "Empire of Hatred" article appeared; others, namely the final section of this book, that could only be written after a new phase of the Revolution had occurred. The last substantive additions to the book were made in 2022. The intellectual climate in which it was begun was far livelier than that of its publication, with all mainstream discourse on liberalism falling into malign idiocy— roughly the same impulse that posits that Joseph Biden could win a fair election, or that he is in any sense ruling over a nation. The general idiocy has tainted radical and dissident thought as well, perhaps from arduous effort of trying to understand the insanity of our present state, perhaps out of despair.

But this book began in a very different environment. President Trump's election spurred a good deal of angst among intellectuals that the rise to power of a duly elected businessman and libertine somehow presaged a failure of *liberal democracy*. Patrick Deneen's *Why Liberalism Failed* found wide readership, or at least discussion. It also found an admirer in Barack Obama. This alone should have provoked more criticism of the thesis of Deneen's book, which attacks a classical liberal or libertarian ethos more than any version of liberalism that has existed in the Twentieth Century, as well as some reflection on how committed a man like Obama is to supposedly liberal tenets as Free Speech and open elections.

Critics and fans of Deneen's book take for granted that, yes, we do live in something called a *liberal democracy*. What they could not do is define liberal democracy. An intellectual battle occurred wherein none of the combatants could define the term over which they feuded. *Liberalism* is simply a sentimental term, and if one likes the way the future is headed, he is a liberal; if not, he is a conservative, communist, or some other creed. That *liberalism* was void of real meaning or content was proven beyond any reasonable doubt by the lockdowns and various coup attempts against Trump in 2020. If perpetual emergency powers are aspects of *republican government*; if employer-mandated vaccinations are part of the *free market*; if the insubordination of the administrative state and the military to the Command-in-Chief is part of *constitutional government*, then the terms simply have no real meaning. They are used as wantonly and meretriciously as references to the *People* behind the Iron Curtain. They are political lies, put forth by political liars. Their only exceptional attribute is that almost none of our intellectuals, even those supposedly critical of the regime, are able to perceive or at least publish this.

But taking these critics seriously, which is perhaps more than they deserve, we find that such criticisms are at best ahistorical, at worst inane. That supposedly conservative and reactionary critics can argue about Locke with a straight face in the Twenty-first Century is pathetic. Classical liberalism would be a great reprieve to modern man, who labors beneath a totalitarian oppression more pervasive and complete than any Twentieth Century dictatorship. Do they see this? If not, they are incompetent. Do they care? Perhaps not, and indeed many antiliberals act in bad faith; their project is not of resurrecting Western liberty but transitioning us into an Eastern slave state, a complete technocratic and Nirvanic hell. Libertarians, for all their faults, are the surest witnesses to the collapse of republican government that occurred in the Twentieth Century, and to diminish their insights for adhering too closely to the ideals of Jefferson is utter idiocy.

A great number of words are wasted finding false similitudes in the past. But Gibbon is little aid in assessing our present state. Collapse into anarchy is an aspiration of those who believe in an intrinsic order to the cosmos, a hope that when the wretched edifices fall away a new growth might spring from the rubble. Yet the harbingers of anarcho-tyranny misinterpret the working of our system for what appears on its face. Anarchy in our system is a weapon of tyrants. It has no native source and could not perdure without a powerful state. A similar Roman delusion exists as to the desire for a Caesar, the general yearning for a man to rise and give order to republican chaos. Americans seem most surprised that they have moved beyond the ideas of their cherished Constitution, though America's Caesar came to power in 1933 and left Praetorian Guard in the form of the administrative bureaucracy. Americans are simply so enamored with their own political notions that they cannot see the state of things.

The right-wing response to Trump's election was pinned on the hopes that he would restore some semblance of personal rule. We will see many times throughout this book that personal rule is always perceived as a threat to the forces of liberal progress, which always operates on the basis of socialization of moral responsibility and leadership. Trump's sundry statements about the manifest corruption of the elite made him a supposed threat to a system that otherwise seemed self-sufficient. Whatever his mediocrity otherwise, Trump truly did seem a man sui generis, benefiting from long access to the propaganda channels and with a personal fortune to draw from. His proposal of sanity towards the issue of immigration could not help but appeal to any voter with even a vague feeling of citizenship, and his persona won him personal devotion without compare. The comparisons of Trump with Hitler are always made in bad faith, but have at least an inkling of truth in the supposed threat of establishing more personal rule over a technocratic state. This is a fact Trump's enemies recognized better than he did, ready as they were to eviscerate the last remnants of constitutional order and democratic respectability in order to deny him his rightful victory. Yet he was too weak to seize power over a system that no longer had any formal legitimacy beyond those facades promoted by the propaganda channels. The opposition party filled his rightful seat with an actual dementia patient, loudly and clearly declaring that personal rule was unnecessary and undesirable over an administrative state that better ruled itself. The antiliberals who called the system insolubly corrupt will now praise Trump for not rocking the boat too much, for fear that a splash might wet their socks atop their tenured perches. The following work is offered as a substitute to their blabber.

Empire of Hatred began as an article in Thermidor and continued in The American Sun. I am thankful especially to Nathan Duffy, Ryan Landy, and Hank Oslo for allowing me to publish there.

Richard Greenhorn
The Feast of Francis Borgia

Empire of Hatred

All glory to God, who has created the earth, the
stars, and the skies; whose creations proclaim His
wisdom, whose light and darkness considered against
themselves indicate His knowledge; who by adoring Him
makes His subjects wise, and who through Wisdom
makes it all the easier to adore Him; whose supplest
truths hold us in gorgeous contemplation; who so loved
the world as to give His creatures selfhoods that speak
of their own glories and through them of God—a
cosmos overflowing with souls.

Yet it is man we turn to—the pinnacle of all creation,
that only creature in all God's visible order who can
discern the glory of the other souls and the glory of all,
yet who is most woefully insufficient unto himself. Only
he is forced by Nature to cultivate his genius for forming
matter anew and creating new distinct things, new souls,
new objects with a spirit and a logic inhering in them.
Our exaltation and our fall is told in this simple truth:
that we cannot construct our own houses or rear our
young without the aid of other men. *The foxes have their
dens and the birds of the air their nests, but the son of man shall
have no place to lay his head*. We were created to be
insufficient, to know the world is not our home. Alone,
we are men only in appearances; apart from common
wisdom we must languish and die as an animal denied
sustenance. Man cannot survive outside a congregation,
the *ekklesia*, the Church. His arts are therefore always a
kind of social creation, however solitarily he might

2

pursue them. Those arts that are pleasing to God are not only a gift of man to his race, but an act of creation offered in tribute to the high Creator, a benefice to those souls of which God is most proud, an act of love rendered unto Love. And where man's works are properly oriented to give the Creator and His creation their due, the simple act of living constitutes a kind of orthodoxy, the right worship of God.

The Empire of Hatred

We find the world unlike this, in form and in spirit. Our world is an empire of hatred, a creation whose logic proclaims its loathing of man and contempt for its Creator. Yet it is inescapable, as universal as God's benevolence, as penetrating as the immanent God's bequeathal of ration and grace: a force of daemonic hatred trouncing all goodness, a vile devil who seems to rule the world, one who oppresses the heart like the Noonday Demon yet gnaws and eviscerates the flesh like a Horseman of the Last Days. There is no rest for the weary, no beauty for the distraught, no wisdom for the yearning. Whatever is good and true and beautiful is wracked, ruined, ground up and reanimated in a dreadful golem, an ape of a just civilization.

Man's life on earth has ever been and ever will be a warfare. But the present assault is not his native struggle, his regular provisioning against flesh and pride but a war against a new order. The enemy has exploded the world into a million fragmented pieces and reordered them into a festering mass—and yet the chaos does not settle or decay, but endures and intensifies from age to age. Order does not bring form, only further oppression, as the horrors lay to rot a host continually revivifying, but without a gleam of life.

The modern world is a stench arising from the etherized corpse of reality, and modern man is a kind of demonic version of what he should be, an incontinent fornicator, a perverse moralizer, an insipid and feeble idealist. The nightmare he is lodged in is immeasurable, indecipherable. Men feel the pangs of honor and the call of their blood, but can find no adequate utterance to bring it to fruition, and traverse the world as half-men, unworthy of the souls inside them. Women are left enwhored, entrapped by the allurements of a femininity without completion, drugged and sterilized with the potions made of the very children they have slain, abandoned without even the consolation of the women of Jerusalem in their flowing tears.

These are not prisoners, these are not slaves. The things before us are *free men*—this we say, this we hear. But they *are slaves*— draped in the habit of cruel oppression, impotent before all honorable dreams, the primary source of his own contempt and the weight of his own hopelessness. But of what material are their chains? Who is the master of the debauched and vile things? Even to be a beast would be a higher state for him, for modern man is a plastic thing, a higher creature of lower material, of animal concupiscence but alien instinct, and his soul hovers over an abyss of some future that will see a final transcending of flesh and blood.

For five centuries this has proceeded. All history comes to us now as a kind of nightmare, a shadow-draped drama of specters and phantasms, a fetter of the individual soul who does not know the why or wherefore of his state, or what sense can explain his immutable fate. One generation is as distant from the last as one species is to another, and the master of the old world is a vagabond in the next. Man once could know from his parents, mentors and neighbors where his talents and dispositions placed him, while the new generations find a world with no niches carved for men and no sympathy for his inevitable suffering. It is a world adapted only to itself, judged against only itself, and considers man only so well as it can act upon him, to imbibe and digest him.

Yet man is enamored by this world: It explodes with demon light, a luminous emptiness. Historical comparison to it must come from the fevered visions of artists and dreamers. His eyes light up; it is electric means that do it. His senses stir, his blood shakes, his eyes mirror an infinite permutation of lights, and he becomes the thought of some other men's collective vision. This man can be led no other way: He has no native song in his heart, nor native strength to resist his mongrelization, nor native creed or culture he might fly to as refuge. He finds in his bitterest moments that he has no selfhood at all—and he drugs himself more, dements the vestiges of his personhood, and searches for final release into the void.

Behold the man: If the soul is the material form of the body as the philosophers have said, his soul is in his pocket. All beauty and truth must be judged by the arbiter of his handheld computer. Like a separate intellect or conscience, it must be referred to before he can act, and the mediated soul of the world speaks to him, whose opinion he craves and against whom—what is he?

In lucid moments, the wise amongst us discern we are falling away from something, even if only an icon or even a mere sensation of comfort, and that we descend towards nothingness. Yet we can do nothing to stop this. An annihilation of the whole race, as intractable as man's own death seems to loom, its inevitability unquestioned and often desired—humanity itself unable to manage the moment, or the future it brings, or contemplate the past that drowned it.

The Revolution

The subject of our study is the Revolution—not any particular revolution, but the general revolution that has advanced on every front for five hundred years.

An alternate name for the Revolution, one which we lapse into at times, is Liberalism. This is a paltry term, a descriptor of thing that should be as loathed as *Nazism* or *Communism* once were loathed, for it is a program just as vile, just as dehumanizing, just as totalitarian as the programs of Hitler and Lenin. Liberalism is putatively bloodless, but only because its brutality is more insidious. Mass murder is conducted not by hired apparatchiks but by mothers against their sons and daughters under the doctrine of *freedom of choice*, and political terror is perpetuated not by jackbooted thugs but by the confluence of criminal underclass and the police state, all while a perpetual imperial war is undertaken against the world, and every man, woman and child is potential enemy combatant without possibility of flight, subject at a whim to incineration by hovering toys. The doctrines of Lenin and Hitler were frail in comparison, mere excrescences of Liberalism, errant branches grafted and proposed as trees of their own, but doomed by their departure to wither and die under the shadow of its progenitor. Nazism and Communism were outgrowths of and reactions to the triumph of liberal capitalism. *Liberalism* is simply the most condensed and pure aspect of the Revolution, one which by its very nature or lack of nature cannot be defeated or unrooted by its bastards.

The Failure to Name the Revolution

Counterrevolutionaries have not adequately judged Liberalism for what it is, as a force more insidious than communism, socialism, and Nazism. They mistake its fluidity and its lack of principles for a liability, not its *coup de grace*.

The great reactionary Juan Donoso Cortés believed liberalism's failure to establish principles would be its downfall, placed as it is "between two seas, whose constantly advancing waves will finally overwhelm it, between socialism and Catholicism. Of all the schools, it is most unsatisfactory, because it is the least learned and the most egotistical. As we have seen, it knows nothing of the nature of good and evil because it detests all bold and absolute negations." [1] Because Cortés was a noble man, because he was an intellectually honest man, and a man of Catholic logic, he was not prone to see the full treachery of liberal thought. He could not see that the failure to establish principles was an asset, not a hindrance, to its monstrous growth. Cortés's was a Latin mind, that which was founded in Athens but cultivated

---

[1] *Catholicism, Liberalism, and Socialism*. (1851) 112.

and perfected by the Medievals, that which abhors contradictions, that which will trace errors back to first principles rather than allow them to sully the pure tint of certainty. Writing in the era he did, when the socialist movement was burgeoning and burbling with intellectual vigor, and the Catholic Church whole-heartedly defended her dogmas and the principles of the Old Regime, the liberals stood amongst them like intellectual pygmies. Christ the Logos had formed the world by reason and arranged all things in an order of justice and love. If the socialist now raised the banner of anarchy against this, the Christian could not fail to acknowledge the implicit tribute, that the order he so proposed was so complete it could only find answer in disorder as a principle. The liberal materialist, in comparison, was navel-gazing.

Cortés was completely wrong, both in the unmerited regard he had for the supposed rigor of the socialists, and more lamentably in his failure to predict disaster in the Church. His fine habits of mind sought logical ends and means, and he could not comprehend that dull-minded Anglicanized pragmatism, that "looking away from first things, principles, 'categories,' supposed necessities; and looking towards last things, fruits, consequences, facts" as William James would herald,[2] was the future of universal respectable thought. The cruel rigor of socialist theory could not ultimately occlude that it was a bourgeois thing, and was ultimately consumed by the materially bourgeois it had spurned. The Catholic Church in her own way embraced liberalism at the Second Vatican Council, and sat

---

[2] *Pragmatism*, Lecture II

sentiment in the place logic had one held. For the Council seemed to assert that pluralism in religions could be a virtue, a thoroughly pleasant notion that vitiated her claims of evangelical mandate and destroyed her logical necessity for existence. The fruits are well known: A decaying Church full of pedophiles and their enablers, now wholly subservient to the atheistic state.

The collapse of both socialist and Catholic political movements affirmed the dominance of the Revolution, the superiority of the alogical creed of the liberal system and the eschewal of fair principles in favor of material progress and a morphing godhead. Its lack of coherence, its absence of a sure moral gestalt and the inconstant application of what sundry morals it possessed, all proved assets rather than hindrances.

The world of the present day, in the two-thousandth and twenty-second year of Our Lord, is one far more anarchic than the socialist contemplated. The order of Nature has been perverted, and all existence, to the rational mind, seems to totter on the weight of the failing logic of the world around us. How can the current state of things endure? The Natural Law has been in countless ways abjured, while the social world has been remade into something the ancients could not recognize, and which the moderns cannot understand. The old structures of domestic and civic life have collapsed so that modern man has only the vaguest conception of the processes that truly govern him, or the means which provide him food, drink, and all other provisions keeping him alive.

How did this come about? How did the worst, the most dishonest in this apery of the feckless few men who spread the gospel and conquered an empire—how did this occur? What grants the liberal system its power?

The Revolution is not Synonymous with Communism

One is tempted to say we labor under a kind of *communist* oppression, and many critics on the Right do so. A basic level of scrutiny must eviscerate the notion—it can hold a place in the mind only because our vocabulary is so paltry and has not kept pace with the level of scorn the Revolution has merited. If the gross oppression so recognizable in communist countries is now present in our own, it is not owing to some particularity of Marxist-Leninist thought. America, the present vanguard of the Revolution, has no serious Communist Party, and scarcely has ever had one, while the Communist parties which once littered Europe have been vanquished, or else are husks vacant of the ideological heart which justified their existences. The modern enemies of Western civilization are not the anarchist fulminators against government, but those who possess and never relinquish the levers of power; her oppressors are not the enemies of capital but its possessors. One might in the present day witness in the streets various bloated beasts, squawking for Black Sodomite Rights in the name of Marx and Proudhon, screeching *Property is Theft* in an orgy of bitter sentiment, but it can never be anything but this—sentiment.

The creed of the United States and the modern Western world is not a Communist one. Insofar that she has one, it is that of the general Revolution—call it *liberal, capitalistic, masonic* or whatever designation we may choose. Communism is something solid, tangible, definable. Marx's historical materialism makes sense only in a system where contradictions can form, and contradictions can only form when something concrete is first said: in the Hegelian *elan*, no antithesis can form without a thesis. The contradictions Marx expected to see in liberal capitalism are actually played out in communist societies, for the communist societies were forced by their very reason for existence to take positions on class structure, on law, on government, on which the passage of time can have an effect. The *liberal*, the unconstrained Revolutionist, faces no such constraints. To the liberal, no contradictions need ever form because no concept merits firm definition. And yet the chaos by which the Revolution destroys and conquers would be unendurable if it came on too fast; the poison of progressivism, without conservatism as a palliative, would soon wear out the body politic, would ossify into something that might be attacked. The liberal yearns for the fleshly desire of concupiscence, the conservative the fleshly desire for rest. Both are looking at the world the same way, bent on maintaining onward course of material progress and spiritual degradation.

Marx was very much a man of his time: Fundamentally bourgeois in his mindset, Eurocentric to a tee, quaintly racist and sexist, and, most crucially, consumed with a notion of class that now seems positively Jurassic in the age of *intellectual capital* and the *ownership economy*. We have become so used to referring to vague, arbitrary terms like "middle class" that we forget Marx's definitions of classes possessed stark clarity—the proletarian worked in the capitalist's factories, and the capitalist exploited his labor. Where are these factories today? Where are the workers? Who can take the labor theory of value seriously in a service economy driven by financial opacity and arbitrage?

Liberalism is far more perverse than Marxism. Marxism made definite claims, but *liberalism* itself is an almost meaningless term: to one man it means free markets, to another statism; it is the scourge of corporations in one generation, their greatest proponent to the next. There is no shaming a liberal with hypocrisy because he has no set objective ends, only a means of attainment. The liberal state and the capitalist economy are, in tandem, the perfect Darwinian replicator: Together they have destroyed all traditional social forms, and what the state cannot crush, the market will. Liberalism is not a belief so much as a virus, holding within it the DNA of all the past *liberalisms* that have ever existed. There is no prior form of leftism which modern liberalism has not outpaced. Even poor Marx is left in the dustbin of history.

And yet to the stalwart mind, to the honest intellect, politics requires radicalism because our lives require radicalism because being itself requires radicalism. We in pride sometimes equivocate owing to the indeterminacy of our senses, and quibble about assuredness when we fear being mistaken, but ultimately reality itself is binary, and our answers to dilemmas of existence can only be *yea, yea* and *no, no*. Either Being exists, or it doesn't; either Truth exists, or it doesn't. It is not only cowardly to stake to existence a halfway point but incoherent, an attempt to place the limitations of the senses within existence itself. The goal of the intellectual is to discover what is True, what is definite, even if it is painful—especially if it is painful—and to live according to the Truth as best as we are able.

The great Belloc used the term *alogos* to describe the modern problem, a fine term for its right philosophical

12

underpinnings, but sadly esoteric and unable to arouse contempt. St. Pius the Tenth called it Modernism, the synthesis of all heresies, an apt statement about liberalism in all its forms, theological, political, economic. But the term, again, carries little imprecatory force, and can be an insult only to one who has adopted the premises of reaction, for it is a laudation to the promoters of the Revolution itself. *Il faut être absolument modern*, proclaimed that demon child of the Third Estate. We might call them *Sadists* after the perpetual revolution proposed by that constant resident of the Bastille, but what could we say but that it has already been appropriated, that the body politick has already been inoculated to so many of his perversions? This is the nature of liberalism, that it has already deconstructed the balustrades of morals which might forestall its approach with ridicule and contempt. We have no adequate term of opprobrium because it has sapped or destroyed all sources of popular judgment from which it might arise.

Attempting a Definition of Liberalism

The first step towards solving any problem is in defining it. Oftentimes this first step is also the last, for once we have defined a problem, its solution follows by logical necessity. And accordingly, many of our most contentious disputes arise when we have not been discussing the same thing at all. The task of defining terms is especially important on the political right. For the forces of conservatism and reaction to be effective, they must not only resurrect arguments thought lost long ago, but recapture the very terms of dispute, the loss of which so often does away with the very notion that there was a controversy in the first place.

The problem we face is that liberalism is by its own functioning something almost beyond definition. An example of this difficulty: Any definition of liberal which cannot hold within it Jefferson, Lincoln, Franklin Roosevelt, and Barack Obama is not an adequate definition, for all these men represented in their day the kind of spirit we now associate with liberalism, even if they were not known as such at the time. And yet even within the public lifespans of these individual men we see a remarkable amount of transformation.

Jefferson at least in his self-conception, represents the paragon of what is now called "classical liberalism," but he who was in 1798 a radical proponent of self-rule and universal peace through trade had by 1808 subjected a huge population to foreign government and dragged his nation close to catastrophic war. Lincoln began his administration as a legalistic attorney protecting the interests of Northern industry, and became the exemplar of the *arc of history*, a patriarch of racial terror. Franklin Roosevelt began as a pragmatic reformer and transformed into the conquering exemplar of international governance and human rights, and destroyer of Old World empires. And Obama the technocratic and post-racial conciliator of 2008 would have been inveighed against as a homophobe in 2016 by the open promoter of degeneracy and racial terrorism. How do we find a principle which can endure the trial of ages when we can scarcely find the principle played out in the lifespans of individual men?

It is tempting to say that liberalism has no underlying principle, no coherent motivation girding one era's liberalism with the next. We see here transitions from pacifism to war, from statism to mob rule. One might

14

take liberalism as the doctrine of change for change's sake, in which case we must concede that liberalism is but another name for chaos, or the desire for chaos. But if this holds, then liberalism is mere anarchy, and no political ethos could have arisen from it. We may also be tempted to say liberalism is about democracy, yet many of its cornerstone reforms are manifestly against democratic forces and individual autonomy. The liberal can spout endlessly about "local democracy" when there is some particular perversion he needs to condone, and claim the need for an international forum when the rights of sovereign states need to be quashed.

Liberalism cannot be guilty of self-contradictions because it lacks a coherent body of ideas. Because it operates as a wrecking ball to every impediment it meets cannot be defined ahistorically, for we cannot know what era's liberalism we are encountering without knowing what era's walls it is trying to smash. For this reason, it seems liberalism is always a reaction to something else. But again, this raises the question whether liberalism has a motive force. We cannot expect to attack liberalism, and certainly not to erect something in its place, with only a fleeting half-knowledge of what it *is*, and thus it seems vain to try to assign a precise definition, and our attacks must be waged against a vaguely defined concept, or worse yet, a feeling. And we are left with the above-stated problem: Whether we can define the monster at all.

Liberalism is not about Liberty

Just as tempting is to accept the self-admissions of liberals that their program is about freedom. Everything liberals say about liberalism is a lie, and this fact inheres to the term itself, for Liberals are the true enemy of liberty, and in all their various forms always have been. With every Revolutionary change comes some new oppression. This is necessarily so, merely as a principle of economy. We know that every legitimate right is founded in Nature, and paid for by God the Creator in the very nature of the object. If we have a *right* to drink, it is only because He has made water abundant; a *right* to property only because He made land and chattels plentiful and man productive and rational; a *right* for man and woman to rear their children because Nature's God through sexual reproduction guaranteed this is how it would be most propitiously done. Every true right is found in the nature of things, the *objective logos* of the thing at hand—true even of those goods created by man. For every *civil right* is to be found in the objective makeup of the social order: the class relations that exist, the moral character of the people, and the physical constraints they face. Those rights guaranteed by Magna Carta could have no foundation or endurance were they not bolstered by the recognized obligations of the men demanding them. Such rights develop as custom proves practicable, as necessity and obligation demand.

Every bogus right must be offered on the altar of a previous right's immolation. Liberalism cannot create anything unless it arises from the ashes of an ancient freedom. And so *freedom of speech*, whose legitimate roots are found in the right to redress the government, has become the refuge for obscenity and pornography; so as modern *Civil Rights* are concerned with eliminating all forms of discrimination and merit and crushing all remnants of a true civil society on bases unproved and unprovable. A true right serves to regiment and rationalize the existing order; liberal rights are designed to pervert this order, and to create dependency on the ruling system by subversion of Nature, society, and man himself.

True liberty is beautiful thing, and is recognized as such by all true men. Dupes can be found who accept the liberals' claims about themselves—that whig history of whiggism—and shriek that liberty itself is the problem. And so we find claims that liberalism is nothing more than enshrining individual autonomy as the highest good of life, and that such pursuit of individual goods is necessarily opposed to the common good. It must be replied that such a dichotomy has never truly existed. The liberal who promoted rational self-interest in market transactions did not do so because he disdained the notion of a common good, but because he believed market efficiency was the truest way of arriving at that good. The classical liberal promoting religious tolerance likewise went about it because it seemed to bring an end to centuries of turmoil and bloodshed, fought over creeds the enlightened mind could no longer recall. His eyes, even if myopic, were aimed towards the higher good, not diverted towards his navel.

No, Liberty is a good thing, and indeed one of the greatest things. Individual autonomy and free choice are the highest goods of terrestrial life. It is simply our state to be free—this we cannot change. As a matter of political philosophy, the only question that concerns us is how this freedom should be employed. It is no wonder that the promoters in political liberty are those who draw greatest distinction between liberty and license: Liberty is our freedom well-ordered; license is this freedom's abuse. Liberty as such is the freedom that makes man happy, and license the lack of bounds that causes him harm. Man is *absolutely free* in his rational will, but he is *practically free* when the order around him is oriented around achieving his happiness. All men are free, and all men will be constrained, whether in just or unjust manner, kind or cruel fashion: by perceiving an action's consequences and adjusting his behavior, or by reaping these consequences in fact. Man is bound by the order around him: the order of his own flesh and blood and psyche; the order of Nature: the stars, the moon, the skies; the order of society, its classes and kings and commerce. All men have near-absolute freedom within this order, just as men have the *freedom* to walk off a building or gargle bleach. But to live according to the order of Truth is to be actually and practically free.

To argue about freedom is inane. The primary political question is not the liberty *per se*, but what constraints must be placed on man to achieve his true happiness. This requires no great theory of freedom, but a study of the nature of reality, those laws imposed by the very makeup of being in both the natural and the social order. There is no freedom for a man outside the law any more than the man on a rooftop can free himself from gravity, or a driver can happily liberate himself from the road. The road is created for the convenience and pleasure of the motorist, and when he uses the road properly, is the most free: he drives most quickly and most safely, and achieves most fully his goal of transit. The man on the road and the man in the ditch are both equally free, but only one has liberty, while the other has only his rut.

A man who does not *know* the universe cannot truly act upon it; and one who cannot act has no practical freedom. It is man's first task on this vale of tears to find the truth of things, to understand the order of creation and to engage appropriately with what existence has revealed to us. *Quid est veritas?*—Pilate's question is the primeval one. That he used this utterance as a way to slay the man who was Truth Himself exposes the central dilemma of human action, the eternal desire to pose the question and the congruent desire to leave it unanswered when it seems to belittle our interests. *Ecce homo*, he declared to the crowd who knew Him to be Truth, and clamored out for an easy damnation instead. Such is *realpolitik*.

The Vacuity of Modern Antiliberals

Again, what cannot be repeated enough: Everything liberals say about liberalism is a lie. It does not foster freedom. It does not foster economic stability. It does not make man more open or enlightened. In all these matters the precise opposite is true: Liberalism fosters subservience, economic dependency, and bigotry—a squalid systemization of the mind.

And yet so many *antiliberals* of the present day, through stupidity or guile, will welcome any curtailment of personal freedom as a triumph. Their enemy is not license but the entire Western tradition. Since the time of the Empiricists, the thrust of *enlightened* opinion has been to deny free will in favor of a mishmash of secondary causes. The rapt admiration in which the Eastern system has held Western intellectuals for generations is but the effect of the progressing

Revolution, the transition of false reason to romantic sentiment and, in our age, shallow nihilism. The blather of the Buddha and the Dao was the general foe at both Thermopylae and Poins; it was not until the Fourth Revolution that this nihilism ran rampant in the West and the rise of electronic media eradicating egos and annihilating the soul in electronic dharma. The Western conception of liberty is nearly synonymous with the *West* itself. It was brought to apotheosis in Christianity and constituted the heightening and completion of the individual, not his erasure in Nirvana; it was the cultivation and perfection of rational desires, not the idiotic mantra to *desire nothing*. Any admiration of Eastern order is the consummation of Western defeat.

These modern *antiliberals* are both lazy in their intellectual pursuits and their choice of enemies, driven by mental sloth and political cowardice. How easy it is now, to turn to the papers and find Harvard professors, compassionate conservatives, and indeed the present Supreme Pontiff ranting against individualism. What is the Classical Liberal in the present day but a patsy? These men inveigh against Jefferson and Voltaire but in this boobery they cannot muster a charge against Lincoln—but for perhaps his blatant racism— and most certainly cannot muster the courage to describe the rapes and calumnies of a monster like Martin Luther King. These men are not only intellectual nonentities but cowards, and some of the actual turncoats, beholden to Oriental tyrants in intellectual if not material sway.

Liberalism and Democracy

Liberalism is not synonymous with democracy, and the Revolution does not presage a tendency towards rule by the people. We see with the progress of the Revolution a devaluing of any just rule by the people, as well as any notion of subsidiary or mixed government. We see, in other words, a clear enmity between what the ancients knew as _democracy_ and what we call _liberal democracy_, practiced today. The subtle difference between the two results in an ultimate incompatibility in the ends of democratic rule and liberal rule. However much it may drape itself in democratic garb, the end of liberal democracy is the subversion of rule by the people such as any true democrat must despise.

To shed light on this fundamental yet subtle distinction, it is worthwhile to return to foundation.

Aristotle recognized three basic forms of government: Monarchy, aristocracy, and _timocracy_,[3] literally meaning rule by property, but often translated as popular rule or, with its opprobrium removed and as we shall use it here, _democracy_. Indeed, to Aristotle "democracy" was the corrupted form of popular rule which, along with tyranny and oligarchy, constituted the corrupt forms of ideal systems.

The ancients everywhere held democracy in distrust. This was only natural, as the democratic form of government is fraught with problems. Yet the critique was almost always a functional one, not one which finds in the democratic ethos an intrinsic sickness, a kind of spiritual iniquity as modern reactionaries are prone to assign to it. Aquinas for example found monarchy to be

---

[3] Thomas Cream, Alan Finister. _Integralism: A Manual of Political Philosophy_. (2019) 146.

the highest form of government because a state as a body is better organized under one head than under fifty; democracy was the lowest form of government by converse logic. Democracy was not in itself against any notion of justice recognized by the philosophers or the Church, but it was merely a pitfall.

Democracy's defects could often be remedied by a proper fitting within the state. Polybius praised the particular genius of the Roman Republic for its equilibrium between monarchy, aristocracy, and democracy. Likewise did Blackstone, in his description of the English constitution, laud the three houses of Parliament as the ideal distribution between king, lords, and commons.[4] Such a constitution was beneficial, not for the sake of governmental forms themselves, but for the representation they provided to the actual estates within the nation, a recognition of their unique attributes and the inherent discrepancies which must exist between them. Accordingly, democracy could most plausibly exist only in small states where custom and Nature had mollified most hierarchies and hardened the people forced now to rule themselves. Such were the Puritans of New England, a flinty and hard-minded people whose collective understanding about the true constitution of their state made them perhaps one of the few in the world that could sustain a true democracy.

It is this attribute—consensus about the constitution of the state by the governed—that guarantees the legitimacy of a system that necessarily ties the people to the government itself. Aristotle's use of the term timocracy, if unduly restrictive in tying the principle of

---

[4] *Commentaries*, Book 1, Ch, 2-II

rule to property alone, acknowledged the need for practical bounds of popular rule. Unmoored from any principle, democracy becomes mere mob rule, a government of anyone who can cry and clamor. A functioning democracy must guard against this by expanding the suffrage only on some fixed principle exogenous to the people themselves. Thus we might propose that every landowner should receive a vote, and as more men rise to the dignity of owning land, the voter roles should increase in like proportion. Whether these landowners govern well or poorly is besides the point. What matters is that the governance of the state is based on a principle independent and superior to the mere composition of the voter rolls. Some conception as to the true and desired material constitution of the state must claim precedence over the say of the voters.

A *liberal democracy* recognizes no set constitution, and indeed recognizes no settled constitutional principle at all. In a liberal democracy the state and the people, or more precisely the *mass*, are synonymous with one another. Where this is the case, governance can no longer be judged against any principle. The primary question is no longer one of the tawdry workings of democracy, and the primary goal in a liberal democracy is not of playing to the base standards of the plebs, but engaging and retaining a supremacy of the mass itself. This is best effected by the abrogation of any previous principles of constitution, whether it be land, intelligence, or citizenship itself. The purpose of liberal democracy is therefore the unmooring of the previous makeup of the state, the evisceration of its previous constitution and in its stead the cultivation and control of a malleable mass. The matter of mass immigration provides the most notorious instance of this. What *principle* could demand that an illiterate Somali three years in Minneapolis should have any say over American taxation, water management, and nuclear weaponry? There is and can be none.

The difference between *democracy* and *liberal democracy* has been underappreciated, and has as such left democracy open to untoward attack. So we read from the great Tocqueville: "I think that the species of oppression by which democratic nations are menaced is unlike anything which ever before existed in the world: our contemporaries will find no prototype for it in their memories. I am trying myself to choose an expression which will accurately convey the whole idea I have formed of it, but in vain…" He continues, "Such a power does not destroy, but it prevents existence; it does not tyrannize, but it compresses, enervates, extinguishes, and stupefies a people, till each nation is reduced to nothing better than a flock of timid, industrious animals, of which the government is the shepherd."[5] One reads Tocqueville's magnum opus and realizes that he is not really describing democracy as Aristotle would decry or Thucydides would define. He is instead witnessing the rise of mass governance and the supremacy of a new kind of state. Indeed, "The democratic nations which have introduced freedom into their political constitution, at the very time when they were augmenting the despotism of their administrative constitution, have led to strange paradoxes."[6] In truth, it was no paradox at all, if we look beyond the façade of popular rule. That lover of hierarchy, the man who felt "religious dread" of the

---

[5] Book II, Part IV, Chapter VI.
[6] Id.

social leveling he saw ineluctably proceeding from the reign of Louis the Eleventh, could not parse the purely democratic from what he saw before him, which was the rise of liberal democracy, or if we speak more particularly, the rule of industrial power by the wielding of the proletariat.

These two theories of rule could not easily abide one another. And so those men who loved so well democracy on the Jeffersonian principle of yeomen and small towns found themselves disenfranchised in the Jacksonian rush towards proletarians and industrial cities. The theory of Jefferson would have been recognized by the ancients as dreamy yet all the while recognizable. The new Jacksonian democracy was a different creature: the management of the masses, power divorced from principle, a democracy navigable or contemplatable only where an industrial apparatus allowed it. As with a native American vis-à-vis the Somali usurper, no principle could be adduced towards the common good or functioning of the state, for the relative power of individuals through their suffrage is always diminished by the unprincipled addition of aliens. Indeed, the suffrage is commonly expanded when the government wants to seize more power. Any notion of *Rule by the People* is vitiated where the *people* can be changed simply for the expediencies of power. A universal law might be established from this: The expansion of the suffrage, unmoored from any principle of expansion, is always by nature undemocratic.

Our modern system is perhaps the least democratic ever to have existed. Man's nominal freedom through the suffrage is immense, but his actual freedom over his proximate and quotidian doings is increasingly miniscule. The liberal state will allow the average man a one-hundred-millionth share over the selection of a president, but precludes him regulating the composition of his own schools or social clubs. The boobyprize of national representation is held out as enlightened, a fair compromise for losing sovereignty over all that is near and dear to him.

Nor is this simply mob rule. The spirit of liberal democracy cries out, *The People are the constitution!* Yet we find as a result of the Nineteenth Century reforms democracies less anarchic than those that preceded them. The burgeoning party system provided less room for political heterodoxy than before. To put most quaintly: The system transformed from one where the voters chose their leaders to one where the leaders chose their voters. In such a circumstance, the only political question of any importance becomes, Who is worthy to contort and control this mass of men? The answer to this is not a matter of government per se, but of the nature of the manipulation of the masses. Howsoever ancient England and Athens voted, whether they were ruled by one or many, whether the government was just or insolvent, whether public order was well or ill-kept, they remained throughout England and Athens. Yet under a liberal democracy it is taken for granted that the people through their votes can change the very essence of the state—how and whether England and Athens should exist at all.

All premodern philosophers recognized the need for a degree of subsidiarity, the allocation of power in the hands of that which is most fit to rule. The question of all good government is, Who is fit to rule a particular thing? The answer to this question is found in the nature of the things themselves. Parents are always and everywhere the natural caretakers of their own children, and property owners are thought most fit to determine how property should be managed. True rights flow from the nature of things as they are, and are known so far as we discern the truth of things. But as we have already said, and we will later show, liberalism is always and everywhere an assault on the rights of true democracy, and this because it is always and everywhere an assault on form and being itself. Where liberal rights are granted to a man, his actual power over the thing at hand is diminished. So we see feminist rights serve to destroy everything that is female in woman; so we see rights of religious liberty only serving to weaken the claims of religion, turning it into a kind of consumer dressing and degrading any legitimacy it has over the spiritual and moral order. So we see the expansion of uninhibited *free speech* laws immerse the public forums with the shrieking of rabble and the dulling of the effect of all legitimate grievance. The result of rights-mongering is inevitable; what is female cannot endure to be tested by the trials of manhood and remain feminine; what is holy cannot be treated with indifference, with anything but love or hate; what is impactful, wounding, incendiary must always be regulated if speech is to have such powers to move us at all. To divorce a right from its nature, whether this nature be imparted by human custom of Nature's God, is to remove a right from its proper power of enforcement and place it in the hands of a usurper, that who governs not by logical force by the sheer power of arbitrary coercion. For this reason, every natural emblem in which liberal rights are allowed to fester must be weakened and destroyed. The order that arises to bolster these spurious rights must be a distortion of logical order and of Nature herself.

Defining Liberalism

Liberalism is the process of enshrining what is unnatural in the body politic, and ultimately the minds and souls of men. Liberalism is not about freedom, it is about license. For liberalism is never concerned with the liberty to do something we ought to do, but to gain the ability to do something we should not do, and as a program of practical change, it ultimately exists only as a justification for vice. It is, in fact, vice turned into a science; it is applied injustice gussied up as justice; it is what is inherently irrational contorted into the boundaries of social rationality, and from there, incoherently posited as a universal principle. That which is not irrational can be adapted without the methods of liberal suasion, but liberalism demands coercion to establish itself. The liberal rights which men come to enjoy, and which may at times lead them to prosperity or indirectly to virtue, nonetheless arise out of the motive of squalor and vice. This is true always and everywhere of liberal change.

The process goes like this.

First, there is a vice or usurpation that needs justification. By vice or usurpation we mean not only a departure from the status quo, for a status quo can be wicked and its transformation or destruction does not necessarily portend a liberal change. This usurpation may take many forms: the desire to exploit others, the desire to let loose one's libido, the desire to usurp power.

The actual course of this usurpation depends on the technical means available to make some threshold level of people to adopt the reforms necessary to achieve the usurpation. Sometimes the social means necessary for its adoption are not present, and the initial attempts to make the change die on the vine. For a liberal cause always requires a special material circumstances to justify itself, because it is a departure from the natural order, from reason, history, and law, and could not perdure on its own. Liberals must always place great reliance on technology and the state to adopt and maintain the social forces necessary to keep the change in place at that threshold level, and as we shall see, technology itself ultimately acts as its own deforming vice and material means of establishment.

But bare social coercion is not enough to effect permanent change, and a theory must be provided to support the vice in terms of logic and law, and the discovery of a new, universal logic justifying the usurpation. A liberal change is not merely political, but one which envisions redefining the rules of Nature. Thus, the newfound principle is used to remake the social body, not merely by material coercion but under the claim that the social body is uniting itself to a higher law. The final stage is the remaking of man himself within the bounds of the new liberal principle, culminating in what Burke called the "complete revolution," that revolution which extends to "the constitution of the mind of man."[7] It is these last stages which complete a liberal revolution, and which make the liberal revolution more pernicious and dangerous than any other. For persistent vice—and again, this is the basis of Revolutionary movements—cannot be justified at the individual level. It can only be justified in the

---

[7] *Letter to a Noble Lord.*

context of license on a society-wide scale, the claim that such a vice is in accord with the new general law, and then the reformation of man through the technical apparatus.

By way of contrast: The freedoms won in the Magna Charta are not liberal freedoms, no matter how often liberals may strive to adopt them under their mantle. Property rights are in no way liberal. Limited government is in no way inherently liberal. But attempting to form a coherent system of justice out of property rights alone, as Jeremy Bentham proposed, is a liberal assertion. Claiming that men have an inherent right to rule themselves, as Jefferson posited, is a liberal claim. Magna Charta was an attempt to solidify well-accepted political rights in the context of a country besought by foreign invasions and made up of discordant peoples. But a liberal claim always makes an assertion for itself that transcends its immediate realm of concern. It takes up the banner of absolute truth while at the same time reserving the right to change that absolute truth when it sees fit. Without taking up the mantel of absolute truth, the usurpation would eventually be found out to be just that, a usurpation.

Additionally, as we noted above, the technical means are not always available for effecting a liberal transformation. Take, for example, the assault on monogamy and Christian marriage. Why marriage must be attacked is plain to see. The family is a little semi-sovereign, the surest defense against universal tyranny, the stalwart of all subsidiary power structures, undergirded most firmly by what was, every century before the last, biological necessity. An attack on the family was a common feature of the four revolutions, though it only succeeded in the middle of the Twentieth Century. This was not for lack of trying. The Protestant Revolt witnessed a great breakdown in sexual morality and explosion of licentiousness, yet the Epicureans faced a stolid citizenry, and sexual anarchy never became codified. During the French Revolution, divorce laws were liberalized to such an extent that by 1796-97 there were more divorces than marriages within the Republic.[8] The same happened during the Russian Revolution, when the legal distinction between marital and promiscuous love was abolished, marriage contracts could be written for the span of one night and need not be registered, and unlimited divorce was allowed. Yet by 1944 the liberty of divorce was denied for most citizens.[9] Why did these attempts against marriage fail? Both the French and Russian radicals, having seized the government by in part using sexual anarchy against the Old Regime, were now forced to walk back their thrusts towards debauchery. Quite simply, they lacked the technical means to effect the change, to instill the vice as a public force, and thence to change the natural behaviors and the hearts of men. The large band of whelps roaming the streets of Paris, and the prevalence of debilitating neuroses in Soviet factories made a total sex revolution unfeasible in those times. It was not until the Twentieth Century that monogamy could finally be destroyed, not by moral progress, certainly not by some Hegelian hogwash about a novel realization of freedom, but by means of the birth control pill. There was no argument won in this process, no real moral development or new insights. Put simply, the technical

---

[8] Pitirim Sorokin, *The American Sex Revolution* (1956) 110
[9] Id. at 113-14.

means the reformers lacked in 1789 and 1917 were available to the generation of 1968.

Socialized Morality

To repeat: A liberal reform is one which cannot be promoted within the bounds of reason or morality or law. Liberalism is wholly dependent on the adoption of a new *socialized morality* in order to justify the vice that has been let loose in the body social. It is this characteristic which makes liberalism ultimately inimical to virtue and true morality. For liberalism does not merely corrupt the morals of one state, of one age. The acceptance of vice as a principle requires the reformation of the Law of Nature in order to justify its changes.

It is worthwhile to draw a distinction between concepts of Natural Law, since both Christian and liberal thinkers use it to justify their respective programs. Natural law's fundamental claim is that we must know man and know his position in the cosmos before we can treat him justly. This understanding constituted a kind of direct relation between the state and man, for rightness and the justice of treatment were geared in relation to individual men. Man had to first know nature in order to develop a material social order that facilitated an individual's personal moral development, from which a good society might spring. This system was respectful of the moral autonomy of man, for it held that if society was to function, it depended on man's own charity and personal probity. To know natural law was to know the way man should be guided towards a good society, but without the concerted act of human will, no such society could arise.

The Natural Law of Enlightenment thinkers was much different. To Rousseau, Hobbes, and Locke, the natural law was necessary and also sufficient for the ordering of a good society. Natural law was not only a rule of how an individual man was to act, but a blueprint of the actual composition of the social order. Whereas man in medieval society could be thought to ensoul the body social because the goodness of that body could only be as good as its constituent men, the Enlightenment's Law of Nature diminished man's role in the social body to the equivalent of a cell in an otherwise self-sufficient organism; it viewed society as a vast ticking watch to which man ultimately could contribute nothing but to relish his place as a cog in the mechanism. "The end of good is the good of mankind," says Locke.[10] The tenets of Enlightenment have long been null and void, but this precedence of that notional thing *mankind* over individual man has remained throughout.

This was the great transformation of liberalism, that from *man* to *mankind*, the one that spurred the reorganization of political philosophy and indeed the great spiritual change in man, that which characterizes him as *modern*.

Usury and Socialized Morality

This great transformation arose most clearly in the economic sphere. To see this progression, we look specifically at the practice of usury. The acceptance of usury is one of the foundations of modern economics,

---

[10] *Essay on the End of Civil Government*, Para. 229.

and had the English not justified the practice, it is difficult to believe the capitalist engine could have ever been revved.

There is no justification for usury, that is, the taking of a profit on unproductive loans. It gives unaccountable power to a class of people who provide no productive labor, subjugates those taking out usurious loans to the prospect of lifelong indemnity, and transforms the character of economic activity from one of industry to that of a roulette wheel. As such, usury was condemned in a single voice by the philosopher as ruinous to the state, and the priest as ultimately destructive of a man's immortal soul. The practice was universally condemned in the medieval world; it was tolerated only amongst wretches, in Cobbett's memorable words, "for the same cause incest is tolerated amongst dogs."

Yet usury found a defender in the English crown, and in the years after Henry the Eighth's usurpation of spiritual matters in England, usury more and more found acceptance. This was an outcome that would have been impossible were it not for the very particular social circumstances of that time, that is, the existence of a large proto-bourgeoisie grown rich from Henry's looting of Church lands, and a large vulnerable underclass created out of the same theft. The continued economic turmoil wrought from the theft, the decline in industry and resulting necessity for state welfare, and the Tudors' financial wantonness created the need for funds, and of course usury was an easy means of acquiring them. Without these particular circumstances, it is difficult to believe the mass of people in England would have allowed such a crime to continue.

And yet none of the bare facts about usury had changed. Surely its growing use was a sign of tyranny? There have been many tyrants in history, yet we know just as well that such tyrants eventually have their fall. But the vices and oppressions of the Sixteenth Century had the benefit of coming about when the English people were in the process of radically redefining themselves as a people. A new philosophy was arising that required men take up the tyrant's yoke and consider it sweet. How could this be justified on the grand scale? We fly to the defense made by Sir Francis Bacon, whose preeminent place in the Age of Reason makes him an authority on any topic he treats, if for his historical importance and not his revealing of truth. Instead of condemning usury, suppression of which will always be vain and enforcement a perpetual nuisance, the state should license certain lenders to commit the crime. He continues:

> Let these licensed lenders be in number indefinite, but restrained to certain principal cities and towns of merchandizing; for then they will be hardly able to colour other men's moneys in the country: so as the licence of nine will not suck away the current rate of five; for no man will lend his moneys far off, nor put them into unknown hands. If it be objected that this doth, in a sort, authorize usury, which before was in some places but permissive; the answer is, it is better to mitigate usury by declaration, that to suffer it to rage by connivance.[11]

---

[11] *Essays*, "Usury."

All states allow certain vices so as to prevent worse behavior to the overall detriment of the social good. Yet in just states, these permissive measures are allowed with the understanding that man's personal faults can never be wholly eradicated, and the harm done in trying would not be worth the meager benefits. But these allowances are in regard to personal vices inherent to man's individual nature, not those vices created or enabled by the social environment itself.

Usury is not a personal vice, but a public one. It has no existence outside social transactions, and cannot but harm other men by its practice. At the same time, no one is so naïve as to claim that medieval loansharks were ever completely without a clientele. Yet there is a great difference between a crime conducted out in the open versus the shadows of Skid Road, a crime which is regulated versus a crime which is allowed, but always with the proviso that its practice could be throttled at any time at the discretion of the state.

In adopting the tactic of regulation, the state acquires financial benefits for allowing such vice: it becomes a necessary partner in the criminal enterprise, and any prior questions about the morality of the practice falls away. It is replaced by an alternate analysis, one in which the total society-wide, revenue-enhancing effect is assessed rather than its intrinsic morality or effect on the individual. We well know that man is prone to crimes like usury. But to accept this fact and even to tolerate some evils in practice, knowing that it is in vain to try to squelch them all, is far different from providing sustenance to the crimes, which all forms of regulation materially must take. And as incentives shift for the state to allow more and more of a vice, it will find that the social body can bear a larger and larger area of that gangrenous growth. Thus, in the case of usury, one can completely admit that much evil will come from it, but also that preventing such evil is costly, and such costs might be spent on other social endeavors. Tolerating the existence of vice has transformed into manifestly aiding them.

In a system which regulates rather than condemns crimes, man's relation to right and wrong—that fulcrum from which our relationship to God and our fellow man depends—is now mediated by our relation to the entire population. And this is the characteristic of liberal morality as compared to individualized assessments of bad and good. Liberal morality is created not by man's rational determination of his situation in the universe, his relation to Nature and the social world, but as a dependent variable in the sea of other dependent variables, something like the way prices are determined in neoclassical economics. Man's moral nature is at the mercy of society at large: it is socialized.

We note that through all this, the idea of usury is still squalid and immoral; but this has been drowned out by the function of the market, the thousand other vices of avarice now regulated by the ballooning state, the specious reasoning of the economists, and the ultimate transformation of man himself into *homo economicus*, who sees the world in eat-or-be-eaten terms, and owes his fellow man no more than the what the Golden Rule demands: That if he is able to commit usury on his neighbor, his neighbor is just as *free* to seek usury from him. This reciprocity in exploitation is called *justice*—and it is steadfastly maintained as a form of justice, for to say that such actions are simply might-equaling-right would be to give away the lie. Though liberal changes always separate us from reason and morality, our most human attributes, they nonetheless will not allow man to be cognizant of that he has descended to the level of animal exploitation. Man must still be assured that he is operating on some basis of some higher ethos, an expanded godhead which miraculously allows for vice.

From this dynamic arose Hobbes's mighty Leviathan, the very notion of which shows the corruption wrought by adoption of liberal mores. Man, the political animal, does not need a great impetus to form tribes, cities, nations. Man is a social being, and is more himself in society than he is apart, and even more himself in a just society than an unjust one. Yet man needs some special impetus to join a covenant of injustice, some mutual assurance that his skirting of moral law will not be punished; that, like criminals in a gang, all have the same motive not to defect lest the crime be exposed. This is what Hobbes envisioned the state to be—and given the state of Seventeenth Century England, that middling heretic was merely being descriptive. The social contract of the Hobbesian Englishman was that he would enter into such a unjust pact; in return would arise the Leviathan—that beast which God holds out to Job as the summit of His awful power.

Liberalism is a Christian Heresy

Liberal causes are never won through argumentation; rather, they are won through transformation of the population as a whole. When these transformations are completed, the question is not whether these changes have been good or bad, but whether or not their reversal is materially feasible.

This is the case with the modern welfare state, which is clearly unsustainable, but is also so well entrenched that its malignancy or goodness is simply irrelevant. The average man rarely bothers to assess the value of the welfare state or its creators; its material intractability transforms the intellect into believing in its inevitability, and this in turn dulls any moral or intellectual impulse to judge its existence in the present and future, or its creation in days past. The same process is effected through technological dependence; once man becomes dependent on technology, its morality becomes basically moot. In other cases the liberal will simply skirt the need for specious argument by transforming the population itself, most notably through immigration and expansion of the suffrage. In the regular course of things, an argument is won on its merits, but under a liberal regime an argument is forgotten after social coercion removes all stakes from the debate. The intellectual justifications which follow are always slipshod, because it was never the logic of an argument which impelled the change, but rather brute force.

But the most pungent feature of liberal revolution is the change made in man himself. Because man is not convinced of a liberal change by reason, the acceptance of a liberal change, which holds itself out as a new facet to the law of nature, transforms man's relation to the world as a whole. The man who acquiesces to a change based on logic retains his relational position to society and the world, but a man is not allowed such autonomy in a world where all material and moral existence is in flux. His liberty and reason are entirely dependent on the new means of arriving at the new socialized rule. And man has become more and more degraded through the centuries as the changes have come with greater rapidity, as he has found himself more and more subservient to technology and completely divorced from the means of materially sustaining himself. It is with the unimpeded acceptance of technology that the Revolution reaches its perfect state and ideal form. It is at this point that we currently find ourselves.

The question arises when this process first began. Because vice is omnipresent, because tyranny is perennial, the operative question is when man was made into a creature amenable to the kind of social subjugation here described. Clearly this was with the Protestant revolt. From a historical perspective, we find the proximate cause of so many of the hallmarks of liberalism in the Reformation that we must begin there. But its meaning lies deeper than this. Because in response to various frauds and usurpations, both ecclesial and political, the Protestant Revolt requires a new man be created—the Protestant Man—who would in the passing centuries become the modern liberal. Man was to be transformed not, by and large, through propaganda or population replacement (though both played a role), but through the mediating institution of the Protestant sect. The Protestant revolt completed the first unmooring of man, that between his immortal soul and the prospect that he might have any ability to work out his own salvation. It created a mass of wretches ineluctably damned, and damned for the benefit of the elect. It, in other words, turns the entire divine economy into matter of socialized morality.

The layout of this book.

We will now chart out the course of the five revolutions. We adopt the paradigm of Plinio Correa de Oliveira, the great Brazilian reactionary who understood the wretched and vile nature of the Revolution in its many stages. From him we even appropriate the term *Revolution*, which encompasses the gradual and unabating crisis. His *Revolution and Counterrevolution* is as concise a description as could be conceived of, and we wish only to expand on his work, and hopefully add further dimensions to it.

We refrain from simply reviewing the literature of well-known liberals and critiquing their work. We refer to figures like Hobbes, Bacon, Hegel, and Rousseau not in order to scrutinize their work, but only with the purpose of navigating the evolution of ideas, shading the edges of the objects of our study, which is the heresy of liberalism—which is a *real* thing, with an independent existence and reality apart from any attempts to conjure it up. This study must be done discursively, for that which is but a perverse mutation of what has gone before it can be understood best not by theory but through effect. We do not endeavor to lay down an exact line of liberal thought and achievements, a task that seems dull and dreary, and has been undertaken by others who can better tolerate it.

A modern attempt to define liberalism sits before us.[12] Liberal platitudes are taken as truth: That liberals distrust power, that liberals have faith in human progress, and belief in "civil respect," and that people have intrinsic worth "whatever they thought and

---

[12] Edmund Fawcett, *Liberalism: The Life of an Idea*. Second Edition.

whoever they were," and that they long for an ethical order without appeal to divine authority. And yet the author is left without a definition. "If a satisfying noncircular definition of 'liberalism' is still wanted, none is available. Looking for liberalism in semantic space or conceptual space is looking in the wrong place... The liberal outlook is not a cohesive structure like the chemistry of a natural element. Some parts of the liberal outlook cohere, some conflict. Nor can the outlook be given intellectual coherence or persuasive appeal by reducing all its requirements to one overriding idea, such as liberty or equality. Liberals give their outlook coherence by pursuing its discordant aims together, and they are not acting like liberals unless they do." In other words, the student can see but not know. The rest of the study takes on the character of a hodgepodge of facts and people, but suffers from the problem noted above, of failing to discover any intrinsic unity to the thing. *The liberal outlook is not a coherent structure*—we agree with the author, because what is intrinsically evil has no positive existence, and because we would not study a tumor, however weighty it may be, without reference to the organ attacked. For this reason, we approach the matter chronologically, to see the progress of this cancer and come to a more coherent understanding of its malignancy.

The Revolution always shares from age to age a certain common trait in that it abstracts away from the good of the individual. The very lifeblood of the Revolution is a kind of transhumanism, a slurring over the human good for the benefit of some notional and social creation. This was as true of the First Revolution as it is the Fifth. If we convince the reader of this claim, than our task will have been accomplished.

The reader may disagree with what we select as the characteristic features of the Revolution in any given era, let alone our attempt at analysis. Such disagreement may not pose a problem in describing the First and Second Revolutions, the Protestant and French, whose characteristics are so well engrained in our common understanding of *History*. But with the Fourth Revolution, that of 1968, the characteristics are not so definite, the effects of the transformation not so clear; our descriptions and analysis must be more open to controversy, without such support of the common knowledge. This cannot be helped.

The Five Revolutions are these: The Protestant Revolution, whose victory was the spiritual splintering of man and the acceptance of positive evil as a component of the polity; the Jacobin Revolution, whose victory was the Age of Reason, but specifically the unmooring of man's political existence, the rise of ideological rule, the establishment of the faceless mass as the new material principle of ruling; the Bolshevik Revolution, whose victory was the fracturing of man's economic existence fostered by the Industrial Revolution, and with this the triumph of capitalist production; the Sorbonne Revolution, whose victory eviscerated man's social existence, seen in the triumph of the technocracy and the all-consuming nature of the Civil Rights Regime; and the Revolution of 2020, that of the Coronavirus, where as a principle man's individual biological needs were made subservient to the advancement of General Health. This is the progress of liberalism, whose enemy is true nature, right order, the set constitution of things as they are. In all its iterations we see the social order perverted, vice enshrined, and perpetual movement towards the obsolescence and eventual eradication of man.

The First Revolution: The Protestant Revolution

The Protestant Revolution

The Revolution itself is a Christian heresy, and can be understood under no other aspect. It is from its nature as heresy that the Revolution derives its universalist claims and its all-consuming character, which establishes the Revolution not as the enemy of any one creed or race or era, but of the Godhead Himself, and His entire human race.

It is tempting to study the Protestant Revolution only on facial terms, as the political conflict it assuredly was between the Roman Pontificate and the princes of the rebellious states. But this analysis must be inadequate, and grossly so. Under such an interpretation, the works of Zwingli, Luther, and Calvin fall to obscurity, as the invidious adoptions of the rebel states, speciously taken up by princes who would have embraced any source of conflict in their pursuit of power. That the conflict was waged on theological grounds, under this theory, was mere accident owing to the nature of one of the disputants, whose legitimacy lay solely in her claims to theological truth and whose power could be fractured only by attacking her thusly. But historical memory easily refutes this charge. The Revolt's philosophers are who we recall, while its princes, with the exception of the Tudors and Hohenzollerns, have fallen out of memory.

A materialist is the most bigoted of men, he who would transform the highest aspirations of men into sublimated political strife, and all human experience into a phenotypic environs for his genes. The result is simply empty, more speculative and trite than the shaman's meanderings. The true importance of the Protestant and Catholic divide cannot be understood but by recourse to theology. The rift created by the Protestant revolters was the greatest ever to split a once-united people, those men and women who formed the grand empire of Christendom. In the proceeding centuries it would yawn wider and wider in every field of human endeavor, in philosophy, anthropology, economics. It is from the rift of Christendom that the weed of Revolution first crawled, and the fertile soil of Catholic philosophy that this weed fed.

Though it is an atheistical thing and a godless abomination, liberalism is a Christian heresy. Its native materialism could not be a motive force were it not attached to a divinization of human action, nor could its optimism remain palatable were it not for its pilfered eschatology. The ancients could not have been duped by the trappings of the liberal creed or possessed by the rank optimism of moderns, nor the rank effeminacy of facile equality. The ancient materialists were not fools, and no classical freeman would have surrendered himself to the yoke of amorphous and notional Liberty for which so many millions of recent centuries have shed their blood. Those men could adhere to a materialist creed, but knew to do so was a form of con-cession, a repudiation of hope in higher gods. The modern materialist, in contrast, sees in the rut of quotidian pleasure a divine thing, a hallowed shallowness of accumulation. The ancients witnessed the tumults of human affairs and contemplated man's miserable state; only the liberal can look at the earth's epochs of blood and claim to see the revealing of a new and higher state, one in which not only tyrants but tyrannies must hang. The Gracchi might through the shedding of blood achieve change in their city, but only the liberal believes such bloodshed can win justice everywhere. The wisdom of the pagan world lay in its pessimism. It was a world that could sometimes shine with a transient magnanimity of certain great men, with the refulgence of certain odd thinkers arriving before Justice through the natural light of reason, and yearning to believe it was established by a benevolence above them. But in this world of pirates and demons there was no true refuge—no refuge of the soul, no general order for those who sought reprieve from life's warfare, no singular creed that could provide rest amongst that cacophony of men who could not find reason to live but merely found themselves alive.

There can be no return to paganism in the present day. Paganism was nothing but a chaos, and chaos cannot be returned to by choice, by a willful devolution of a mind once ordered. Attempts at an instauration of the old pagan forms are unavailing, and always must give way to facile Satanism, a shameful rebellion against the truth of Oneness the Church established and the order of the Logos that she cherished. There can be no return to paganism, only a deformation of the Christianity that fully and totally destroyed and replaced it.

What was Christendom?

Because liberalism is a Christian heresy, it can only be adequately defined in relation to orthodoxy. And so we must begin by asking what that Faith was or, from the social aspect, what was this thing, Christendom, which the Catholic Faith created?

To speak of Christendom is to speak of Rome. It is from her that all great things of the West find if not their genesis, then their tutelage and fruition. As the glories of Hellenic art, science, and philosophy could find their due only under universal promulgation through the Empire, so the blood of the first martyrs was given effect in the normalized and perfected ritual worship granted by the protection of Constantine. That reforms that would facilitate the rise of the renewed empire were doom to the administrative apparatus of the West, which would decline and eventually be formally erased. In the disorder of the decaying apparatus the men once recognized as the empire's administrators and generals took upon themselves the titles of lords and king. And they remained loyal to Rome, not by virtue of pay or political expediency, but through the waters of baptism and the chrism of their coronation. Through the Dark Ages the imperial head remained in Rome, but its mandate was no longer the will of Praetorian Guard, but the Christian Faith. As the antique Roman had terraformed the landscape and regimented the laws of the land, so the Church went about the task of baptism, capturing every soul for God and thereby gaining another subject within her jurisdiction.

The new empire's borders were always in flux, growing beyond the Danube and raising her minarets and spires in Germany, in Poland, in Ireland; and contracting under the successful heretical rising of the Mohammedans. Yet through the centuries, the notion of the empire, even if just a notion, was sustained: The campaigns of Belisarius are inexplicable otherwise, as is the fervor the Crusaders outside the walls of Jerusalem, and the odes of Dante atop the mountain of Purgatory. In their dark temples strewn across the continent, monks daily sang the language of Rome, and transferred its letters in the hope that literate ages might again be able to enjoy them. The slave economy of the Caesars endured, but through the pacific conquest of Christ it was softened to serfdom into peasantry, and from that into nations of free-holders and free men. If this thing, Christendom, was a dead empire, then scarcely any other the world has seen could be considered alive.

Her emperors were the Supreme Pontiffs, the popes. By virtue of baptism, the Church asserted jurisdiction over the souls of all her adherents. In matters of the Faith her jurisdiction was universal, her power total. In the immiserated nations the Church may easily have claimed a similar power over the material realm, yet largely stayed true her own adage of leaving to Caesar what was Caesar's, and civil affairs were broadly left to the princes. The Christian did not take worldly goods as intrinsically evil, but viewed them as sorry substitutes for the treasury of moral virtues and the expanse of the world to come. But no serious man alleged the Church could exist without establishing her own claim to worldly power. The extensive properties owned and managed by the ecclesial power often provoked disputes with the temporal powers over merely temporal things, and this was always an embarrassment to an institution of such celestial creed. But the unenviable prospect of the Church owning property was worsted only by the

alternative: that the Church be owned by somebody else.
And if the Church found herself balancing the demands
of her spiritual existence with a need to make friends
with the Mammon of iniquity, she found herself in the
same state as every man on this vale of tears, whose
primary occupation is to reconcile his material life with
his ideals, to find a way for Mammon to serve God.

Secular princes did not dispute the supremacy of the
Church in spiritual affairs or question its temporal
jurisdiction over its own lands. Yet power must ever vie
for power. The conflicts over the civil and ecclesiastical
jurisdiction provided a source of constant disputes,
disputes which provided the impetus of so much
Protestant wrecking. England in particular saw an array
of monasteries grown exorbitantly wealthy through the
civil wars of the Fifteenth Century, when they served as
a kind of refuge for wealth of nobles otherwise
consumed with slaughtering one another. The resulting
system, administered by monks, priests, and nuns,
served as the most wholistic form of *social welfare* that has
ever existed, and with it wealth and freedom.

"All historians agree, that they were 'easy landlords;'
that they let their lands at low rents, and on leases of
long terms of years; so that, says even Hume, the
farmers regarded themselves as a species of proprietors,
always taking care to renew their leases before they
expired. And was there no good in a class of landlords
of this sort? Did not they naturally and necessarily
create, by slow degrees, men of property? Did they not
thus cause a class of yeomen to exist, real yeomen,
independent of the aristocracy? The country people
spoke of them with great reverence, and most grievously
deplored the loss of them. They had large estates, were

easy landlords, and they wholly provided for all the indigent within miles of their monastery. The Monasteries set the example, as masters and landlords; an example that others were, in a great degree, compelled to follow. And thus, all ranks and degrees were benefited by these institutions, which, with malignant historians, have been a subject of endless abuse, and the destruction of which they have recorded with so much delight, as being one of the brightest features in the *Reformation!*"[13]

The Magisterium

But the Church as a purely political entity is scarcely of interest to us. The especial jurisdiction the Church claimed for herself was over those who accepted the Faith. From her adherents she required assent of the will to her creed, embodied in the total body of her substantive doctrines called the Magisterium. The Magisterium constitutes not a formal code of laws, but is best understood as a collection of statements about the makeup of God and Nature that the Church takes as objective fact. Such statements are more profound than mere external laws, which are only prescriptions of conduct, but instead form a body of received truths about the nature of existence from which principles of practical conduct may be extrapolated. Most simply, the Magisterium is a claim about the universal nature of existence to which the laws of every Christian nation must conform, and the conduct of every Christian man must be guided. As a result, the Magisterium served to

[13] Cobbett, *The Protestant Reformation in England and Ireland*, paras. 151, 59, 154

cultivate the Western mind, propagating one philosophy, one epistemology, one view of the social body, and one vision of man.

The Magisterium consisted of the testimony of God as received by His one Church. Much of this was explicit testimony. The Ten Commandments were clear prescriptions of conduct received through Moses from God Himself. Yet the Christian did not hold that these were mere laws, as if promulgated by local council or petty tyrant. Instead, they were to be viewed in the context of the entirety of creation, and indeed the Doctors of the Church held that the Ten Commandments could be deduced without any explicit testimony from God at all. The prohibitions against theft and murder were derivable from observing the objective makeup of the world—which was, after all, a statement of God's will, though provided in a deeper medium than words—and through the use of the natural light of reason to discover what benefited man. The Christian could hold this because he believed God was the *Logos*, that He has formed all things in an orderly fashion, and even as a gesture of His love constrained His own conduct to make it explicable to the creatures He had given powers of reason so alike to His own. So the Christian held on faith that the earth is not inscrutable chaos, not a snare to beguile man but something to be understood, and through such understanding a means to make him happy. The divine revelations bequeathed in Scripture and through tradition could never be opposed to the order of reason God had established. In crude terms, this meant that those things called *faith* and *reason* could never be opposed, for both were the gifts of an omnipresent and beneficent God. He had willed the sun to daily rise and the sparrow to fall, just as He had willed His Son to die for the sins of man and to miraculously rise again—and all as statements of His greatness, and His desire to make Himself known to man.

The necessity of reconciling faith and reason may not be clear at first pass. It certainly stands as offensive to the modern mind, that holds along with Kant that religion and the Divine are at most emotive things, separate and different from notions of science and ethics, and not a matter for rational discernment. Nor is this rejection a purely modern mode. Mohammad had posited a God unhinged from necessary order, a God who willed to bind himself to no laws, and who therefore at times could be found to act contrary to the order he had enshrined. *Omnipotence will do what it will* is perhaps the natural mindset of lowly man, bound like mites in a cosmos of rotting wood, at all times tossed on the depredations of fate. But the Christian did not believe this. The God he knew as Love Itself had given man a creation worthy of his rational state, one that could be known and understood, and through knowing and through understanding, better loved, as all the greatness of creation testified to He who had created it. God was the Logos, the universal order. Centuries of shallow skepticism have done nothing to dislodge this belief from the Western mind; the scoffing empiricist cannot contemplate the universe where his discovered laws are anything but universal, nor can the ideologue bode the thought that his chosen prejudices provide anything but a universal guide of conduct. Like all first principles, this tenet of universal order is an *act of faith*, but one which even the vilest atheists are disposed to keep, though assuredly because they have never bothered to contemplate it.

The fruits of this atmosphere were readily apparent. Critics would later abuse the Scholastics and doctors for their overreliance on deductive reasoning, their supposed quibbling over how many angels can dance on the head of a pin. But the very practice of deduction attested to the breadth of the Christian's intellectual project, the fact that he grounded his precepts in first principles, that he recognized no rational divide in God's great cosmos, and no incompatibility between divine commands and man's reason. The form of inquiry he developed was as rigorous as that established by the greatest of Athens, and had to be. For where no incompatibility exists between reason and faith—where the world seen is fundamentally no different from the world unseen—to have knowledge of one is to proceed towards knowledge of the other.

To the Christian, there are no scientific questions that are not in some sense theological. His God had declared *sum Ego sum*, Being Itself indited in the immanent Word. As such, all questions of metaphysics, anthropology, and philosophy reduced themselves to questions about a living God. The cosmos in his eyes was vivacious; in its every aspect it spoke to the nature of the divine. From the highest to lowest things, reality was strung with webs of interdependence and order. "A Church which embraced, with equal sympathy, and within a hundred years, the Virgin, Saint Bernard, William of Champeaux and the school of Saint Victor, Peter the Venerable, Saint Francis of Assisi, Saint Dominic, Saint Thomas Aquinas and Saint Bonaventure, was more liberal than any modern state could afford to

54

be. Radical contradictions the State may perhaps tolerate, though hardly, but never embrace or profess."[14] The elasticity of Medieval thought came from the depth of which the Church made her claims, which partake of the nature of the Logos and all the created universe, the nature of which she jealously guarded. A vast array of practice could prevail where morals and belief were uniform, and sprung from such deep soil.

But this interdependence was won only by an absolute jealousy of doctrine. Where first principles were determinative, the structure could only stand where they were defended from assaults, and where the slightest hint of the solvent of heterodoxy was rooted out and exterminated. In the modern day we are amazed at the content of the controversies which the Church expended so many resources and sacrificed so much goodwill: That of the mere syllable, between Arius' *homoiousios* and Athanasius' *homoousios*, or the controversies of Abelard, whose claims about the Holy Ghost are so subtle and facially innocuous that the modern mind can scarcely track them. What to call this but the ravings of a bigot?—and in her parsing of diphthongs, who could proffer otherwise than that she is history's worst?

The Arian controversy, which burst forth almost as suddenly as the persecution against the Church had ended, seems surest sign of this. Yet the vigilance was necessary. For even in the fledgling days, the Church well knew that the adoption of one notion of God inevitably suggested changes to how the rest of the world, including the makeup of society, would be organized. Aruis had posited that Christ was not quite

---

[14] Henry Adams, *Mont St. Michel and Chartres*, Ch. XVI.

the Godhead, but still quite like a god, as Ares or Apollo or Julius Caesar, those demons or men who ruled by virtue of strength rather than justice. If this was true, then Christ's passion and resurrection, otherwise so poignant as a story *sui generis* of the actual Creator coming to earth only to be murdered and rise again, became merely the tale of a great man such as the pagans already well knew, a man gifted by Divine favor to overcome death and lead his people—the Empire's gentiles—to glory. It was no coincidence that the most notable of Arius' adherents were members of the Roman legions, the imperial guard who thought themselves superior to the general population, as in plain political fact they were. A victory for the Arians threatened to establish that a mere creature could through his own force of will rise to the level of divinity, that simply to be exalted as a great man was to give one power over the very order of reality; it threatened to establish that the civil religionists of the old pagan order had, in their deifying of mere tyrants, come closer to the Truth than they ever could have imagined. It was this catastrophe that the Catholic victory averted, the fate that would have followed had not so many suffered martyrdom for the sake of one syllable. That *might makes right* is a conceit as old as time, one that appeals to the indolent perception of the senses, but against which the mind and heart always recoil. It was this conceit the Catholic victory forestalled: reaffirming that Christ was not creature but Creator, and with this protecting the mystery of the Incarnation.

The Church's jealousy and the Catholic victory had spared civil society the debates about Caesarism as a principle. The social order that followed was undergirded by a moral consensus such that humanity has never seen. Tyrants still occasionally rose, but they also fell, and the course of their tyrannies was never confused with the positive will of God who deserved only what was good and just. We might contrast this with our own age, where there is no political brutality, however severe, that cannot find a measure of applause amongst the defenders of decency and order; where there is no moral perversion so profane that it cannot find rationalizers in respectable society, and sacrifices to it in the dregs. It was only with the Protestant Revolt that the consensus wrought by the Church and her Magisterium failed—with attendant evils we shall soon see.

Catholic Doctrines

For the purposes of understanding the Revolution, we draw attention only to certain aspects of Christian belief, with special focus on how they affected Christian rule.

All Christians believed that God was good, and that His creations partook of His goodness. This found witness in the Book of Genesis, where God looking at the cosmos He had created through the first five days of creation declared it good, until the creation of man on the sixth day, whom He proclaimed even better than all the rest. The stars, the earth, the light and the darkness, the animals and plants and microbes were all positively good, and man was foremost amongst the universe of goodness, a little less than the angels.

But who can believe this? Who has not witnessed such evils that make our residence in this world such torture? Who has been immune from the wounds and the scarring of creation?—or fail to see the decay and disease of the years, the indeterminable process of breaking up, the stain of human treachery and the blight of death which can spur even the Lord to weep? It is only the doctrine of *Original Sin* that makes the world's putative goodness all but a bitter joke. This doctrine holds that because of man's disobedience towards the will of God all of Nature was perverted, from man's innermost desire to the stars in the heavens. Yet at the same time the Christian affirmed that sin was in a sense not *real*, that it had no affirmative existence but was only a perversion or deprivation of the good. He asserted that God had not created evil, and insofar that evil *was*, it was a lacuna of what properly should have been. Evil was only the absence of a good fitted for some object, like disease attached to an organ. It was because of this that depravity attached to man's will and that decay lurked in all things beneath the sun. The true goodness of man and the true goodness of reality could not be directly perceived by the five senses, which saw, tasted, heard, smelled, and touched the decay about them. Belief in the world's goodness required an act of faith.

Knowledge enlivened by faith told man that the world was good; but this could never be in full accord with the senses, which found the world manifestly bad. It was no surprise the Christian was naturally drawn to the philosophy of Idealism, and with this an implicit acceptance of the doctrine of Platonic Forms. For if existence was intrinsically good, as the Faith did aver, and yet existence was most latently rotting with evil, then a truer reality must exist apart from the observable incidents of creation. Man saw the world through a dark glass, one of fleeting sensation and decaying matter, yet he could be assured that on the last day, when he saw as God did, all things would be made clear: The Forms of the seen and unseen would then be whole and entire before him, and man's corporeal vision would be united to the knowledge he retained in mind and heart.

The doctrine of Original Sin was tightly united to that of *Free Will*. As a practical matter, Original Sin could not have any persuasive application nor its doctrine any binding effect where the evil of sin was seen as intractable, as the cruel imposition of God and not the effect of man's volitionally defiling His order. Better simply to ignore a God so wicked than to relinquish oneself to such tyranny. No, the Christian argued that God was wholly good, and evil had entered the world only through the defection of man from what God and his own heart told him was right. As a strictly logical point, the existence of Free Will cannot be proven. One cannot amputate all the ages' arguments that man's soul is nothing but an agglomeration of secondary causes, that the moment's contemplations are not the residual effect of some distant Madeleine bite, or that man's life is fundamentally any different from a tossed stone's, rattling about the earth. One cannot through logic abolish determinism. The Church was forced to take free will on faith, or more precisely, to adopt the metaphysical supposition her creed required. As she often did to intractable philosophical questions, the Church wielded the sword of Faith where reason found only a Gordian Knot, and by bursting through allowed truly free thought to prosper.

The principles so briefly here defined found their fulfilment and material form in the Eucharist. The Church declared that the Eucharist was truly the body and blood of Christ, that through the sacrifice of the mass and the miracle of transubstantiation, the objects that appeared as bread and wine were not so, but were veils cast over their true nature which was the actual personhood of Christ. As such, the Church's Eucharistic theology could not endure for a moment without some recourse to the doctrine of Forms, for the man who recognized no difference between accident and essence, between sense and actuality, could not accept the Eucharist as what the Church claimed, for the senses declare the host to be merely bread. Put simply, a man who relied on his senses alone could not be Catholic.

As the source and summit of the Faith, the Eucharist was the sun around which the orbs of her philosophy and practice turned. The priesthood existed to confect this gift; the hierarchy of bishops to guide the priests. The Magisterium existed to guard against unworthy reception of the Eucharist, its moral prescriptions designed to conform man's will to the Almighty's and to reject the enticements of errant dogma, which were but a perversion of the true Incarnation and thus a blasphemy against God. This was, in part, the meaning of the Eucharist, the hope it provided and the significance it held, so long as man strove to make himself worthy of it. For the Eucharist was the reproduction of the actual Incarnation itself, and sufficient to provide justification for Christ's coming to earth. It found Christ as both God and man, and required a recognition of man's nature as much as God's to do it justice. And if man was nothing but a cruel biped, if he truly was a wretch without hope of redemption, he never could have been a worthy receptacle of the Godhead. That man was a craving, cowardly, sniveling creature bound by the chains of concupiscence to a restless and tumultuous existence seemed clear. Yet another existence resided within him as a potentiality, a literally godlike one, the man washed clean of Original Sin, the Form of lost perfection taken on by Christ Himself, which alone can provide man hope for his own existence.

The Eucharist was very literally the Incarnation brought forth endlessly, and in the ways we have discussed, a reification of the Church's doctrine itself. Understand the Incarnation, and one could understand the Church; understand the Church, and understand Christendom.

The Citizenship of Christendom

What is there to say about this world? Man was the same as he has ever been, harassed by disease, war, and ignorance. The same pitfalls of governance ruled, though the dourest sage might in honest moments concede that if philosophers could not be kings, then at least they could be Christians. Vice was ever-present, but mediated. Wars erupted, but were tempered by Christian values. The nihilism that at regular intervals allowed millions of Orientals to be slaughtered as if snuffing out a match was impossible in the West. The man of Christendom was sure of his soul as an everlasting thing, an individual thing—this conception of the soul *was* the West, one that provided motivation for his morals, moderation of his vices, and grounded his will for power.

The average man has no problem blending in with others, of accepting the ease and false solace of social conformity. To yearn for individuality, to force man to cultivate his own soul, can only be a burden to a fallen creature prone to sloth and intellectual torpor such that the idiocy of *Nirvana* can hold appeal. Yet this was the task imposed on every Christian. In the battle for his own soul, where the Oriental sage taught him to cast aside his soul altogether; the Church promised man a relentless warfare; the sage promised him an end of all suffering on earth, while the Christian told him pain could not be evaded, and that not even God Himself could avoid suffering on the face of the earth. What greater contrast between the fates of men could be envisioned?

There has never been a more individualistic people than those great men of Christendom. It is man's soul that makes him an individual, and the Church regularly forced man to confront his soul in the starkest of terms—to ask if it was fit to receive God in the Eucharist, to weigh his actions in a manner that they would one day be judged by Christ and exposed to man. These confrontations were a burden and a relief to him : a burden as considered against his concupiscence and intellectual sloth, a relief for the soul he knew he possessed and which could be made divine. And Christendom was above all things an empire of souls.

If Christianity was false, it was a bizarre and monumental fraud. It was one to which its own churchmen constantly added accoutrements, new flanks on which its legitimacy could be attacked. The debates of the Scholastics could be derided for their esotericism precisely because they had laid out as clearly as any philosophers have ever done the great questions of morality.

What were the fruits of this environment? Was this a black age, a myopic era, a charnelhouse for man's true

potential? If man of this age was uniquely deluded, his
delusion was one that adored wisdom, his abject state
one that most made him like a god. These men were
enamored with a dream of life which united his highest
faculties with the heights of creation, which saw his
pitiful miseries as kin to the suffering of God Himself.
His sins had the power to damn him, and his virtue the
power to save him, but he was not alone; the universe
labored along with him in this travail, and nature
groaned at his side.

But this study is not an encomium of that era. The
reader does not need to accept this place as a unique
height, only as a departure point for our decline. We
have described a theory of life universally eradicated, a
full five centuries dead. To mark its decay is where we
now turn.

When was the Protestant Revolution?

When did the Protestant Revolution occur? The date
most commonly cited is 1517, the year Luther allegedly
pinned his thesis to the Wittenberg Cathedral. But this
raises certain difficulties in studying the appearances of
Protestantism. For one, Luther in 1517 was not yet
recognizably a Protestant. His protest against the abuses
of indulgences was largely just, and complained-of
abuses were abhorrent, more so to those Catholic who
believed in their propriety than those who came to
deride them in principle. Though called the father of the
Reformation, Luther's assaults on the Church were *ad
hoc* rather than systematic. And even if that great
songwriter's oeuvre could stand as a consistent and
meaningful intellectual impetus, we would blanch in

assigning it as a determinate date any more than we would take 1762, the year of *Le Contrat Social*, as the beginning of the French Revolution, or 1847 as the year of the Communist Revolution. A given work may lay the intellectual basis for a revolution, but a revolution itself is a result of a complex interplay of material events, not a mere matter of the mind. And thus even if Luther's ramshackle theology had been in other than an inchoate state in 1517, the year would be inappropriate for defining the start of the revolution.

Nor can Luther's rebellion be considered itself a completed revolution. A helpful comparison is of the Albigensian heresy of the Thirteenth Century, the proponents of which dominated the south of France and threatened to deform all of Christendom. The Albigensian promulgated beliefs easily recognized as what is called Manicheism, the notion that God's power of good is confronted and equaled by a positive force of evil. As we noted before, the Catholic did not recognize any positive nature to evil at all, instead seeing all travails on the earth as an absence of a complete and proper good. But the Manichee saw evil not as an absence but an independent demonic host, lodged against God in perpetual strife. The Albigensian in particular believed that the evil element was associated with the material side of reality, whereas the principle of good was entirely spiritual. The natural effect of this was to discourage the goods of the world, such as animal meat, spirits, and marriage, and which in a jumbled reaction allowed for the taking of concubines and the endorsement of suicide. The heretics entrenched their beliefs deep in the ruling classes. It was only through years of bloody war and the Dominicans' constant application that the

Albigensians were defeated. Their name is now all but forgotten.

Why, then, did Luther and his ilk succeed? It is beyond any dispute that the revolt occurred when the Church was primed for a fall: corpulent with wealth, and the worldliness of her churchmen notorious. A true *reform* was undoubtedly necessary, but the mad orgy of heresies, treasons, and apostacies that made up the *Reformation* functioned only to scar the world rather than remake the Church. No claims of novelty can serve as explanation, for there is no germane *protest* in all the huge mass of works whose essential points had not been broached, argued about, and defeated by council and doctor centuries prior.

We cannot live in a world untainted by Protestantism's stain, and so cannot parse out the world receptive to the heresies from the world that resulted from them. Suffice it to say that we find in the work of the Protestants the theological and philosophical justifications of mechanism and determinacy. Luther and Calvin lived in a world poised for technical break-through. Centuries of internal stability and the failure of the Crusades had turned wealth and ambition inwards, and allowed more consideration of the economic and material. The rise of capitalist production in the wealthier merchant states and the continued advance of tinkerers and empiricists stand before us now as dread omens of things to come, but in fact they were only signs of regular progress and not inflection points in the course of Western progress. It was in how these technical advances would be employed that would truly transform the West and begin in earnest the course of the Revolution, and such employment was dependent on the character of the people. And it was Luther and

Calvin who formed this character, who in their sundry disparagements of Catholic philosophy provided unlimited license to the rising class of mechanists who would replace the priest as the spiritual emblem of the West. The Protestant Revolution only really found completion when its particular creeds were tossed aside and its lasting effect, the moral dissolution of Christendom, could be exploited by men who had no use for creeds, or indeed for anything human in particular.

What is Protestantism?

What universal definition of Protestantism could we attempt here? Its unitive force is based entirely on its opposition to the juridical and spiritual authority of the Catholic Church. The length and breadth of this opposition varies with each sect, but the opposition is universal. Among that fifty-thousand sects, one finds similarities between them the way one finds similarities between men, likenesses of a particular eye or hair color, unities of height and race, and yet in the end all of them individuals, an array one can organize against the Church but who have no necessary relationship otherwise.

If any positive element can be assigned to Protestantism as a whole, it exists in being weighed against the doctrines of John Calvin, whose *Institutes of the Christian Religion* provide the most advanced and rigid of the dissident theologies. How much a particular creed drinks from the cup of Calvin's doctrine can be considered proof of its Protestant orthodoxy. Within the Anglican sect, for example, those most adhering to imitations of Catholic sacraments, called high churchmen, do not consider their creed a Protestant sect at all, but a branch of the Universal Church of which the Roman has an equal but separate part, while those tending towards Puritanism will identify the Anglican creed with the general reforms of Calvin and gladly call themselves Protestant. Yet even the work of Calvin is imperfect as a common thread, for where so many of the fifty-thousand sects have nothing to them besides sentiment and prejudice, the rigor and cruelty of Calvin's work can only tenuously adhere.

We have no endurance to enter into a close study of Calvin's teaching. It is sufficient to note its operative evils. The central distinction of Calvin's theology concerns God's foreknowledge of election, that is, which souls will go to Heaven and which will go to Hell. There is no debate among Christians that God has such knowledge: It arises from His omniscience and His existence outside time. God at any moment knows which men will reach salvation and which will meet hellfire. God likewise wills it to be this way: it follows as a result of His omnipotence, His power to determine everything across all of creation. Again, no Christian can seriously argue with these conclusions.

The controversy opened by Calvin stole its tenor from the Manichee. At essence it was a dispute between the powers of God's *permissive will*, or the toleration God endured to see man justly suffering for his chosen sins, and God's *active will*, which was His positive personal desire as effected through the order of reality. The Catholic maintained that God's will towards the damned was permissive: Because of the power of free will given to man, He would allow man to choose his damnation, and would tolerate this choice as a corollary gift of the free will God had provided from the beginning. God willed man to exist and be sustained from moment to moment, and God positively willed into being the outward material circumstances of man's life. But it was man alone who freely chose his own sin, and man alone who reaped the just consequence of his sin once committed. So God, through his permissive will, allowed.

The Calvinist could not find in God a force of univocal good. He did not, like the Manichee or the Albigensian, openly proclaim the parity or coexistence of good and evil as two separate and distinct forces. Instead, Calvin placed the forces of good and evil within the Godhead Himself. The Calvinist God was a god of two active and positive wills, one that willed the goods of creation such as any Christian could perceive, and the other that pursued evil for His glory. The Calvinist did not deny the testimony of Genesis that existence was *good*. But goodness itself was achieved through the active encouragement of evil on the theory that the damned, through their preordained example, played a necessary part in redeeming the saved. "I confess that all descendants of Adam fell by the Divine will," said the man, "and into that state of wretchedness in which they are now involved; and this is just what I said at the first, that we must always return to the mere pleasure of the divine will, the cause of which is hidden in himself. Therefore, some men are born devoted from the womb to certain death, that His name may be glorified in their destruction." [15] This cannot be confused with the operation of God's permissive will but a result of active conniving. "It ought not seem absurd when I say, that

---

[15] The *Institutes*, III, 23, 4.

God not only foresaw the fall of the first man, and in him the ruin of his posterity; but also at his own pleasure arranged it. For as it belongs to his wisdom to foreknow all future events, so it belongs to his power to rule and govern them by his hand."[16]

For Calvin, the faculty of free will had not truly been bequeathed to Adam or to his progeny. What evil befell him was not the result of his free choice, but of God's affirmative and active will. Evil thus took on the aspect not of an absence of some good, but a positive force itself—and how could it be otherwise, begotten from He who alone was Good, as was all His creation? But the makeup and tendency of this force was not often clear. To properly discern God's will now went beyond a study of the divine law, provided in Scripture and Tradition, or the Natural Law indited in the cosmos. Study fell to this dark and shadowy thing: God's Hidden Will, his latent promotion of evil throughout history. This Hidden Will, once acknowledged as theological principle, could not but consume all other considerations of the Godhead; it became the last recourse and seemingly the determinative power over all. In this sense we see the resurrection of the Manichees' controversy, for again positive forces of good and evil are pitted against each other. Yet unlike the Manichees, both good and evil forces reside within God himself, with the force of evil serving as a kind of hidden key behind all existence.

One might wish that Calvin had utterly destroyed the Christian God, that he succeeded as well as Mohammad and Lucifer had, or had enthroned a Kronos or Moloch in His stead. One wishes Calvin's God were truly bad, an honest villain, for we would then be free to thrust him

---

[16] Id. at 7.

aside. Yet this was not Calvin's Godhead; this god could not be escaped by leaving town walls or offering specious sacrifice on his altars. Calvin's God is universal, and so the world becomes a sanctuary of holy despair. Sacraments can benefit man nothing: the elect do not need them, and the damned can only waste or defile them. The cathedral spire that draws the eyes upward in hope must be toppled, for it spurs the damned to false hope and deprives the elect of their proper thoughts, which lay in their own sanctification. The tyrant, once he resolves to be hated and feared, has no honest use of emblems of false love.

True virtue cannot prosper in such an atmosphere. In the Calvinist mode, the hierarchy of Heaven is destroyed, and with it any notion of spiritual greatness. Heroic virtues are slurred across that primary distinction of *damned* and *elect*. The damned ware no longer cautionary tales like Judas and Dives, who by their evil wills deprived themselves of their proper place in the communion of saints. No, in the Calvinist world the damned are in their proper place. They suffered, and their spiritual rot provided the loam on which the sanctified grew. It was good they were damned: it was God's personal intent to make them so. The true glory of God and the good of mankind could not be achieved without this mass of the preterit, those sad wretches who were an eternal afterthought to Providence, that miserable class who had been luckier to be born without souls at all.

We spoke before of Bacon's support for regulating the evil of usury towards the public good. Calvin addresses the matter in like terms. "It could be wished that all usury and the name itself were first banished from the earth. But as this cannot be accomplished it should be seen what can be done for the public good."[17] Bacon's practicality was only Calvin's theology applied to the social sphere, and the logic of the politician and the divine were effectively the same: Since evil exists, and it is impossible to eradicate it, that evil should be regulated and culled to the common weal. We might question why a man who had so great a distrust in material wealth could even tolerate this vice; the sin of adultery has never been quashed and never will be, yet we see nothing to suggest Calvin would liberate the brothels on the same logic. The answer to this went to the new notions of social wealth. Usury was not only a bellwether of the changing moral attitude towards evil, but an active implement of the blessed princes and thieves who had drunk of Calvin's theology. For by heaven's sake it happened that the *hidden will* of God, so seemingly inscrutable, in fact might be known by the terrestrial amassing of riches. Where God possesses an evil will, one hidden from His explicit pronouncements or the Natural Law, and where a huge mass must be damned to let shine His goodness, Christian duty seemed to require some attempt to discern this hidden will, a means by which one could separate the goats and the sheep. The hidden will of Providence seemed most naturally to appear in the form of material wealth.

Capitalism and the Protestant Spirit.

Max Weber's claims about a Protestant work ethic, which have risen to the level of modern folklore, are not immediately apparent. Outwardly, there is not much of

---

[17] *De Usuris Responsum.*

the materialistic in Protestant theology, which in large part called for the smashing of icons and deprecation of the material form of the sacraments. But Calvin's project was never limited to his scholarship, and the fact that he had a significant role in a thieving operation was never really obscure. Where were the invocations of the Sixth Commandment against the organized thefts being conducted against Catholic property? The Reformation was simply, at its basest level, a process of thieving, and the princes who partook of the varying heresies were made richer than those who did not. Calvin's theology, for all its rigor, was no better or worse than any specious dogma an arch-thief might have dreamed to justify his crimes.

But in most practical terms, the Protestant Revolt was a necessary condition for later capitalist development. The land and lucre stolen through the course of the revolt provided the resources for the initial capital investments so necessary for the system to prosper. Likewise, the huge populations of people thrown off the ecclesial land created that unfortunate mass that would later be known as the proletariat, the large reserve army of labor that could be exploited without moral qualm. The exact working of this process is not relevant to us here. It is enough to note this fact in broadest terms: That industrialist capitalist development prospered where the Protestant revolt was most successful.

Weber does not concern himself with a broad history of capitalism. His concern is largely psychological, an inquiry into how the new attitude to wealth dovetailed with the new attitude of salvation. Weber places great emphasis on the concept of a *calling*. It is by one's calling that a man finds his place in the secular sphere, and it is by one's calling that man might faintly hear the song of election from Heaven. "The question, *Am I one of the elect?* must sooner or later have arisen for every believer and have forced all other interests into the background. And how can I be sure of this state of grace?"[18] Girded by asceticism, man set himself to task in fear and trembling to see if God would grant him sign of benefice.

By what fruits the Calvinist thought himself able to identify true faith? the answer is: by a type of Christian conduct which served to increase the glory of God. Just what does so serve is to be seen in his own will as revealed either directly through the Bible or indirectly through the purposeful order of the world which he has created. Especially by comparing the condition of one's own soul with that of the elect, for instance the patriarchs, according to the Bible, could the state of one's own grace be known. Only one of the elect really has the *fides efficax*, only he is able by virtue of his rebirth and the resulting sanctification of his whole life, to augment the glory of God by real, and not merely apparent, good works. However useless good works might be as a means of attaining salvation, nevertheless, they are indispensable as a sign of election. They are the technical means, not of purchasing salvation, but of getting rid of the fear of damnation. In this sense they are occasionally referred to as directly necessary for salvation is made conditional on them.[19]

---

[18] Weber p. 65 (Ch. 4(A))
[19] Id.

73

Outward proof of election became necessary for one to participate in the political community. "From that followed for the individual an incentive methodically to supervise his own state of grace in his own conduct, and thus to penetrate it with asceticism. The religious life of the saints, as distinguished from the natural life, was— the most important point—no longer lived outside the world in monastic communities, but within the world and its institutions. This rationalization of conduct within this world, but for the sake of the world beyond, was the consequence of the concept of calling of ascetic Protestantism."[20] If Mammon was not exactly divine in this framework, it clearly had the power of divining.

Weber concerns his study only with the positive aspect of the Protestant attitude towards wealth. But an obverse negative aspect must exist alongside it: the Protestant attitude towards the poor. If the wealthy are to be classed among the elect, it can only follow that poverty is a sign of damnation. If riches are a sign of God's preference, then poverty is a cold brunt statement about the spiritual gifts God chooses not to bestow. A pitiful irony must sicken one: That a movement arisen out of the slander that Catholics were *buying their way into Heaven* had now apotheosized and nearly deified the material—the Protestants had eradicated an *abuse* by making such practice a creed.

How simple this all is!—to unite the natural disgust of poverty with the throbbing desire for vengeance. Who can look upon the sallow and scarred face of the beggar and not recoil, or withhold a shudder at the tales

---

[20] Id. at D.

of saints kissing the leper's wounds? Disgust is too natural to a creature of strong senses and weak hearts, a feeling that can do nothing but defile man's humanity in the terrestrial world and dull his wisdom towards approaching the next. The new Protestant perspective was license for cruelty. It presaged a vile marriage, a new unity of the gut's revulsion with the hidden will of God. Nothing is more natural than to turn back upon the approach of the beggar, but the Catholic was forced by his creed to look upon this pitiful fellow and love him if only by grace, if only by acting above Nature—indeed in seeing *beyond* nature, into hearts as God saw them, to the souls and flesh that on the last day might be made perfect again.

Yet to the Calvinist there is no remedy of Grace. The terrible specter of the beggar was the same to man's native sight as he was to God's perfect wisdom. The wretchedness of the earth seemed no façade of the wounded cosmos, but wretched *per se*, at the deepest cores God had founded in them. As the unelect existed but to mollify and instruct the saved, so the poor existed only to be used by the rich. Why should they not be? What alternate role should they serve but to give their lives to some greater good, as God had given them souls to be incinerated only for the elects' edification?

We find in this transformation the first roots of the *mass*, that body which would form the material force of all modern political movements. Later generations would learn to wield this preterit mass as political materiel. "What signify a few lives lost in a century or two?" asked the noble Jefferson. "The tree of liberty must be refreshed from time to time with the blood of patriots and tyrants. It is their natural manure." Jefferson was neither a Calvinist nor a Christian, yet the very sentiment would have been alien and abhorrent and unutterable to the man of a united Christendom. *What signify a few lives?* To the old man they were everything, even more when illuminated by the heroism and justice of martyrdom. The Western mind in Jefferson's time had moved far onwards towards an instrumentalist view of man, but the initial step had been taken with Calvin's economizing of sanctity, and was the natural effect of the theology and practice of the First Revolution.

The Protestant Revolt in England

At its summit, Calvin's *Institutes* is barely recognizable as Christian. In practice it was spread like rags over the shame and wounds inflicted by a hateful ruling class, used in much the same way *Das Kapital* would be used by governments partaking of the communist form: One could adopt as much Calvinism as necessary to effect the desired thieving, and when the system could not bear the hard medicines of the theorist, it could be applied in halves and parts, however much necessary to protect the crime.

So it was in England, where the Calvinists were allowed to prosper so far as their zeal aligned with the underlying policy of the day, which was the lawful theft of Church property. For the Protestant Revolution in England was nothing but theft and subsequent coverup; its religious claims were made after the fact, and cannot be understood but as a secondary effect, and not an impetus. To understand the process as anything but theft is to be duped; it is to lack the faculties of perceiving cause and effect. A man can confront the true Protestants, Luther, Zwingli, Calvin and recognize in them the sparks of manly energy, even when defects of pride consume their souls. But the figures of the English Reformation are cads, men of little or no moral courage and of physical discipline even less. Their creeds rise rather as excuses than organic intellectual conceptions, red-handed sophistries and half-witted amalgamations.

It is always worth revisiting Henry's affair, for its critical points of contention are often elided, and its full import often drowned in bathos and the slippery logic Anglican supremacy encouraged. The first plain fact is that Henry was not seeking a divorce from Catherine of Aragon. His queen had previously been vowed to Henry's older brother, but he had died before the marriage could be consummated. Under Henry's specious theory, his marriage to Catherine was incestuous and illegitimate; an annulment, certifying Henry's claims, was in order. But Pope Clement could not agree. Catherine's previous union had been *ratum* but not *consummatum*, and as such was not a completed marriage. The prior annulment had been properly granted, and Catherine's marriage to Henry was firm and indivisible. Perhaps given the English domestic turmoil and the Lutheran treason abroad, the pontiff would have preferred to grant Henry his severance. But he did not and he could not. The pope lacked jurisdiction to contradict the vows of two laymen, those vows that stood higher than every earthly sovereign and Christ's own vicar on earth.

There is only one true guarantor of practical freedom: That no man attempt to place his powers above his right estate. And in his actions, Clement, weak and vacuous as he was, stood as one of the emblems of real liberty. For he, the most powerful man on earth, would not usurp power he did not have. Marriage as a sacrament everywhere stands as an example of the highest use of man's free will, the binding of oneself in perpetuity to the form of one's desire, just as God has bound reality to His. And with this troth the man's will became God's, and so deserving of His great protection. According to the version told by Henry and his attendant usurpers, the entire affair was one of an almighty usurping pope denying a king his rightful sovereignty. But the wonderful fact of the affair was the pope's impotency against the sacrament: the wills of a man and a woman, a covenant susceptible to no legislation and subservient to no miter or crown. Henry's usurpation, his claim of jurisdiction over vows freely made, was not of the pope's power but of God's. Henry struck at the institutional church when he could not strike God Himself.

There was much to be won in this terrestrial strife. The monasteries in England were inordinately rich, having served as refuge for wealth during the civil wars. Valid complaints might be made for the reform of these monasteries, though none could be proffered for their destruction. The tale of indulgences still provides a lazy basis for the Lutheran revolt, but Henry's specious claims of reform cannot be borne even by Protestant historians. However much they strayed from Benedictine rigor in practice, their contribution to social welfare has no parallel in the modern world. The monasteries provided rest for the weary vagabond, succor for the indigent wastrel, a generous landlord for the impecunious. They were a balm on a fallen race. Their ransacking was a disaster.

The Character of the Anglican

The English thieves were not native Calvinists; few men could be. Yet the Calvinist cause in England grew by necessity, a reaction to the theft and impoverishing of a great mass of their fellow men. The parasite class could not damn so many men to penury under the old Catholic view of mankind, while the Calvinist system provided the greatest justification for the theft ever conceived: The victims were unworthy, the unelect, the damned. Direct lines of descent form between the pilferers who enriched themselves on the Church theft and those who most fervently promoted the Calvinist creed, the name Cromwell foremost among them.

This explains the tincture of Calvinism in what became known as the Anglican church. The greatness of Anglicanism lay in its cowardice and incoherence: It was both Catholic and Calvinist, democratic and hierarchical, poetically accoutremented and philosophically squalid; a lily-livered heap which operates on one principle: That it will never oppose a Protestant king and it will always oppose the Pope. What the needs of the time demanded was all Anglicanism had to give.

The Anglican sect's one redeeming feature was its service of civil peace, and towards this its mechanism was simple: Toleration would prevail for Methodist and Puritan, Jew and Unitarian, for all creeds but the Catholic. The practical purpose of this is not obscure. The Jew, the Methodist, the Unitarian—they could pose no risk to the political state, no threat to the wicked distinction between elect and non-elect or the hallowing of Mammon called the *Protestant spirit*. Meanwhile, the Catholic still claimed possession of an ever-present miracle of the Incarnation which threatened to singe a hole in the otherwise seamless garment of the new superstructure, to expose as illegitimate what was so clearly illegitimate. It was the Incarnation that no heresiarch could tolerate, and so it was the Catholic Church he would always flay.

The Anglican sect is perhaps the most perfect *geist* of liberalism, the longest thread running across the centuries, a barometer of the liberal sensibility: Inconstant, unphilosophical, alogical, blatantly bought and sold, unzealous even in its zeal, an institution driven by no truth but human impetuosity. It was from compromise that the "Church of England sprang. In many respects, indeed, it has been well for her that, in an age of exuberant zeal, her principal founders were mere politicians."[21] So said one of its advocates, who could not help noting that from its earliest days it was a tool of realpolitik. In its craven moderation it played a more fundamental role than any other institution in shaping English character after the death of Cromwell. First and foremost, it recognized the Faith as the ideal tool for civil accord and popular appeal. Patriotism and civic duty were allowed a place above the old Catholic virtues of humility and piety. Outward manners in turn became synonymous with morality.

This is not to suggest that no Anglican could be found with an especial love for Christ, that the sect could not hold within its boundaries men striving for holiness. But a church inoculated against zeal could never hold out these men as exemplars. The ideal Anglican neither flayed himself for his imperfections nor succumbed to the infamy of vice. The perfect Anglican

---

[21] Macaulay's Essays, "Hallam"

was he who weighed his soul upon the collection plate, who bowed to the hum of current manners—no more than could be sought for as paragons by *mere politicians*. In their hands, the Faith became not an interaction between man and God, but a means of integration into social etiquette. So testifies one thoroughly acquainted with this character: "We find men possessed of many virtues, but proud, bashful, fastidious, and reserved. Their conscience has become a mere self-respect. When they do wrong, they feel, not contrition, of which God is the object, but remorse, and a sense of degradation. They call themselves fools, not sinners; they are angry and impatient, not humble. As to confession, which is so natural to the Catholic, to them it is impossible; unless indeed, in cases where they have been guilty, an apology is due to their own character, is expected of them, and will be satisfactory to look back upon."[22]

Who is this man described? Is it not the noble pagan—the man we read about in Plutarch as complete unto himself? This man is scarcely new, but his place in the order of creation assuredly is. For this man, however much he resembles the pagan, is not a stoic in an indifferent universe or a Faustian striver in a crepuscular reality, but a baptized Christian soul who placed himself in his own kind of Communion of Saints. The Anglian sect allowed the man who strove only for the pagan virtues to retain his place within the Christian eschatology. It gave the man lived by the principles of his own personal morality the ability to foist his own alleged goodness on the shoulders of a loving yet

---

[22] John Henry Newman, *The Scope and Nature of University Education*, "Philosophical Knowledge in Relation to Religion."

indiscriminate God. For no matter how egregious a particular heresy, no heresiarch ever sought to expel the attributes of benevolence and supreme charity the Catholic God displayed in jealously guarding His right worship.

So many of the great men Protestant England produced were essentially pagans. The ethos of Edmund Burke and Lord Chesterfield was little different from that of Cicero or Marcus Aurelius, or the vast number of pagan civil religionists who saw politick virtue as synonymous with sanctification. Their minds did not tend towards any supernatural light. Nonetheless they felt they could trust their acts and lives to the guidance of Benevolent Providence, though they had no use for grace, or the actual participation of the Divine in the actions of men. Meanwhile the worst men England produced were essentially trash, bound by the ethos of a lingering Calvinism that could not be exhumed with Cromwell's corpse: a huge mass allegedly forgotten by God as it had been betrayed by man. They were the ones who would be shoved into sweltering factories, and given the suffrage as a means to deform the state. And between these two was an acquisitive middle class, who judged their wealth as a sign of God's eventual eternal favor, when they could be bothered to think of their future state at all.

Tolerance and the Liberal

It was from this atmosphere that the positive principle of _tolerance_ arose. From this we do not mean practical acceptance of a vice or imperfection for the sake of avoiding some greater evil that might arise by quashing it; for it is inevitable that imperfections exist among us that cannot be realistically combatted, and that we endure only because we are impotent to practically change them. We mean by *tolerance* the acceptance of some vice or imperfection not as a necessary evil, but as a positive good, a sign of some higher virtue in diversity. The Anglican persuasion was the exemplar of this principle. A sect that could not fully decide whether it was Catholic or Calvinist had no choice but to tolerate diversity in worship; that same sect, to retain whatever goodwill and legitimacy it had, could not claim one faction was holier than the other. A loving God now stood by to support individual pride and prejudice, to assure man that in matters of worship and creed, what was personally right for him was in accord with the Divine Will, and thus the order of creation.

The adoption of tolerance as a positive principle could not be reconciled with the old faith. Christ had warned, "he that shall deny me before men, I will also deny him before my Father who is in heaven." He had told men that not a jot or tittle of the law would pass till all would be fulfilled. He had dictated most firmly and unequivocally that His followers must baptize all nations, and that those who did not partake of His body would not be saved. It could not be otherwise, for neither God nor the Church made localized claims, and to hold contrary would defile the omnipresent object of veneration. The pagan could be tolerant about his local gods because of their limited jurisdiction, but the God who made and sustains the universe could not accept but that His worship be universal.

It was for this that the Christian's evangelization was so fervent, and the accordant reason why his intolerance of heresy was so absolute. This jealousy was never explicable in material terms. To the Mohammedan, schism and heresy were closely tied to political power; the armies of Aisha and Ali fully explain the rise of the two sects of Islam which they birthed. But the ancient Christian, persecuted and pathetic as he was, had little material reason to guard his dogmas as strictly as he did. Political hatred is never a costless commodity; it is purchased and used at great price. And that such a hunted and meaningless flock of souls would dedicate such resources to the inessential is beyond what logic bears. Why did these fishers of men not cast a broader net?—these unlearned disciples so wise in philosophy and ontology and cosmology, yet stupid enough to make these superfluities essential to their communion?

But as we have already observed, all questions of philosophy to a Christian ultimately reduce to a matter of theology. A heresy to the Christian is not merely an intellectual error but a false icon, a deformation of beauty of the face of the cosmos. So it has ever been that those who posit a *Zeitgeist* and transforming World Soul cannot endure the Catholic position that Truth is as surely posited as a man's flesh, blood and soul. The liberal can set his intellect to the highest heavens and expatiate on them as long as he has breath, but he cannot acknowledge that the order of the cosmos is set, impermeable to any incessant theorizing—he cannot endure that the Logos is the furthest thing from an ever-changing spirit, but had in fact a face and mouth and spoke. The liberal cannot endure the *person* of Christ. As a theory, Christ is no threat: a spirit of the universal godhead no more significant than any a theorizer may propose. But the Catholic knew it was a person who made the cosmos, just as it was a person that must be worshipped and glorified. It was through His Incarnation that the rank theorizer was put to shame, that the order of God's justice was reified and protected, and which made absolute truth no more a matter of question than a man's physical existence could be.

"I esteem that tolerance to be the chief characteristic member of the true Church," proclaimed Locke, expressing the consensus of the entire humane Protestant world. As long as a man acted as he thought fit towards his Creator and put up with his neighbor practicing in a manner he saw fit, that man could be assured of finding pleasure before God. A notion once condemned as anathema by every knowing Christian was now held up as the highest encomium of the Faith.

No better instance could be provided of the new moral code supplanting the old. What modern principle is so lauded as that of toleration? It is synonymous with civilized life and enlightened taste. A longing for it is presumed to exist in the hearts of all honest men, and he who does not accept it stands like the feeble and brutish pagan worshiping his household gods against the Alpha and Omega. Who but a bigot can concern himself with every jot and tittle of the law when offered a comfortable and careless benevolence towards his neighbor? What apter sign is there of the evil of the old ways, the chains of sin that Luther had so beneficently cast off from the human race? The intolerance of the Catholic Church has always been recognized as the pressure point where the Revolutionist most concertedly directed his attack. At the Second Vatican Council, the Protestant, liberal, and Communist all sought the same decree from the Council Fathers, declaring the morality and positive goodness of religious freedom as a principle. They won—and the doctrine of tolerance was accepted by the Council to the applause of the entire civilized world. In close succession the moral legitimacy of the Church collapsed, and the last organized bastion of counterrevolution lost all relevancy to the world's conduct.

But this we will treat in its proper place. By the end of the wars of religion, Tolerance had conquered most dissident creeds. The individual Protestant still adhered to the tenets of his own beliefs, perhaps with such fervor as to give his life for it. At the same time, he looked upon his neighbor engaged in a radically different creed and practice and not only tolerated him as acceptable sacrifice to civil peace, but in fact declared that if the aberrant practice was sufficient for his neighbor, it must thereby be pleasing to his Creator. This was cognitive dissonance, a systemized irrationality disguised as the practice of Christian meekness and nicety. In truth, the man who accepted Tolerance as a principle no longer followed Christ as a He was, and not even Christ as his personal creed proclaimed Him to be. This man might struggle for his creed to the point of shedding blood, but he could not honestly proclaim that the God of his creed was the life and logic behind all things. In practice there was a god higher than that of his chosen creed, an unnamed god such as St. Paul had spoken of to the men of Athens.

That *Agnostos Theos* was the Revolution itself. It was the universal order unmoored from actual reality, the nebulous and progressive development of dogmas, the insane proffer that multiple contradictory truths can coexist and, along with this, the implicit existence of some nobler principle guiding the divine order. Any order of the cosmos was conceptually possible with this mindset. The root of this was not so much a false notion of Christ, as manifold heretics have promoted through the ages, as the notion once unendurable to every singular sect: That the exact nature of the Logos did not matter, nor did the manner in which He was to be acknowledged and worshipped. Those ancient pagans who had accepted chaos had presumed it could not be ordered, while those who accepted order had presumed that such order must have a form. Yet under the new theology chaos did not necessarily contradict order; a mishmash of truths could endure because a Supreme Truth watched over this flurry in benevolence. It was from this atmosphere that the universe would be filled with creeds and theories and ideologies which, however contradictory, could still posit they were guided by a benevolent god. It was in such an atmosphere that the ideologue could claim without blushing that his own system was indeed universal, and worthy of consideration amongst a catalogue of other universal systems. It was in this atmosphere that the liberal intellect found itself able to abjure a stolid belief in any particular order, all while relying on a belief in some higher Order which somehow remained. It was in this atmosphere that a divinized belief in *Progress* rose from the sludge, that some Order higher than logical order smiled upon creation, and blessed the chaos that was to come.

Modern Liberties

We now turn our attention to the principle of tolerance in a much smaller sphere, that of the fledgling liberal state. What we know as *liberal rights* have their genesis in this era; the revolts of 1688 and 1776 are both fruits of this new mode of being. These rights are not derived from the order of Nature or a given social form, but exist only on the basis of incoherent coexistence of differing principles. After the Protestant Revolt, the English constitution was a tottering thing, as incoherent and self-contradictory as her ruling sect; it aroused dreams of greatness in politicians whose only goal was to keep it standing aloft. But this could not be helped. Those rights which are won by theft, those rights possessed not by the bequeathal of Nature but by the usurpation of one class from another, can never settle into equilibrium. Every true right flows from the logic of thing, from the nature of the world as understood and rationalized by man. And where nature and logic are held to be immutable, those rights can be posited as eternal as the actual Law of Nature. The English Common Law had arisen on these premises, and stood as a blessing to the nation until the previous century, Christendom's most brilliant expression of the Natural Law, of principles arising out of right reason.

Yet the modern liberties of Englishman were not obtained by reasoning to natural right. They were the specious attempts to tilt the hand of state towards the Protestant thieves, who achieved permanent success in killing a king and thereafter would rule in gentler and specious form, though on the same regicidal principle. One could take Cromwell's crusade seriously or not, but there was nothing inconsistent in his proclamations of his own rights and the fact that he murdered a king, as many a fledgling aristocrat had done or dreamt to do. It was the men of the Restoration and who sought to establish as universal principles what Cromwell's brute force had won. But these new rights had a special character. They were the enshrinement of a political form that could never resolve itself in logical consistency. As a baseline fact, a monarch that served at the good graces of his Parliament was not really a monarch, for such a monarch has no rights but for those recognized by the true sovereign. Out of this inherent inconsistency all others rose.

Of course, no right can have a practical effect if not recognized by the powers that be. But the new conception of the monarch could not in principle hold against itself. The notion of sovereignty and self-rule that arose in 1688 set the king's rights as contingent on the will of Parliament. Any notions of justice and right based on the principles of 1688 could at best be *entitlements*, granted by the sovereign so long as that sovereign remained in power. They were not Natural Rights, as the defenders of the revolution often held, but could only exist so long as the powers that be desired to grant them. By their very nature such entitlements presumed a superior, some mediator to give order to how these entitlements could be granted. If the new battalion of rights was truly to be perpetual, it was only because the new sovereigns were presumed to rule forever.

To take only one sample of the compendium of rising entitlements so often confused with natural right: *Free speech* can only ever be an entitlement granted, not a right sustained on positive principle. So far as free speech can be lauded or even reasonably exist at all, it must be constrained and oriented towards one established goal. The allowance of free debate in Parliament is of this type, and even this was only an instrumental right rather than a moral one, a guard against the wrath of the king. No *absolute* right to free speech can ever be envisaged any more than the promotion of sedition can rise to the level of positive principle. As such, free speech can only ever be a relative right. Where the figment of absolute free speech is lauded, it is and always must be a means of the ruling power to attack its enemies: an intrinsically anarchic means to be wielded by inchoate powers against the establishment, or to bolster the conspiracy of those who have already toppled their foe. The ability to wield to one's advantage forces of the inherently anarchic is the modern sign of true sovereignty, the display that even where one does not possess the levers of government or the economic means of production, he nonetheless has the force of operative power on his side. The sovereign of a state is not necessarily he who possesses the institutions, but he who has the ability to dissolve them.

So were those primitive principles of Speech wielded by the oligarchs of England and their defenders. So it was with the matter of the Seven Bishops, where the fundamental laws of libel could be perverted so as to meet the specious demands of those preaching treason. We might rehearse other principles of 1688, so similarly askew, but to parse the components is but to note a corruption in part of what is corrupt in the whole: that the English constitution, as it was now so set, could never reach true equilibrium. Further dethronements could only be stalled by the perpetual complaisance of the king and the total supremacy of Parliament, and further Revolution could only be stalled by the perpetual enshrinement of the oligarchs in their power. Whenever the specter of the royal prerogative rose its head, the parables of rebellion become the principles of the conservative and, later on, the colonial. But this was an unstable thing, one that must inevitably fall towards either anarchy or tyranny—or perhaps both. Only men of genius like Burke could aspire to keep it upright at all.

Burke and the Englishman

It is sad fault, though perhaps a Providential one, that the lovers of modern republicanism place such special interest on the crises and death of the Roman republic. Men of supposedly sure principle admire and adore Cato the Younger for his stalwartness, and Cicero for his wisdom. But such admiration suggests more than such tribute intends. Cicero's sagacity was spurred by his witness to a tottering government, and his particular genius is recognized largely because it was essential to making the Republic seem to be a salvageable thing, which of course it was not. He was of that class of men who stood up for personal principle and failed, and who should come to us as cautionary examples just as much as moral ones.

The character of Edmund Burke, if considered rightly, must be placed in a similar role, a true Parallel Life between the Classical Age and Christendom. Born of an Irish father who apostatized in order to practice law, Burke embraced Christianity but in the mode of the polite Anglican, as a tenet of civil peace, as creed worth little more than poesy in capturing the mind and heart. One might blind oneself looking for a passage of Burke's that exalts Christianity for more than its bare moral prescriptions, as a sign of faith that glows with the tenderness of the Christ child in his bed or sorrows beneath the torrent of a pierced heart on the cross. He was not above the specious use of Natural Law when it served him against his enemies, most notably in the scurrilous Hastings affair, but he could never let it take him too far lest it stand in judgment of his existing ideal state. That ideal state, that exemplar that so possessed his prejudices, was that uncanny disequilibrium called the English constitution: that means to keep a feckless king on the throne and the oligarchs in power. As such, he seemed never to lose an opportunity to pull up the king's glory while starving him of power, or to pass off prejudice as a principle because prejudice was really the only principle he had.

The man whose virtues and faults formed and have ever accompanied the conservative movement was at heart an atheist. He loved Christianity for its fruits, but like all liberals disdained that Christ had ever lived. In the end, he was so terrified of the material aspect of his own death that he would not allow the site of his grave be disclosed lest a Jacobin desecrate his corpse.[23] He held himself out as a martyr against his enemies, happily writing himself off as a patsy trembling at the Jacobin mob before him, yet he could not face the possible indignity that might occur to a vessel that could no longer do him any good. The fatuity and cowardice of all conservatives is written in this last will and testament.

There is no innate virtue in fighting for a lost cause. But the entire premise of Burke's conservatism was that defeat could be noble and martyrdom honorable even when the cause was nothing but one's own prejudices. This kind of inversion of values which so well characterizes the propulsion of conservatism, could

---

[23] Russell Kirk, *Edmund Burke: A Genius Reconsidered*.

92

only be lauded on the basis of the First Revolution's vaunted tolerance; that the conservative's bathetic messianism, maintained on the basis of prejudice beautifully possessed, possessed any moral weight whatsoever. Burke's eyes could not really be turned to the Heavens, he who used the Faith only for the maintenance of secular comfort. And he could decry the effects of the Second Revolution but not really understand them, because he did not really understand the effects the First Revolution had had on his nation or on himself.

Westphalia

What was true within nations prevailed between them. In Germany, the power stolen from Rome was placed in the hands of local kings and princes. Lutheran moralists quivered yet to depart too far from their Roman guides, and the moral law varied little across borders—usury being the notable exception. And yet the order of things was profoundly and deeply changed. Europe had become a continent much as it had been under the Roman Empire, with every town possessing its own God, though nominally He was the same in all. What changed as man passed from state to state was man's relationship to Him. In one state he was a creature that might achieve spiritual greatness, while across the border he found himself Luther's thing, for whom achieving good was impossible and the moral law was designed only to make man despair.

Westphalia accepted this multiplicity of man's existence as a principle. Tolerance between states meant that man's very nature was, as a premise of international and natural law, always in flux.[24] As the holy fire of the Thirty Years War faded, even the Catholic powers were forced to accept the new reality. Though they held the old Faith and its venerable conception of man, it was the new state that would prevail, one with an implied power to define the essence of God and man, and to rewrite the moral code to the sovereign's liking. Men like Richelieu and Louis the Fourteenth could not scoff at such a premise.

It was with the Treaty of Westphalia that the forces of the First Revolution were definitively victorious. What may have ended as a reconquest for Christendom, as a mere chapter in the book of heresies alongside the Cathars and Arians, now stood as a fetid and extant thing with which all world history must ail. It was with Westphalia that the principles of the First Revolution could no longer curtailed or driven back, when it was clear that the stolen monasteries would never be recovered, when the ransacked churches and defiled altars would never be restored, when the moral consensus forged through the previous millennium would never be resurrected. This was the moment of Protestant victory, the definitive and decisive first step in Modernity's long walk through our culture. The disputes between princes and popes of the Middle Ages cannot provide us with this starting-point, for disputes between powers are perpetual, and must be—what concerns us is when those disputes can no longer be mitigated, when the legitimacy of one side's existence is no longer accepted, and therefore their pleas for justice can be

---

[24] Blackstone's *Commentaries* Book II; *quod naturalis ratio inter omnes homines constituit, vocatur jus gentium*

ignored. For all the supposed worldliness of that Greek-worship miscalled a Renaissance, there was nothing irreversible in its excesses and much to be adored in its excellencies. That Luther himself saw his work as a palliative to the era only highlights how obvious was the need for a reaction, and how plentiful history is in supplying them. And for all the homage paid to what are called the principles of Machiavelli, a mere book could not enshrine new principles of bastardy against the Christian standard. Vice is omnipresent, but so is the law in man's heart. As such, the operative question regarding any moral transformation can never be the existence of vice itself, but how such vice somehow won moral favor.

No, the Protestant revolt was the genuine break in human history, the poisoning of the streams that watered Christendom and a perversion of natural development. Only the principle of toleration could inaugurate the belief that a king possesses a kind of absolute moral sovereignty, the ability to implicitly or explicitly remake the moral gestalt of his state. Only Calvin could actually do the work of etching into Christian moral code the principle that the strong would do as they will, and the weak must suffer as they must. It was only by the deformation of Christianity that Christian principles could be weakened, and later usurped and overthrown.

Treatise on Liberal Christianity

What was the Protestant Revolution? It was Christendom's destruction won at the moment of its final triumph. For with their usurpation, the Protestant

revolters proved the obsolescence of the pagan
worldview. The Reformation had been wholly between
Christians on Christian terms, one assuredly infected by
heresy but otherwise bereft of any recourse to the old
demon gods. The Protestant usurper spent no time
looking to the age before Bethlehem, but gazed ever
aloft to where the Spirit was taking him, to a new
Pentecost and sanctification.

Yet victory over the pagan was bought at great cost
For it was to the pagan world that the ancient Christian
appealed in his evangelization, and the pagan world
which the early Christian disciples converted. It was by
God's ordering and to the Christian's immortal
advantage that the Roman pagan stood as the height and
consummation of the world without God. The Roman's
gods were the incarnations of the wickedness and glories
of existence, and he was through them exposed to this
world's malignancy and enthralled by its joys. He strove
for virtue haphazardly, and did not abjure the testaments
of his senses, though he felt the shadow lurking behind
them, and felt dimly at times the Light shining above
him. It was a world that could bode no contradiction,
and therefore could scarcely accept an almighty God
murdered wretchedly on a cross, or that miracles might
be an act of goodness rather than the conjuring of
demons and the invidious playacting of magi. But the
noble pagan was nonetheless at home in creation, as far
as he could be at home without knowing its Creator.

It was in this aspect that the pagans found an ally in
the new Christians. For the Catholic loved creation. He
knew that while Mammon would corrupt him, the
apparent goods of the world were actually *good*. In fact,
the Catholic believed that material was better than the

materialists could ever conceive of it. He witnessed a baptism and proclaimed that the liquid element most necessary to his body was just as needful to his soul. He took up bread and wine, without which not even the rudest civilization could endure, and declared them worthy homes for the physical and spiritual presence of the Son of God. The Catholic proposed that all of the true joys of the pagan world be retained: feasts would continue, now held for God and His saints, while the pomp and ceremony of the emperors would be heightened by recognition of its imitation of the celestial court, presided over by Christ the King. Even the marital act, so often the blunder and oppression of man, was raised by Christ to the integral testament of a sacrament, one that divinized the very propagation of the world. The pagan world was transformed, completed, raised but not replaced: its excesses trimmed, its demons exorcized and driven out of the temples wherein a mightier God would now dwell. This was the beauty and promise of the material, and the sacramental nature of worship: The corporeal spiritualized, and so more heartily embraced.

The ancient evangelist had proposed his arguments to the man of good will: he presumed he was talking to what Diedrich von Hildebrand called the Classical Man, "the spiritually healthy man, the man who stands in full primal relation to spheres of life, who knows the world in its true dimensions, whose response to values possesses inner plenitude, and is heroically unconditional."[25] The Classical Man acknowledges the greatness and culpability of his own soul, and his ability to act freely according to his soul's desires. His actions

---

[25] *Liturgy and Personality.*

and beliefs are affected by the social context he finds himself in, but he knows his mind and soul exist independently of these. The recognition of one's independent selfhood and completeness is critical, for only when we recognize the distinct nature of our own selfhood can we fully engage with other beings and ultimately engage with Being Himself. The evangelist presumed he was appealing to such a man as this, a man reactive to his own soul, that soul which on Judgment Day would stand alone.

Our Lord, in speaking of the road to salvation, addressed the individual. For the Church's extraordinary moral precepts, those that expose and resolve the deficiencies of existence, are nothing if not applied against the individual. His teachings presume to be dealing with individual men with individual proclivities and desires. This does not mean the law was not meant to be applied on a societal basis. The Ten Commandments clearly were, as were the other elements of Hebrew law. Yet man could not be saved by simple adherence to this law; it did not alone make him *good*, it only left him in a state that might be saved. The Ten Commandments recognized the foundations of natural justice, but they could not raise man to the supernatural heights he was destined for. For it is only through the working of grace that man becomes truly blessed. The Beatitudes for that reason are not commands, but are rather descriptions, aspirations for the man who lives his life in grace, risen above the natural plane. To abide by the Ten Commandments was required of civil virtue, but to achieve the beatitudes is to be worthy of the heavenly city.

It is the doctrine of grace which surpasses in every way the old pagan morality. It is by and for grace that the Christian is expected to suffer, not only against the unjust but even against the just: expected to wither under insult, to forgive trespasses, to turn the other cheek. It is in these things that man submits to Divinity and thereby becomes divine. It is in these things that infidels declare the Christian religion to be inhuman—a charge the Christian can only partly deny, if the *human* is all there is. But the Christian's task is to rise above human pomp and artifice, to see water and recognize it as spiritual water, to consume bread and recognize it as Godly food: to see the sacral order behind all being, and to know that on the last day our sickly and weak bodies will be glorified and made eternal, just as all being was meant for.

But Our Lord's adjurations to blessedness were not general laws. They pertained to the individual alone. Our Lord's admonition to lay aside both cloak and coat was a personal plea directed towards selflessness, individual sanctity, and an understanding of the transitory nature of material goods: Applied on a society-wide scale, that is, taken as a commandment, the admonition is a demand for socialism, and the abjuration of even a moral claim to the rights of property. Our Lord's cry to turn the other cheek is a personal admonition to show mercy, mercy which is only meaningful if man possesses a natural proclivity, desire, and innate need for just retribution; on a society-wide scale, this is a call for pacifism necessarily verging into anarchy, an abjuration of all legal rights, a negation of all law and, as a natural consequence, a call for the acceptance of rape, murder, and pillage as a matter of course. Sin neither paid for nor punished is subject to no law, and ensures that injustice becomes more free than justice, and the basis of Godly order is abjured.[26] Such moral nihilism cannot be reconciled with the Commandments, and no one can accept such a position without sin, without enabling and tacitly justifying it.

Such is the difference between the commandments prescribed by Nature and the supernatural ideals impossible but for grace. The latter cannot be achieved in a man who does not first accept the former, for grace is the perfection of nature, not its supplantation. In like way, Christian doctrine presumes and perfects the classical man: presumes in the sense that doctrine presupposes it is dealing with a creature prone to all the strengths and weaknesses which we encounter in pagan literature—the pettiness, jealously, greed, pride, honor, self-love; perfects, because doctrine moderates man's strengths and diminishes his weaknesses, and exposes to him the true celestial plane on which he is waging his earthly battles.

Nature is perfected through grace, and grace presumes Nature. Yet following the Protestant Revolt we find again and again men who understand themselves as talking to a society of the elect, of men already saved by grace, men who have presumptively overcome nature, and are saved apart from strict adherence to the commandments. "The Law and the Gospel are two contrary things which cannot be in harmony with one another," Luther had proclaimed. "The Law points out what man has to do, whereas the Gospel unfolds the gifts God is willing to confer on man. The former we

---

[26] St. Anselm, *Why God Became Man* I-12

cannot observe; the latter we receive and apprehend by faith."[27]

Already in Luther's writings we find a growing contradiction between Nature, reflected in the Law, and grace found in the Gospel. To a member of the elect, that man who was presumptively saved, all that mattered was the speaking of the Gospel. And so to the presumptively saved man and to the *a priori* saved people, the Beatitudes served not as adjurations to holiness, but positive prescriptions that supplanted the Old Law. These were men entitled to the merits of this grace without the extraordinary virtue the Catholic understood as prerequisite. Now grace was cheap, and heavenly blessing presumed among the entire host of the presumptive elect; such are the workings of Our Lord's words when addressed to the self-proclaimed saints as versus a world of sinners.

A revolution in morality had occurred, howevermuch explicit moral tenets appeared the same. In old legal terms, the courts of equity had overtaken the courts of law. In the judicial system, mercy is replaced by statutory lenience; in the economic sphere, alms-giving is replaced by socialism; in the domestic sphere, chivalry is transformed into feminism. All such sacrifices presume a departure from the rule of nature and justice—this is precisely why, on an individual level, they are acts of especial charity. But to impose them on a society-wide basis foists a kind of exterior Christian revolution on the social body, and obviates the need for personal struggle and transformation in such a way that true Christian sacrifice is unnecessary or impossible. Such changes presume weakness rather than strength as the rule: they

---

[27] Luther, Tisch. I.C. 12 S17

presume, paradoxically, that man's soul is too feeble to offer real sacrifice, but that his backbone is strong enough to bear the brunt of the tyrannical government that must arise from the inversion of justice; they presume that man is so deeply bad that personal transformation is vain, and yet that the universe full of such men is not a cruel and hostile one which we must fight and tame, but one which has a kind of benevolence written into its fabric if we will only craft social programs to realize it.

This is the kind of thinking aptly called *slave morality*. Nietzsche, that son of a Lutheran pastor, did not understand the inherently masculine quality of Christian sacrifice, but he well understood liberal Christianity which, by denying any inner life in man and looking only upon the outward meekness and servility of Christian teaching, raises weakness into a virtue in itself. Those apparent concessions to weakness—turning the other cheek, comforting the destitute, recognizing the frailty of human intellect—are not meant to make us worship weakness, but to position ourselves rightly in the hierarchy of values, rightly before the God, *Agios ischyros*, from whom all our terrestrial strength comes. These shows of humility are not meant to have us deprecate the hierarchy of being. On the contrary, one's obedience is meant to acknowledge this hierarchy, and that it is a hierarchy greater than the earthbound fool can see. The strength embodied in turning the other cheek arises from accepting humiliation on the terrestrial plane in order to recognize the more excellent greatness of the spiritual. There is no virtue, anywhere in the universe, to weakness per se. The masochist freak engages in no virtuous act when turns the other cheek; only the man who recognizes the hierarchy of Nature can shine with any virtue when suffering abasement, when he affirms in his acceptance that this hierarchy extends from the dust beneath his feet upwards to the heavenly hosts. The strength in turning the other cheek comes from submitting ourselves to the will of God, who is higher and stronger than any of our tormentors.

The modern world is overrun with phony grace. It is grace whose effects are always inhuman, for it can never be wise or just to require a man to achieve divinity before he be governable. Yet this is the operation of the regime of modern rights and entitlements, whose adoption would be intolerable but that Western men had already been acclimated for such constant insult, such demeaning and detestable subjugation, impressed into thinking that this base servility was a *Christian* thing— this perversion of hierarchy and Nature by fraudulent grace. From this inversion arises all the errors of ideology, which is always a kind of regimented socialized morality. Hence the specious tone adopted often unwittingly by those who do not believe a jot of the Christian creed, yet whose program could not arise or endure if not for this inversion of Christian belief. The revolutionist will always revert to pseudo-Christian banality towards the moderates, those unconvinced of the full zeal and dogma of the forefront demagogues, yet whose sentimentality cannot let them to abjure this new working of the age's holy ghost.

The hierarchy of the universe is made by God, and His law is nothing but a rational response to the order He has created. The Protestant inverter takes advantage of a paradox, one that arises in the fact that a saint has less practical need for the law than the sinner. For grace often carries such a holy man over difficulties which the sinner must wage perpetual war against, and in his blessed state is able to transcend the law, to live and fulfil its entire spirit and not merely its outward forms. So we find in the holiest of saints men and women who have seemed to abjure the claims of justice altogether, as they in their sanctity and gifts of grace easily could.

And we return to that problem we cited before: Where does this leave men who presume themselves to be saints, who take their election as a point established? What need has this man for the rigor of the law? For that matter, why must a host of the elect engage in commerce on the same terms as those unleavened by grace—why bother to impose any law on the commerce of saints? All revolutionary idiocy arises out of such questions, on the assumption that the Old Law and the tenets of the Old Regime are not necessary for the New Man. The implications of the Lutheran revolution were no different, and amply clear to those who wished to pursue them. "There are to be no serfs because Christ has liberated us all" said the revolting peasants' manifesto, that bastard child that Luther could not bear to legitimate. But why should the old hierarchies hold? Why should these men, presumably saved by grace, presumably risen above Nature, not abjure the old laws of serfdom, enlivened by the new spirit as they were? These questions the Protestant could not easily answer, at least not without reference to the hidden will of Mammon, which of course was waiting to be revealed by whomever willed for its power.

The Protestant Revolution had transformed the world from a universe of strength to a universe of weakness. The hierarchies from priest to bishop to pope and thus unto Christ were struck down. This hierarchy of strength was in ruins, and in its midst stood God alone. And who was He? He was a lawgiver, assuredly. But that His laws arose from His creation was no longer so clear. For the law exists only to make men despair, Luther claimed, and so to drive men to the Gospel. Nor was it clear that He was a jealous God, for in fact under Protestant rule He could tolerate any fable told about Him so long as it lent weight to no papist hierarch. Why should not the dregs revolt under the standards of anarchy? Why should the Law apply to those who were saved? Why should the Old Order be respected when all men were priests?

The inversion of values harped upon by Nietzsche are those that rearrange the order of justice and mercy. They are not Christianity's values in a broad sense, they are the Lutherans' abjuration of saintly heroism and the Calvinist rejection of divine matter. Christ took man as he was. He said that through struggle and perseverance, against enemies internal and external, he could partake of God's glory. The Catholic creed took upon itself the literal deification of matter, of the apotheosis of taste and touch. It glorified the sensible and raised up the natural, and never thought to abjure either. No, Nietzsche did not know the old Faith, the Faith of the Incarnation, the Faith that carried the hierarchies of the world into the celestial sphere, that established freedom as a principle of Divine Love. The rule of the universe is strength. We adore Christ because He made Himself weak who was Strength itself. There is no feat of virtue in all the universe that does not require strength, and the greater the strength, the greater the virtue, and the greater the standard to be won. And if strength have no merit over weakness, if all honor be akin to degradation, then Our Lord's sacrifice was no sacrifice at all, and a gesture bereft of all meaning. For a Christian to propose a universe without hierarchy, without virtuous strength, is to deny the central act of his very redemption, to make the entire thing incoherent.

Nietzsche squawks—"The Church combats passion by means of excision of all kinds: its practice, its 'remedy,' is castration. It never inquires 'how can a desire be spiritualized, beautified, deified?'—In all ages it has laid the weight of discipline in the process of extirpation (the extirpation of sensuality, pride, lust of dominion, lust of property, and revenge).—But to attack the passions at their roots, means attacking life itself at its source: the method of the Church is hostile to life." Hence he could conclude *morality is the enemy of nature.* "The saint in whom God is well pleased, is the ideal eunuch. Life terminates where the *Kingdom of God* begins."[28]

Refutation of this is hardly necessary. That Christ had raised the marital act to a sacrament and in vows trothed *with my body I thee worship* provides immunity against all such banal complaints. That thing of Nietzsche's inveighing, that *inversion of values* was a Protestant thing, not an innately Christian one. It was a liberal thing, one that worshipped weakness, castrated the passions, whitewashed the beautiful, raised up the banal, and succeeded in uprooting reverence for the law of Nature's God; it was a thing which established as rule that a man could walk outside the natural hierarchy so long as he assured himself he was a child of grace. However much the Western Revolutionist has fallen

---

[28] *Twilight of the Idols*, "Morality as the Enemy of Nature," 4

away from theism, this primary and primordial characteristic has ever been retained: this confidence in unearned grace, the result of which is the abjuration of the Natural Law. Nietzsche was a damaged man, striving in vain to reestablish a value system in an age of moral and industrial chaos. He could not understand the Faith, but he knew the oppression rising against all men of high spirit and strong will. "Liberal institutions straightway cease from being liberal, the moment they are soundly established: once this is attained no more grievous and more thorough enemies of freedom exist than liberal institutions! One knows, of course, what they bring about: they undermine the Will to Power, they are the levelling of mountain and valley exalted to a morality, they make people small, cowardly and pleasure-loving,—by means of them the gregarious animal invariably triumphs. Liberalism: in other words, herd-animalization."[29]

Nietzsche wrote of the bourgeois of his time, but his complaints cut as sharp and deep against the Revolution in all its courses, including the First, whose perverse characteristics against the Faith he could not discern. The Revolutionist has always warred against freedom and against the will. The Revolutionist along with the Catholic conceded that error entered the cosmos by the abuse of free will. The difference between them lay in response to the dilemma. To the Catholic, free will was an indescribable gift, proof of the highest participation in the glory of creation and the medium for his own salvation. But to the Revolutionist free will is a blight; rather than hone and cultivate this source of disorder, he seeks to root it out entirely, and to remake the cosmos in

---

[29] *Twilight of the Idols* 38

such a way that he cannot be harmed by its abuse. Such is the marriage between the hatred of liberty and adulation of false order. Calvinist, Jacobin, and Bolshevik saw the ugliness of defiled order and proposed that not the error but the capacity to err be excised from their models of the world: They saw the faulty hand that had marred the portrait and declared the hand must not be corrected, but lopped off.

Conclusion: Liberalism as an Attack on the Incarnation

We earlier asked if any motive force could be assigned to the Revolution—a question we evaded by describing the process of liberal change. But in analyzing the mechanism of change and looking at its history, we come across the answer to our question. For all its changes, all its inconsistencies and incoherence, the Revolution as a force must always be opposed to the Catholic notion of the Incarnation of Christ and the continued assertion of the Incarnation in the Eucharist and the mass. The Protestant revolt succeeded as the first proto-liberal revolution precisely because it remade the mind and soul of Christian man into one that accepted a fungible and indeterminate nature of God, and a new position for men in the world classed either amongst the intractably elect and damned. Liberalism has long since relinquished explicitly Protestant theology as a means for promoting itself, but the Protestant attack on the Eucharist has always been part and parcel with the Revolution, and is intrinsic to it.

This may strike the reader as too convenient, a recourse again to easy nostalgia. In the Western world, there is no institution like the Catholic Church which, aside from the truthfulness of the claims she makes, has maintained her values so consistently throughout the centuries. If liberalism is inherently a tendency to change, then its antipode must be that institution which is changeless, and the Church emerges as its opposite by default. Yet it was not mere circumstance which resulted in this duel: The Catholic Church makes claims about God and man which are more fundamentally opposed to liberal change than any blind adherence to tradition. These claims are embodied in the Incarnation of Christ, and the central practice of this truth is the continued reenactment of this in the mass.

We will not loom on the religious claims made by the Church about the Incarnation and the Eucharist, though of course they are true. We mean only to state the logical consequences that must result from a belief in the Incarnation, whether we take the event as historical fact or not. The Incarnation grounds, firstly, the notion of an immutable, omnipotent, single God. By asserting that the Word was made flesh, man is no longer allowed the creation of new gods. God is not localized, and one town's god cannot be said to have superiority over another's. There is no development of God as we see in Hegel's notion of the Zeitgeist, and there can exist in concept no great divisions about His nature or the nature of His works, as we see in the embarrassment of Protestant sects. God is the Word, but in being made flesh, He is not merely an idea capable of being expanded and contorted to meet the desires of the age, but a single essence, *et nunc, et in saecula saeculorum.*

Secondly, the Incarnation grounded the nature of man. It both raised the possibility of the divinization of the flesh and stated that an individual man was valuable without relation to any exterior circumstance. These huge, unproveable, and seemingly preposterous claims required a project of man's betterment, one not arising out of any innate bosom feeling but of divine necessity. In twenty centuries of Christian practice we have become acclimated to treating benevolence as somehow natural to man, but in unloosing our notion of manhood from the divine, we find there is no inherent reason to treat other men well. The only reason for man to do anything is for the service of his own interest. Charity arises when we adjust our understanding of what those interests are. If other men are nothing but flesh, there is no reason for us not to use them self-servingly; in fact, it is the height of foolishness to do otherwise. And while there can be a détente from time to time arisen out of reciprocity, there can never be any lasting charity when our neighbor is but a means to a material end. The Incarnation posits that every individual soul is unique, and our flesh is not an indistinct part of a mass or some limb which can be amputated for the good of the whole but rather, in a lesser form, holds the same importance as Christ's flesh held: the carrier of a thing great and immortal.

It is incredibly easy to see why these facts should be not only distasteful but despicable to those with worldly power. And accordingly, heresies generally rise out of a powerful class attempting to weaken the doctrines of the Incarnation. The Arian heresy, which proposed Christ was a creature of God rather than the Divinity itself, understandably dominated in the ranks of the Roman army, that which had controlled the empire for centuries on no basis of legitimacy but brute force. If Christ was merely a great man, raised through his acts to divinity by some higher godhead, he was no different from Julius or Augustus—or Tiberius and Claudius, for that matter. But if the claims of the orthodox were true, and Christ was divine apart from His great actions and words, and men had the power to be sons of God solely by receiving Him, the entire basis of the legions' legitimacy was threatened. The bare exercise of authority could no longer suffice as reason to rule—and in the Christian era, it never has.

For all intents and purposes, the conception of God and man as required by the Incarnation is humanly impossible: Man will always be anxious to change the nature of truth to conform to his selfish desires, and he will always be anxious to use his fellow men as wantonly as his desires dictate. The Church's greatest weapon in fighting this tendency has been and always will be the Eucharist. In practice, reception of the Eucharist requires constant assent to the dogmas and moral code of the Church, which is in itself a great protector of orthodoxy. Yet the very existence of the Eucharist is as critical as the obligations it imposes. It stands against the Protestant notion that the completeness of Christ's sacrifice on Calvary rendered the rest of time essentially superfluous, and man's striving in that period equally vain. It is an affront to the Calvinist notion of foreknown election, for if not all men have the capability to receive the Eucharist, then Christ was a liar in claiming to have come to be received by the entire human race. And it is a guard against the tendency to turn Christianity into nothing but a philosophy, for there is no better guard against thinking God is a mere idea that His physical presence in worship. The unity of Christian will and action is found in the Eucharist, just as is found the unity of Christ's divinity and manhood.

This is why Christ left mankind the Eucharist: this is why it cannot be attacked without eventually destroying Christianity as a whole.

The Protestant Revolt was everywhere an attack on the Real Presence, and with it the Incarnation. The natural outgrowth of this was the liberal Christianity we described above, the unenunciated creed of most modern sects, including what are called Modernists within the Catholic Church, and from which the entire liberal mindset springs, even among the putative atheists. We see this in its embrace of weakness as a virtue, its inversion of objective order, thereby comprising the psychology of the liberal and his practical philosophy. Liberalism is a Christian heresy—from the Protestant Revolution onwards, man has suffered beneath this storm of ideological chaos. The human race has been worse than a stranger to itself.

We will follow the Revolution in its later stages, but the attack on the Incarnation remains implicit throughout. An ordered hierarchy of Nature cannot be had, and the Revolutionist finds order only through the toys of the intellect, just as the Lutheran deigned to find God only through spirit and not the lowly matter of the sacraments. Where the personhood of Christ could be denied so could the solidity of Nature, all without falling back to the chaos of the pagans, the pessimism of the stoics, or the waywardness of the savage. What better proof could be offered that liberalism is a heresy than this? That a loving god has always looked over the Revolutionary order, however inconsistently this might track with the revolutionary mantra of the day, however much this god in Molochean fury demands the blood of his followers in expiation.

Hence why the Revolution is universal, one, and total,[30] because it is a shadow image of a God that is universal, one, and almighty. However much the Revolutionist may usurp elements of the old pagan world, it is not fundamentally pagan; it is a movement born out of the Catholic religion, not the instauration of Baal. Its purpose is not to erect singular temples but to reform the God of Nature, the Logos. Any attempt to call it a pagan thing is incomplete. It would be a blessing were the Revolution localized, a deified thug or a town's beneficent demon. No modern religion based on paganism can oppose Christianity; it does not have the power, to be *part* and wage war against *all*. Nor does the Revolution conceive of itself as anything but the new Godhead.

The Reformers' claims that they had forged a direct connection between God and man is the first of the many primary falsehoods told by the forces of the Revolution. Under the Protestant system, man's connection to God was tenuous, unstable, obscure, and insecure. The Catholic God willed at every moment the personal salvation of each human soul, and at each moment gave man the power and the grace to achieve this. To the Protestant this channel was foreclosed to all but the few elect: the damned did not factor. For a majority of the human race there was no inner grace or possibility of its acquirement. The entirety of the spiritual order was seemingly arbitrary, founded in cruel chaos.

The French Revolution made each man a featureless citizen, a mere grain of mammalian matter in the all-

---

[30] Plinio Corrêa de Oliveira, *Revolution and Counterrevolution*, Ch. III.

consuming mass; the Industrial revolutions made man a homogenous productive unit in the vast machine of the economy; the modern revolutions deny man even his animal and physical characteristics, leaving him in appearances uninhabited husk of flesh, at other times an incorporeal spirit that can choose its own sex, race, and species. Yet it was the Protestant Revolt that began this process, the one that ensured that man would never more be at home with himself. That about his soul he could never be sure if it was like a god, or if he was an irreparably damaged and miserable thing, dependent nonetheless wholly on a cruel, capricious, and total tyrant. This was the first great transformation of the Revolution. And as man's highest faculties are rational and spiritual, the First Revolution attacked him in his highest attributes. Man could no longer trust that he could train his spirit like an athlete for a race, that he could struggle for spiritual greatness through his rational will and the aid of God's sacraments. This element of his nature was now alienated from him, his native powers and very selfhood less than what it was before. In this sense, at the deepest core of man's self, the Protestant world was already a profoundly alien one. The fruits of the First Revolution were already *transhuman*.

The Second Revolution: The French Revolution

A singular revolution, considered as the series of events that topple and replace an existing social order, is not of great interest in a study of the Revolution as a whole. Far more interesting are the intendant changes that make the revolution possible. Revolutions are never conjured out of air; they are in fact amazing in their predictability, even if only in retrospect. Individual revolutions are notable not for the cataclysmic changes that adhere to their names, but for the stasis they achieve. We are concerned in this study not with the storm, but with the landform that remains when the torrent subsides. On the old continent of the prerevolutionary landmass, the winds of progress and conservatism blew against one another. On the new continent the old conservatism is impossible, and any opposition must take the form of an attack on the new gestalt; it must operate by building new bridges to the past, and not merely conserving those which the cataract has washed away. Against the Revolution, once must always be reactionary.

No, because we are concerned with the Revolution as a whole, we approach 1789 not with eyes to the orgy of violence it unleashed, but to the atmosphere which allowed the beast to grow. The Jacobins were but a small part of the ferment of the long and horrible Eighteenth Century. The tenets of the Jacobins are now forgotten or practically moot, but these tenets were never anything more but a small facet of the deluge that was the French Revolution, a token ideology serving as calvary for the actual ideological charge that occurred.

A man who will impose his character on history is always a mostly receptive figure, however great he may be in intellect and valor. His greatness is only ever formed where there is fissure or lacuna, where some imbecility subsists upon which he can impose his mettle. The revolutionist is of this type, seeking to impose his personality at the moment of cataclysm and unrest. The unrest of the French Revolution is of course what makes it compelling: that which allowed for the statecraft of Marat and Danton, and furnished the genocidal movements of armies across Europe. But the tumult did not have to occur; the poor players may have kept their native parts of lawyers and journalist rubbish. How would history have been changed if King Louis had not confronted the Assembly under the shadow of a dead son? Or if Pope Clement had not suppressed the Jesuits in the febrile years before the deluge? How would the course change had Mirabeau lived, or if the States General had not been called at all? We might answer all these questions with drastic difference and yet we would still find the course of the Nineteenth Century largely the same. Some events are so guided in their courses, so inextricably bound as effect to cause, that we cannot separate a discrete event from the current. But the French Revolution was not one of these events. What it accomplished in a burst would have been as inevitable with a steady application of force.

The significance of the French Revolution's reforms is often overstated. As Tocqueville noted, the social leveling that the French Revolution enshrined in law had already been half-accomplished under Louis the Fourteenth and his grandson, including the diminution of noble title and the capturing of the Church as a national force. The actual reforms achieved by the Jacobins were in large part a rationalization of the government to the material form the Sun King had created. The polity had been leveled, and it was rational that the nation's politics should be as well. That this exploded in such violent fashion is a testament to the fatuity of the revolutionary and his ability to attach bloody metaphysical significance to administrative reform.

The tenets of Jacobinism are not crucial to our study. The general spirit that sect promoted is what make them our present interest, the attitude they fostered in the people to be employed as a leveled populace in service of the state. It was, in other words, the self-possessed desire for the creation of the *mass*. This was the metaphysical difference of the French Revolution, the revelation that the wielding of the masses would be the principle of statecraft and the corollary desire of the people to be so wielded. This was the *spirit* of Jacobinism, the acknowledgement and positive desire to be made materiel of the Leviathan state and wielded by the forces of ideology towards the creation of a new order. It was a rising of the people demanding to be subjugated to the purely notional, this liberation from the order of material reality into the slavey of the *philosophes*. Such was the "pure and general freedom" Hegel envisioned the French Revolution to be.

Such are the terms of the Jacobin conquest, or in more precise terms, the tendencies this lot laid bare. For the Second Revolution is above all the revolution of Scientism, the progress of unmaking man's understanding of Nature while purportedly growing wise from its study. So we will show here the Second Revolution was most distinctly the application of the principles of Scientism to the social sphere. With this fact in mind, we turn our attention to the tenets of Scientism, the mode of thought that characterizes more than any other the modern mind vis-à-vis that of antiquity, the half-philosophy that dominates us still, that imposes itself on all learning and vanquishes the hope of systemic wisdom.

But Scientism is the psychic aspect of the change, the making of the ideologue. We start with the material for the change, the atoms of the new atomistic reality, the transformation of men into a *mass*. To understand this, we turn to one of the primeval works of the new atomism, the study of the Leviathan.

The Leviathan

Hobbes' *Leviathan* is a handbook in tyranny. That it is not more often inveighed against owes to its being more often cited than read. That Hobbes does not loom as a darker specter over modernity, as Marx in his numinous materialism or Nietzsche in his anti-democratic fever dreams, is owed to his smaller stature, the fact that he was a paltry antichrist in comparison. Yet it is also proof positive of the Leviathan state's universal triumph, the near superfluity of acknowledging its existence. Marx and Nietzsche confront us from outside the super-structure they lambasted, while Hobbes seeks to woo the creature he describes, to justify the guiles of the demon who has captured him. There are no self-avowed Hobbesians, for how could there be? No school can form around mere servility or before the mettle of a gasping toady. No ruler could find use for Hobbes' works but *ex post facto*, for there is no course of instruction as one might find in Machiavelli, Clausewitz, Sun Tzu or any other of the writers who so openly confuse politics and war. His work perdures not for its own sake, but for the intellectual vacuity it obscures, the evil and pernicious foundations on which the modern state rests. The work marks a break in Western political thought, akin to Bacon's scouring of true knowledge in the sciences. It is a book as sick as Sade's, as demented as Rousseau's, as vile as Freud's, but without their prurient allure. Its ancestors are the economists and evolutionary biologists who endeavor to try to build human society from the irrational greed of slobbering brutes.

Yet it serves us well to begin our discussion with the *Leviathan*, for it is the most worthy and appropriate successor to the Protestant school. The purely negative character of the Protestant cause meant that it could never be static, and Hobbes' bizarre theosophy was but a natural outgrowth of the principles of Westphalia. That Hobbes was a materialist—a wicked and venial one unbound by basic humanitarian values—cannot occlude the fact that he was in self-conception and practice a theologian. His work serves as a tipping point between the specious thievery of the Protestant movement and the universal principles of thievery called *statecraft* established in its wake. Hobbes was a man who followed and felt the revolutions of his time most fervently, and unlike others content merely to profit from them, he attempted to justify the ways of Lucifer to men. He turned himself to human prehistory to find the necessary antecedents to these crimes, and followed them forward to theological hokum.

Hobbes has one fundamental thesis: That the commonwealth is always right. Around this point he most speciously plasters on whatever of philosophy and religion he can. The bastardized Christianity he proposes provides no salvation outside state-worship. The *Leviathan* described what Westphalia held as self-evident: That the sovereign of a nation had implicit sway over the nature of God, and in being coeval with Him, standing as an earthy god himself. Our purpose of looking at this book is not its incisiveness, though Hobbes' attempts at cataloguing suggests he thought his work as a kind of *Summa* of the social sciences. Where Hobbes is not demented he is dull. Hobbes is a fabulist, not a scholar, and a reader derives little pleasure or knowledge from those sections that are most rigorous. Hobbes was not a deep thinker; his first principles foreclose the possibility of the profound. What we turn to him for is the irrational, is the wicked and brutish, the despicable attributes of vice which he raises to principle.

Hobbes' State of Nature

Man in a state of nature is engaged in a war of all against all, *omnia contra omnes*. What is the *state of nature*? It is the state of man as he has never existed, without social organization and thusly lowered to the level of a brute. And the brute is the natural state of Adam and his sons, for to Hobbes man is a creature of feeling and sense and imagination, but no native ratiocination. Aristotle posited that it is man's possession of the *intellective soul* and its ability to reason which positions him above all

120

other creatures on earth. To Hobbes man possesses nothing more than a sensitive and imaginative appetite, a soul reactive to hunger, fear, and the travails of the animal, but nothing more. Man is naturally a beast, and if it were not for the organizational structure of the commonwealth, whose order bequeaths to man something like the ability to reason, he would be impotent to raise his material condition, and his life could be nothing but brutish and short. It is critical to understand how intrinsic the inherently bestial state of man is to Hobbes' claims, for a creature who possessed rational soul and active intellect could have no use for the Leviathan state. The moment the reader concedes to man faculties greater than sense and imagination, Hobbes's thesis must crumble to dust.

Hobbes' commonwealth holds all the keys of culture and all potential for man's redemption, yet is nothing more than brutes contracting. Such contracting arises out man's sole natural right of self-defense, which man has the choice to employ as an individual or barter away in return for protective leagues with others. Larger leagues form. A sovereign is put in place; his rights are total, his power is plenary and arbitrary. Complete submission is owed to him, for it is he who organizes the new league of safety and delivers man from the state of perpetual war. The quality of his leadership does not matter. "The name of tyranny signifieth nothing more nor less than the name of sovereignty."[31] Hobbes' commonwealth is, in modern terms, totalitarian.

There is accordingly no recourse to higher power, for conscience properly belongs only to the ruler. The nexus between God and man does not run through the

[31] Concl.

conscience, but through the sovereign Leviathan, *that mortal god to which we owe our peace and defense.* "Aristotle and other heathen philosophers define good and evil by the appetite of men; and well enough, as long as we consider them governed every one by his own law but their own appetites, there can be no general rule of good and evil actions. But in a Commonwealth this measure is false: not the appetite of private men but the law, which is the will and appoint of the state, is the measure."[32] Such measure trumps the individual.

And so God approves. For the only true dictate of the Divine Law is that man obey his terrestrial sovereigns, and bow to the dictates of civil peace. Hobbes's Supreme Deity does not care if we believe in Him; He asks of us in faith not even the pithy lines of the Apostles Creed, but only that we be able to declare "Jesus is the Christ" for our souls to be guaranteed saved.[33] For as Hobbes declares, Christ's ministers have no power over other men as opposed to the crown nor any established doctrine. Natural Law crumbles alongside individual conscience. The sacraments of course are meaningless. The worship owed to God seems an insult to any serious creed, though in fact Hobbes' God is no crueler than Calvin's: Hobbes merely lowered man's estate so far as to make his subjugation seem an act of mercy rather than what Calvin made a reign of wrath.

The bonds of Natural Law and conscience destroyed, moral instruction must be in vain. "The infliction of what evil soever on an innocent man that is

---

[32] Ch. 46
[33] Ch. 34

122

not a subject, if it be for the benefit of the Commonwealth, and without violation of any former covenant, is no breach of the law of nature. For all men that are not subjects are either enemies, or else they have ceased from being so by some precedent covenants. But against enemies, whom the Commonwealth judgeth capable to do them hurt, it is lawful by the original right of nature to make war; wherein the sword judgeth not, nor doth the victor make distinction of nocent and innocent as to the time past, nor has other respect of mercy than as it conduceth to the good of his own people."[34] Accordingly, any hope for peace relies on recourse to expansion of the Commonwealth. Man is not safe until tyranny is universal.

The State of Nature

Hobbes perhaps more than any other individual helped unleash that great blight on the intellectual discourse, promulgated throughout the Age of Reason: The *State of Nature*. This *state* stands as the most brilliant conceit of the Enlightened theorist, allowing him to apply the most ludicrous of his notions on the palate of an undefiled world, one otherwise hidden beneath the veneer of civilization and its trappings, to erect a social vision like a child with blocks, and to state that because the blocks exist that the vision might be true. In an intellectual atmosphere formed in honesty rather than regimented delusion, such a conceit could never gain legitimacy. But as we find again and again in the

---

[34] Ch. 28

tournament of the *philosophes*, the cosmos belongs to who lends it its best fables.

Darwin's inane speculating is found here *in utero*. All vintages of the *State of Nature* are an exercise in positing a mere animal and adding whatever features the fabulist deems necessary to raise him to the level of civilized man. That these Just-So Stories can be diverting and worthy of the tenure-track cannot be denied, but it is all garbage. If anything at all can be known about man, it is that he is not a mere animal. His sociality is intrinsic to him—this fact is so plain that it wants only notice, not proof. For we do not know ourselves apart from other men. It is no strait to us to associate with one another; it is harder for us to be long apart. In our very physiology we find the first years of our lives are effectively prenatal, by impulse knowing nothing but to suck. Our mothers, however wise, have almost no native knowledge themselves, and were it not for the existing sorority of a mothers, a woman's life would be nothing but tragedy, the pain of watching her most precious things die in her arms nearly as soon as they arrive. No, we are creatures of intellect, creatures of logic, creatures of social wisdom, because God has not given us strength to live by animal spirits alone. We are not men if we are not social creatures; we must fail and die intellectually, spiritually, and physically the moment we abjure the communal wisdom of the race.

Bogus as science, impotent as explanation, why is *State of Nature* discourse maintained? In short, all such discourse is an attempt to transfer order and reason out of man's natural faculties to the very social order itself, which the theorist is then free to modify to his whims. The veil of this conceit cast, the theorist may egregiously ignore the very real creature in front of him, and just as egregiously make the commonwealth not the means of man's fullest happiness, but the actual cause-in-fact of his humanity, the progenitor of his rational soul. Moreover, because man is nothing but a creature of sentiment, society need not possess any kind of intrinsic form reflective of man's attributes. For of course those who cannot be made to see the clear rationality of man will never be forced to concede a logic to mere *things* that are man's creations. Both man and society thus take on whatever characteristics the theorist attributes to him, and the theorist can do what he will.

Against these rank speculators one can only fall back to truth as he finds it: That man is a rational creature, and social order arises from this fact, not conversely. Let us consider this fact in relation to the institution of property. All civil government exists for the regulation and protection of property. Government arises out of property because property is a rational and necessary outgrowth of man's need to protect himself against the forces of Nature. Animals have notions of territoriality, even when their material needs are few. Man, the naked and vulnerable thing, needs more, and in his capacity as a reasoning being can raise the mere act of possession into a principle. In seeing the same situation among his neighbors, he finds that his own needs will be better protected when the neighbor is afforded a similar protection, and in acknowledging this, a principle rises to the level of universal right. All peoples, however primitive, recognize this right, even where their backwardness and poverty see it reach only partial fruition. The institution of property is no creation of the state, but an indubitable fact of man's relation to Nature and realized by the application of reason, one which allows man to create a system of ownership which meets his own needs and provides for those of others. Indigenously the state arises as a servant to the rational interests of its people. This is the heart of a true commonwealth: the common goods, *res publicae* that men cannot survive without, whether the state exists or not. These include all the social knowledge necessary to meet man's rational needs, for as man cannot survive without clothes, he cannot survive without a social knowledge of how to make them; and as man cannot survive without shelter, he cannot survive without the social knowledge of how to construct a house. These rational goods predate and perdure without the city, though it is in the city that these arts can be perfected and man's happiness best effected. This was the true natural state of man, the true *state of nature* as understood by the ancients, not as the fable of the Enlightenment, but by the true scientific observation of man. Man's state of nature is the commonwealth, for if left to his own rational impulses, the city will naturally follow.

These facts must be wicked poison to Hobbes, and so they are. For to Hobbes property is not an outgrowth of man's native desires, not even a phenotype of his particular genetic order as later Darwinists might posit it. Property is a creation of the commonwealth, an after-effect of established order. Naturally, what the commonwealth may give the commonwealth may take away, and so property, no more than any other good within the Leviathan state, can never be a natural right against the desires of the sovereign. A state so conceived cannot commit theft, for obvious reasons.

Whether the rights of property precedes or owes its existence to the commonwealth is a bellwether—

126

perhaps the fundamental political question. It demands us to answer whether reason precedes the state, or if the state somehow creates human reason. All fables of the State of Nature theorists are an attempt to enshrine on scientific grounds that the latter holds. And this is what we find in Hobbes and Locke and Rousseau; such do we see in the modern socio-biologists, ever anxious to fit man into the beehive of capitalist organization.[35] Its purpose is always to pose the question of how man can be bastardized, compartmentalized are reordered into a larger social construction.

No *rational* animal can be made into a skincell of the Leviathan. Its constituents must be brutes, malleable subjects dependent on the commonwealth not only for their material subsistence but for their rational organization of selfhood. Plato too constructed an ideal state *a priori*, but he began by approaching man in his rational needs and asking how they might be fulfilled through the state. Hobbes, in contrast, begins by dissolving man into a kind of *prima materia* of the social order, a clay to mold into a larger form of his liking. Hobbes' vision of man is the most depraved of any promoted by the stalwarts of the Canon, a fodder for tyrants and social scientists alike.

France Before the Revolution

As we noted above, France was a nation that had already been brought together under one central power. It was Louis the Fourteenth who long before had sought to impose the Leviathan state, who treated society and

---

[35] See e.g. Matt Ridley, *The Origins of Virtue.*

polity like a Zeus from whose head the rights of property and conscience flowed.[36] Well before the revolution, the larger structure of feudal relations had been supplanted, and the name of noble often meant one possessed nothing but a privileged position within the state. The great edifices of the feudal structure had been razed, and though among individual lords and peasants the rights remained, commercial activity had given a large part of the new bourgeoisie and the peasantry a taste of the international market economy. Louis' war machine contributed to the growth of a centralized and bureaucratized state, inside which no faction could raise protest. France was not a Protestant society, but the Westphalian doctrine that religion would be a matter of statecraft and not of fact was propitious to strong kings and a national church proudly defiant of Rome. Not even the manifestly intolerant Revocation of the Edict of Nantes could be justified on grounds other than tyranny, directed as it was towards those upon whom coercive influence was unlikely to have any propitious evangelical effect. All movement, even the ecclesiastical, was oriented towards the state. In its wake one found a growing class of political and philosophic enemies, of rationalists, Cartesians and Spinozans, along with a burgeoning proto-capitalist class of Huguenots justly resentful of the state.

This was the atmosphere which fostered the paradigmatic liberal revolution. The aficionados of chaos can turn to it for the purity of Jacobin fervor, felt and hoped for by all men of refinement, a new secular creed assuring all races and generations that a new world lay

---

[36] Lord Acton's Lectures of History, "Louis the Fourteenth."

just beyond the pasteboard mask of the Old Regime, and like Ahab one need only break through the mask for enlightenment to follow. The English had already murdered a king on republican principles and savaged an established church; the Americans had thrown aside another king on the same principles. But these still retained a character of political disputes, of aristocratic vying on principles only a small number truly cared about or understood. The French revolt looks like a general rising, though this is deceptive. The mind of the World Revolution resides in the elites, even when its ostensible will seems to lie with the rabble and the sans-culottes. It was the use of the rabble in the French Revolution that distinguishes it from those revolutions that preceded it, in the ability of its architects to wield for their purposes all classes and forces from top to bottom of society. Unique to the new Jacobinism was the audacity of the architects. They were the first to use the people as *prima materia* as Hobbes understood them. They went about upending a house and rebuilding it with no mind for which bricks served as masonry or foundation, and finally asserting there was no difference.

The Mob and the Mass

We must recall some characteristics about the mob that are often occluded in political discourse. The mob is not an inherently democratic thing. It has no necessary desire to remake the state around itself, only to make manifest the power it has in the existing order. Nat Turner's men were villains of every bastion of decency, but they ultimately turned their plaints to the king, for they knew they were not a force sufficient in themselves.

For their cries to be realized and their desires to be effected, they knew they needed benefactors within the state. Such was the role they commonly found in king in clergy, the clergy who could cool the tempers of the aristocrats through moral suasion, and the king who in raw political terms benefited from having an ally against the usurping aristocracy directly below him. The kings who best guarded royal authority were those who best protected the poor.

The mob's contention with the Bourbons was unique. The Parisian rabble were no longer a force recognizable by its status as subordinate class, and indeed was no longer a recognizable class at all. In the contentions between the Old Regime and the new aristocrats of commerce and science, the Parisian mob was a bulwark of power, a territory to be conquered, a force synonymous with control of the state: The power to wield the mob was the power of sovereignty itself.

A fundamental transformation had occurred: The mob had become a *mass*. Even to refer to this body as a distinct class would be inapt. *Proletarian* or *serf* carries with it a distinct relation to the social order, men defined by their concrete roles and thus distinguishable from one another. The mass has no ingrained or necessary will. It is a politically indistinct group, a group propelled by no particular logic or necessity but from the common call to be wielded as part of a greater movement. The mass comes together knowing it is indistinct, and is powerful precisely for this indistinctness. It serves as a homogenous clay out of which the state can be built, material which was the object of dispute during the French Revolution.

The distinction between a mere group of men and the mass is commonly ignored. Gustav Le Bon makes none at all in *The Crowd*, where he describes the crowd's common characteristics: its effeminacy, its suggestibility, its inability to be guided by reason. But Le Bon's analysis can only take us so far, because he is unable to distinguish between a crowd, which is merely a "gathering of individuals" for whatever purpose, and the *mass*, which is a politically fungible group with existence only within the modern state. A crowd such as a jury or an army battalion, still has a rational purpose for its existence. A mob of men clamoring for bread act in concert with one another, all of them rational agents seeking benefits that are personal and real, however low the mob's conduct might descend to in practice, however much the infatuation of numbers makes its individual members irrational and effeminate. When all is told, the mob is still a group rationally oriented towards the formal purpose of its members.

The mass is a congregation of men with no rational ends outside their act of formation. Its ends are communal, not personal, and notional, not real. The mass does not have any particularized purpose or role within a community. It is a group that recognizes its ability to influence the community not for its constituents' characteristics, but for its size and bulk, and with this its inherent significance within the state. That the mass is undifferentiated and incoherent is no liability but an asset, a sign of malleability and fungibility of purpose. The masses are conscious chattel of the superstructure, the skincells of the Leviathan.

We find the same facts put differently by Pius the Twelfth. "The people, and a shapeless multitude (or, as it is called, *the masses*) are two distinct concepts. The

people lives and moves by its own life energy; the
masses are inert of themselves and can only be moved
from outside. The people lives by the fullness of life in
the men that compose it, each of whom—at his proper
place and in his own way—is a person conscious of his
own responsibility and of his own views. The masses, on
the contrary, wait for the impulse from outside, an easy
plaything in the hands of anyone who exploits their
instincts and impressions, ready to follow in turn, today
this flag, tomorrow another."[37] And so in a unforgettable address the holy pope grasps what Le Bon
could not.

The Mass and the French Revolution

Just a year after the Revolution's outbreak, Mirabeau
wrote to the king: "The modern idea of a single class of
citizens on an equal footing would certainly have pleased
Richelieu, since surface equality of this kind facilitates
the exercise of power. Absolute government during the
several successive reigns could not have done as much
as this one year of revolution to make good the King's
authority."[38] The government was now a free-for-all, a
neutral space whose only rule was power. The king was
still ostensibly a party in the vying, though he could
never again be a monarch in the old form. It was the
mass, and indeed the self-conscious presence of the
mass, that provided the Revolution with its primary
characteristic and its material propulsion.

---

[37] Christmas Message 1944
[38] Tocqueville, *The Old Regime and the French Revolution*.
Part 1, Ch. 2.

But by what was this mass to be led? This was the force of *ideology*. We mean by this not the study of ideas, as the word might imply, nor even rule by idea. *Property* is an idea; *monogamy* is an idea; *habeas corpus* is an idea, one of many that directs our lives just as the streets and buildings of a city guide our travel and commerce. But the ideologue does not seek a concrete end, but through the medium of a particular idea seeks to reimagine the makeup of society as a whole, a process in which the mass of people function as the material propulsion of any desire ideological change.

To understand this process, which so clearly came to life in the late Eighteenth Century, we must return to the Seventeenth. For the rise of ideology was only the social manifestation of Scientism, the fallacy of thought that replaced deductive and theological reasoning following the Reformation. It is a fallacy that has never been supplanted, and which allows modern men to be ruled by the flimsiest suppositions, the baldest of bald-faced lies so long as they are numeric. The Protestant could rewrite the *Logos* as he crossed from town to town; the progenitors of Scientism could remake the cosmos with the ticks of their rulers. This was the central conceit of the Age of Reason, and no one in the modern world has succeeded in dethroning it.

The Protestant Revolution had already divorced matter from idea, sacrament from spirit. The new divines believed they had so benefited from the increase in human wit and ingenuity that the Gospel no longer demanded zeal so much as education to be spread. The Church, so long bolstered by miracle-mongers, stigmatists and a haughty priesthood, for long had been nothing but a scourge of the credulous against the wise. The Catholic posited that the Creator played an active role in maintaining all being in the universe, and without the constant application of His active will, all matter would break down and all existence would end. The Protestant had no particular need for God's continued enlivenment, just as it had no need for the external aids of sacraments once Scripture had been indited. *Salvation through Faith Alone* made the act of salvation an intellectual one. So long as man assented to Faith, he could effectively assent to his own salvation. The meaning of the few sacraments the Protestant retained was wholly interior, utile only as an aid to his assent. As such, the Protestant was not strictly bound to a claim that essence could be different from appearance where the outward form of sacrament had no significance but to man's inward disposition. The Catholic could not deny that what appeared to be bread was actually God lest he be called anathema, but the Protestant could believe what he liked so long as that mere bread well disposed him towards his faith. Where the Eucharist was a mere thanksgiving, a heightened feeling of its practitioners was enough.

It was this atmosphere of scattered essences and subjectivized salvation that fostered the rise of Scientism. Aristotle declared that the end of science was to pursue "knowledge of the essence of a thing."[39] By the end of the Seventeenth Century the best minds in science would declare that knowledge of the essence of a thing was undesirable, if not impossible. To understand this sentiment, simultaneously so humble and haughty, we must understand the intellectual revolt that occurred. The rise of Scientism constituted the great unmaking of

---

[39] *Posterior Analytics*, 79a-22

the Western mind, a perversion and unmooring of the progress of reason which had developed from the Age of Ionic philosophy and flowered through the Medieval Era. Our former sanctity of mind has never been recovered, and so we now turn to a study of its perversion.

Treatise on Scientism

"What science cannot tell us, mankind cannot know." This proclamation, Bertrand Russell's, might be written over the Temple of Scientism, for like the Delphic admonition, it provides the key to all the age's wisdom, the only rule by which moderns may know themselves.

By *science*, we can be assured Lord Russell did not refer to ethics or ontology or any other hobby horse of the rank deducers of the Middle Ages. What he meant was undoubtedly *empirical* science, the use of observed measurements and inductive reasoning as the means of arriving at knowledge. We might then amend Russell's statement, What cannot be *measured* mankind cannot know. And with this bold assertion Russell captured the revolution in thought that overtook the Seventeenth Century. For while man's logic is often flawed and his senses often fail, the new regime of measurement suggested a new objectivity was to be had, a smashing of mental fetters the West had worn since the time of the Peripatetics. The old philosophers were indeed nothing but religious dogmatists.

Announced the sage Voltaire:

Sect and error are synonymous. You are Peripatetic
and I Platonician; we are therefore both wrong, for
you combat Plato only because his fantasies have
revolted you, and I am alienated from Aristotle only
because it seems to me that he does not know what
he is talking about. If one or the other had
demonstrated the truth, there would be a sect no
longer. To declare oneself for the opinion of the one
or the other is to take their side in a civil war. There are
no sects in mathematics, in experimental physics. A
man who examines the relations between a cone and
a sphere is not of the sect of Archimedes: he who
sees that the square of the hypotenuse of a right-
angled triangle is equal to the square of the two other
sides is not of the sect of Pythagoras. When you say
that the blood circulates, that the air is heavy, that
the sun's rays are pencils of seven refrangible rays,
you are not either of the sect of Harvey, or the sect
of Torricelli, or the sect of Newton; you agree merely
with the truth demonstrated by them, and the entire
universe will ever be of your opinion. This is the
character of truth; it is of all time; it is for all men; it
has only to show itself to be recognized; one cannot
argue against it. A long dispute signifies this: *that both
parties are wrong.*[40]

The true man of the Enlightenment could not be
troubled with the quibbling of schools. The Gordian
Knot had been split by the bleeding edge of the
instrument. Freed of old fetters, the mind's-eye no
longer scanning the clouds of Ideas and metaphysics, an

---

[40] The *Philosophical Dictionary*, definition of "Sect."

increase in human welfare had to follow. Advances in learning might even defeat the last remnants of original sin. "No man can doubt that, as preventative medicine improves and food and housing become healthier, as a way of life is established that develops our physical powers by exercise without ruining them by excess, a the two most virulent causes of deterioration, misery and excessive wealth, are eliminated, the average length of human life will be increased and a better heath and a stronger physical constitution will be ensured... Would it be absurd then to suppose that this perfection of the human species might be capable of indefinite progress; that the day will come when death will be due only to extraordinary accidents, and that ultimately the average span between birth and decay will have no assignable value?"[41]

Let us not confuse this optimism with the naïve idealist's, with the undergraduate's unlearned and untoward belief in paltry and ephemeral *progress*. The rise of empiricism had enraptured the sophisticated world. The above statements are from eminent men, serious and well-regarded men. And we find in them a fervent belief in the lifting of the pall of death, the unveiling of the intellect by empiricism and the possibilities an infinite amount of data points supplied. "If only freedom is granted," Immanuel Kant proclaimed, "enlightenment is sure to follow."[42] *Freedom* was freedom from the old metaphysics, liberation from the tutelage of the ancient sages and recourse to one's own reason, liberated and exalted by the new empirical mode.

---

[41] Condorcet, *Sketch for a Historical Picture of the Human Mind*. Tenth Stage.

[42] "What is Enlightenment?"

Descartes

The man who gave solidity to this dream was Rene Descartes—"Great Descartes! if to find truth has not always been given to you, you have at least destroyed tyranny and error that obscured it."[43] The philosophical opposition he put forth, called ever afterwards *Cartesian bifurcation*, set in stark terms the superiority of empirical science against all other learning. Taken to its logical conclusion, it posited that all that was immeasurable was a figment, and that it was only the measurable that was in any sense *real*; it established the metaphysical rule that put empirical science as the apogee of all learning and the process of quantification the supreme end of man.

One cannot do better in describing the new mode of science than Wolfgang Smith.

> Descartes conceived of the external or objective world as made up of so-called *res extensae*, extended things bereft of sensible qualities, which can be fully described by fully quantitative or mathematical terms. Besides the *res extensae*, he posits also the *res cogitantes* or thinking entities, and it is to these that he consigns the sensible qualities, along with whatever else in the universe which might be recalcitrant to mathematical definition." According to Descartes, "the red apple we perceive exists—not in the external world, as mankind has believed all along—but in the mind, the *res cogitans*; in short it is a mental

---

[43] Turgot, "Discourse at the Sorbonne."

138

phantasm which we have naively mistaken for the external entity. Descartes admits, of course, that in normal sense perception the phantasm is causally related to an external object, a *res extensa;* but the fact remains that it is not the *res extensa*, but the phantasm that is actually perceived. What was previously conceived as a single object—and what in daily life is invariably regarded as such—has now been split in two; as Whitehead has put it: 'Thus there would be two natures, one is the conjecture and the other is the dream.'[44]

Descartes had himself given expression to this: "We can easily conceive how the motion of one body can be caused by that of another, and diversified by the size, figure, and situation of its parts, but we are wholly unable to conceive how the same things can produce something else of a nature entirely different from themselves, as for example, those substantial forms and real qualities which many philosophers suppose to be in bodies."[45] It is those measurable attributes—motion, size, figure, situation—that can be conceived; the actual object, so apparently like a form or essence, cannot possibly arise out of these measurable attributes and thus are most safely understood as mental constructs.

With the acceptance of bifurcation, we find that a divide exists between what Smith calls the *molecular apple* and the red, glossy, delicious thing we believe we see before us. The glossy thing does not actually exist: it has no objective reality, but is a mental creation, an

---

[44] *Ancient Wisdom and Modern Misconceptions*, pp 19-20; quoting Whitehead's *The Concept of Nature*, 1964 p. 30.
[45] Descartes, *Principia Philosophiae*

agglomeration and organization of real traits taken in through the senses, but not a thing with independent existence itself. The glossy delicious apple is a *mental thing*, one which happily shares a like form with what we believe other men perceive, but a thing which is nonetheless a creation of man through his cognitive faculties. All the while it is the measurable aspects of the apple that alone are *real*. We know the apple only through our senses, and those characteristics it possesses beyond our five talents are hidden from us.

One might be tempted to ascribe the entire Cartesian system to the temperament of genius, that which revels in intellectual trickery against the straightforward approach of truth. Yet in all, the Cartesian system was no parlor game of the fledgling *philosophes*, but a powerful new way of seeing reality. Essences vanished from the study of physics, but relationships between phenomena remained and, at times, seemed the only subject worthy of the field. The fruits of this method allowed for an increased and improved study of motion. Newton could scarcely have functioned under the old paradigms of physics, and his *Principia* was enough to justify this profound transformation of thought. The Aristotelian view held that substances have intrinsic properties: The rubber ball, owing to its nature, has a tendency, even a *desire* to travel to the ground when left in the air. Under the Cartesian or Newtonian system, the rubber ball had no such intrinsic characteristics, at least none relevant to the question of physical systems. Instead, the ball was a passive partaker of the laws of motion, which were extrinsic to any individual substance and universal in their jurisdiction. The essence of the ball no longer mattered at all, for any object with such measurable characteristics would be acted upon by the laws of physics and behave the same way. It was no surprise that men of the era began to conceive of the universe as a vast machine, whose every cog and lever was interchangeable.

This is all to say that Cartesian bifurcation was in fact excellent in its proper context. But our enthusiasm must be tempered by the metaphysical constraint Cartesian bifurcation imposes. Under the Cartesian supposition, man achieves mechanical mastery precisely because he denies knowledge of actual reality. If essences did in fact exist, it was not the role of physics to understand them.

The objectivity of the universe itself might be called into question now, if what appeared to be real before man was anything but a mental figment. The universe became a stranger to man. His instruments lent him a putatively greater knowledge about it, yet at the same time what appeared the most manifest and obvious fact—the unities he perceived in each individual tree, book, or blade of grass—were figments of his senses and imagination. Alone amongst mankind is the scientist who can delve into the true nature of things. And yet these shamans cannot guarantee the things they measure and the relationships have anything to do with the substances that actually exist. Pure science is wholly relational, an academic habit, its truths not necessarily more impactful than any study of other figments, like the happenings of a novel. For where those things called essences are only creatures of the mind, we are left with quantifications that have meaning only with relation to other quantities. Science in the true Aristotelian sense has disappeared. Gone was any true knowledge of things or even the *ability to know* them even as a concept.

This was the metaphysics that had dissolved all sects—capable of doing so because it had cast aside the very existence of objective truth. And yet no scientist dared to call himself what he was: a professor of figments. No scientist could abandon LaPlace's creed that physical laws were universal, though of course such statement could not be proven on any terms that LaPlace would have accepted. Newton's faith in a Deity was strengthened by his mechanical work, but there was no necessary connection between the new physics and the Logos. The Blind Watchmaker had set his machine in motion and nothing more need be contributed to it. For where essences were removed, made exogenous in the theoretical model, so God who imparted them also could be.

Francis Bacon

We put the figure of Francis Bacon back before us: not as a scientist, for he gave nothing to the new empiricists that they did not possess before. No, we approach him in his most exalted form, as the arch-prophet of Scientism, the man who forged a new path in thought by uniting technical advances and material utility and miscalling it all *scientific progress*. The most pathetic researcher, lodged in counting wooly aphids on the corner of a leaf, performing work any ape could do, can look to the mantras of Lord Bacon and confirm himself in a pursuit worthy as the saint contemplating God. Bacon's fruits were found in the salons of Paris, in the discourses of Voltaire. This *prince of philosophers* is the greatest extoller of departure of Western rationalism and the decline of the Western mind.

A biographical note is helpful, for Bacon was a rare man history has positioned to be no mere philosopher, but a philosopher-king. It was a role he failed at phenomenally, as if his lifelong crusade against Plato needed not only his words but his life's testimony. He rose to the position of Lord Chancellor under reforming and liberal-minded monarchs, and he disgraced himself miserably, needlessly betraying his political benefactors, deceiving his allies, and taking bribes in number too great to count until Parliament could not help but censure him. This would have been shameful in the most degenerate jobber, but for the *prince of philosophers* to behave in such a way calls his work to task. We might not take umbrage were we to find that Schopenhauer or Nietzsche had been made a public minister and brought down the government, but that Bacon, the most self-avowedly practical of philosophers, proved so dissolute and profligate in a post given him so propitiously speaks to a deep failure of his work and his manhood.

We proffer testimony from one of his greatest proponents: "The years in which Bacon held the Great Seal were among the darkest and most shameful in English history. Had his life been passed in literary retirement, he would, in all probability, have deserved to be considered, not only as a great philosopher, but as a worthy and good-natured member of society. But neither his principles nor his spirit were such as could be trusted, when strong temptations were to be resisted, and serious dangers to be braved."[46] Had his method been one of universal morals, of first principles rather than utility, is it unfair to suggest he might have held himself to a higher standard of conduct? He died, in

---

[46] Maccaulay "Bacon."

good empiricist fashion, trying to stuff snow into a chicken.

Whatever the practical failures of that most practical of philosophers, Bacon clearly saw himself as a light in the darkness, an accelerative force pushing forward the practice of physical sciences out of the Dark Ages inaugurated by Aristotle's application of logic to natural philosophy. "[An] instauration must be made from the very foundations, if we do not wish to revolve forever in a circle, making only some slight and contemptible progress."[47] Slight progress had been thought the only kind that might be had from inductive learning, for our observations are useless to us if we cannot make them conform to some antecedent understanding of the things and relationships observed. Bacon seemed to offer another course altogether.

Bacon's contemplated instauration can be reduced to two elements, both of which interest us greatly, here and later: The enshrinement and apotheosis of instruments—in fact a seeming self-sufficiency of instruments in the cause of empirical science—and the replacement of utility as the highest good of scientific inquiry. While seemingly disparate, these ends were actually quite closely related. For the program proposed by Bacon, so reliant on observation and seemingly oblivious to concern of theory, could make no claim to be discovering essences. Where reality could not be known, utility stood in as replacement for a final end of doing science at all.

The guiding influence of instruments allows us to approach scientific problems without theory, without

---

[47] Novum Organum. I-31.

models, without initial paradigms. "The subtlety of nature is far beyond that of sense or of the understanding, so that the specious meditations, speculations, and theories of mankind are but a kind of insanity, only there is no one to stand by and observe it."[48] The intellective power is so inclined to Descartes' *res cogitantes* that it simply cannot be trusted. Elsewhere the retrenchment is but a return to atomism. "The human understanding is, by its own nature, prone to abstraction, and supposes that which is fluctuating to be fixed. But it is better to dissect than abstract nature; such was the method employed by the school of Democritus, which made greater progress in penetrating nature than the rest... Forms are a mere fiction of the human mind, unless you call the laws of action by that name."[49] The critique at times is so radical as to apparently make all inquiry fruitless. "Human understanding easily supposes a greater degree of order and equality in things than it really finds; and though many things in nature be *sui generis* and most irregular, will yet invent parallels and conjugates and reflexives, where no such thing is."[50] The radicalism of this statement should shock us, for that which is *sui generis* is beyond the study of causation, and beyond the scientist's purview altogether.

It takes no great philosopher of science to see how perilous this is. The process of science always requires some kind of model, some kind of logic or theory, even if this model be only a habit of thought. Truly our common sense provides the first paradigm for the most rudimentary science we practice, those first laws we

---

[48] Id. 10th Aphorism.
[49] I-51
[50] I-45

discern in our attempts to discern cause and effect. The readings of an instrument, in a sense, do not give us any wholly new knowledge; they cannot, like a divining rod, lead us to the springs of real understanding, for they are, in themselves, incomprehensible if not closely tied to our own native faculties or the guidance of a predictive model. Data alone, whether gathered through the senses or through advanced instruments, tell us nothing. We cannot strictly know anything without some ability to filter data, synthesize a relationship between relevant data, and make causal claims based on this synthesis. If science is anything, it is the knowledge of cause and effect. And while Bacon's method may expand the scope of observations we take in under the onus of science, his denigration of theory requires that these observations will never be anything but a compendium of events, teaching us nothing.

Models and the Empirical Sciences

To abstract away from the essences of things is the very nature of science. For science is not a general wisdom or an ingrained knowledge, but a process by which we come to know better certain attributes of a thing. Every science imposes on the object of its study a particular epistemic closure, a self-imposed limitation on what matters it investigates. As such, every particular science abjures the ability to gain the kind of knowledge found by the practice of another particular science; it likewise forecloses any knowledge of true the essences of things.[51]

We come before an apple tree: The theologian sees in it the beneficence of God, and perhaps the mechanism of the Fall; the biologist sees in it a living organism, drawing fuel from the earth and sun and air; the ecologist sees its respiration, the complex system springing even from its detritus; the economist sees a source of sustenance, the lives improved by its cultivation and use. Every branch of science casts a new light on the object of study. All these perspectives are necessary and good, for all these needs are human. We can take a ruler and measure the tree's height in meters, or take a spectrometer and quantify the redness of its fruits, or take a scale and measure its weight. But we can never meet a necessary end of such studies; we can never come to the bottom of the thing we think we grok, for our inquiries and methods are infinite in number, as manifold as human genius can contrive method. It is left to the philosopher to reconcile the different aspects of a thing and to attempt to understand its essence through our various modes of acquiring knowledge, that is, through the different branches of science. While God may know all things at once, man is forced to be discursive. We humans must parse.

Within any given branch of science we are not able to perceive causation without a preexisting mental construct, even if this construct be nothing but commonsense. Broadly, we can call this a theory or a paradigm, a "universally recognized scientific achievement that for a time provide model problems

---

[51] Wolfgang Smith, *Science and Myth* 50, citing Jean Borella's *Symbolism and Reality*.

and solutions to a community of practitioners."[52] Even more particular are models, those constructs which take into account the paradigmatic assumptions of the field and create a mechanism for the direct application of principles. A model may be simple or complex; it may not be explicit, and may occupy our minds as a simple heuristic. And yet in call cases it is through the use of models that scientists directly test hypotheses and impose parameters on a specific causal relationship.

The particular sciences differ from one another based on the abstractions they impose through their methodologies. Indeed the distinguishing characteristic of any given science is not in the nature of the specific facts they study, but the methods or models employed. The fact that a biologist finds himself investigating the cell walls of a tree's leaf and the economist an orchard's yearly produce is not owing to the subject of study but the formal ends of the methods they employ, those which compel the practitioner towards a particular datum. In sum, it is the method of the practitioner that finds the data. For this reason, there can be no thing as an "empirical fact" separate from the role of theory.[53] The very act of measuring a thing presumes a causal importance or such measurement would not be made. But such causal importance can only be derived by theory, by employment of a model.

---

[52] Thomas Kuhn, *The Structure of Scientific Revolutions*. x
[53] *The Quantum Enigma*, 33 "Strictly speaking, there is no such thing as an 'empirical fact'—so long, of course, as the term is understood to exclude the concomitant role of theory"

Given the foregoing, we might offer another definition of Scientism to accompany Lord Russell's above: Scientism is the reification of models, their transformation from predictive tools to actual mirrors of reality or, in an abuse of terms, a raising of the model's terms to the level of essences, to confuse our mode of perception with the actual thing itself.[54] For even to measure a thing is to subjectivize it, to make it conform to a particular chosen form of analysis, to abstract away from its essence in order to know it better in this one particular way. It is the epistemic closure imposed to make a given branch of science comprehensible.

The thought processes which we employ in the process of science are more important than our data, because data themselves can constitute no true knowledge. Advanced instruments can enhance our ability to collect and refine the data we possess, but the foundations of logic hold however complex the edifice might be placed atop it. Sound theory indeed becomes more critical when instruments become more complex, because our intuitions become less secure the more we move away from common experience.

No competent practitioner ever approaches an empirical problem without first establishing a theory. "Perhaps it is not apparent that a paradigm is prerequisite to the discovery of laws. We often hear that they are found by examining measurements undertaken for their own sake and without theoretical commitment. But history provides no support of so Baconian a method."[55] And yet for all intents and purposes, the Baconian method dominates. Man's natural intelligence

---

[54] See Smith, *Science and Myth*, 60
[55] Kuhn, *Structure of Scientific Revolutions*, 28

has been replaced by products of his intelligence, those mechanisms which compile data as if they could exist apart from a theory that demands them. The modern scientist has more data points than ever before, more nominal understanding of things than the ancient world could comprehend. Yet he has no assurance that the object of his studies has anything but the most tenuous relation to reality. We consider the tremendous popularity of Kant's great critique, the unanimous acknowledgement of crisis, and yet the complete inability to reform the system, and we must come to the conclusion that the problem is not intellectual error but a kind of existential malady, a funk of half-knowing that our race cannot extricate itself from.

The crisis of modern science, much like the crisis of the modern mind, has been long acknowledged, its criticisms never rebutted, its errors never ameliorated. The system is not honest, but it is useful, and so it is allowed to remain. Cartesian bifurcation has conquered all; measurement and instrumentation are our only lights.

The problem is that we *know* an apple is an apple; we know essences exist. If we do not know this, we know nothing; if we do not think rightly in this, we cannot be really sure that we think at all, or that our experiences are not the flatulent vapors of a debauched god or a brain in a jar. We are free to speculate about any matter we wish, but where our speculations destroy the ability to speculate, we cannot help but destroy thought itself.

And here we come to the second aspect of Bacon's proposed instauration, the apotheosis of utility. Where science is synonymous with what is measurable, technology will be determinative within any epistemic system. Scientific progress, so far as it is possible, must tend to become synonymous with technical improvements. And as the empirical sciences rise to the apex of what is considered wisdom as a whole, the progress of technology becomes consubstantial with intellectual advance. If all we can know is what we can measure, then what we can better measure we better know. The end of scientific advance becomes the progress of technology.

The Galileo Affair

"To make a model for mathematicians is what I have endeavored to do." This was the apparently humble claim of Copernicus, the rest of whose *De Revolutionibus* would be used to upend the old science and enshrine the new as the apex of modern knowledge. Indeed, Copernicus had pursued the model for the most pragmatic purposes. The lights of St. Lucy's Day had once shone against the darkness of the solstice, yet under the Julian calendar the great martyr's feast lay eight days before the longest night of the year. The regress was plodding, a day lost every century, but for an institution guaranteed by her Founder to be perpetual under the sun, the problem was more than a nagging one. The pope turned to the astronomers, the *mathematicians* as Copernicus called his ilk. The Pole's monumental labors arose out of this fertile environment, of a liberal and confident Church seeking to unite the worship of God with the order of the spheres. Copernicus' self-understood task was to give order to the era, not to herald a new one.

The distinguishing characteristic of the Copernican system is its placement of the sun in the center of the galaxy. Yet other aspects of the model were conservative, borrowing from the Ptolemaists and Scholastics in the mechanics of terrestrial movement and in the general cosmology of the spheres. It was not an elegant model: Its predictive power was not greatly superior to those models it replaced, nor could Copernicus remove from it the epicycle, the revolution-within-a-revolution that made the old geocentric models so frustrating to the natural historians of his day and laughable to the scientist of ours. But with such an attitude we risk falling into the modern mindset, the habit of reifying models and attaching to them a solidity that is not there. The Ptolemaists did not attach to their models the attribute of absolute and immutable truth. The ad hoc modifications of equants and epicycles, which left the planets moving like playing children in the sky, could be well justified for predictive purposes, inelegant though they may be. The astronomer who believed his model exactly reflected the movements of the spheres might shy away from having Jove do the waltz in his traverse, but in that case he would have no model and be left without even equivocal light of understanding. Copernicus' stark assumption of heliocentricity cannot but shock us now, but this is only after four centuries of exposure to what Copernicus could not and did not claim. There is no reason to believe he abjured the practice of the ancients, that a model was a *potency* rather than *manifestation* of reality, a mental construct forged to better understand the phenomena observed, not a complete and total image of God's creation.[56]

---

[56] "One must remember that prior to Descartes the geometric

And there was one thing that Copernicus' model definitively could not do: It could not prove that the sun was at the center of the solar system. It could not have, for the model itself presumed heliocentrism, and that which is assumed in a model cannot be proven by that same model. Copernicus showed that his heliocentric model worked tolerably well—perhaps not as well as the reigning Ptolemaic models of the day, certainly not as well as Tyco Brahe's subsequent geocentric model—but tolerably well. His endeavor had been undertaken on the behest of the Holy Father and it was enough to win his gratulation in response. But to repeat: Copernicus' model did not and could not prove that the earth moved around the sun. It took this movement as a given and proceeded from there. Apart from one revolutionary assumption, there was nothing in his work that might be accused of seeking revolutionary consequence.

In the meantime, the Church and the rest of the world took for granted a cosmos that was geocentric. To gaze upwards was to see stars, moons, planets moving around the earth and to perceive no sign of terrestrial movement below. The great minds of science supported

---

continuum—the Euclidian plane, for example—was conceived as an entity in its own right, and not simply as the totality of points. According to the pre-Cartesian view, there *are* in fact no points in the plain—until, that is, they are brought into existence through geometric construction. Classically conceived, the plane as such is a void; in itself it constitutes a kind of emptiness, a mere potency, in which nothing has yet been actualized... Geometric construction, classically conceived, is thus suggestive of cosmogenesis. One could say that it imitates or exemplifies the creative act itself within the mathematical domain." *The Quantum Enigma*, 56.

common sense's conclusions; Ptolemy had won the battle of models between the ancients and, most importantly, it was in accord with the rational cosmology of Aristotle, which found the natural ordering of the universe reflected in the ordering of the spheres. The Church, with the added testament of Holy Scripture, did little but hold and protect what all the world knew. The learned man of the time believed he grasped the essential makeup of the universe. He knew that the planets went around the earth, and he also knew why they did so. He knew how their motion related to the essences of things terrestrial, and he knew from the most learned of the scientists, by the most thorough of the metaphysicians, by the attestations of religious truth, that the cosmos was ordered as he perceived it was. From the highest lights to the lowest minds man found in the cosmos a feeling of an ordered home. No one thought that one assumption of a technical model could alter the gestalt of the universe.

It was this universe that Galileo sought to destroy. It was he, and not Copernicus, who converted all enlightened minds to heliocentrism, and with this upended the old metaphysical reality. As Erasmus is called the first of the Reformers, Galileo may be the last. That both men lived and died Catholics is of no mind, nor that the Thirty Years' War had not yet commenced when Galileo's controversy was at its peak. Galileo's victory over the Church was the last and greatest of new fields to be won; the subsequent wars of religion and political intriguing only decided if the captured terrains could be kept. While moderns may relish the destruction done by the Reformers, most of the men who did the wrecking cannot be accepted on their own terms:

Luther, Zwingli, Calvin are now damned as intolerant middle-species on evolutionary course of higher life; a vile saint like Bruno can barely withstand scrutiny into anything beyond his name. But the name of Galileo in the vernacular of science can mean nothing but a triumph of light over darkness. His was the genius who so insouciantly brought shame to the Church, who called the pope an idiot, fell into an easy martyrdom on his estate, and though he recanted from his heliocentric evangelism in the end, is still held up as the height of moral courage and scientific integrity.

In truth, the movement of the earth was unimportant next to the intellectual conceit that Galileo promoted, which was the worship of empirical science. Galileo's project could in no way be confused with one of a disinterested practitioner. A kind of malice must be imputed to averments so far from the facts at hand that to make them is a pestering show of wit rather than a display of proof. And this is what Galileo achieved. For none of his work, none of his inventions, none of his discoveries or discourses could prove the claim Galileo made: That Copernicus' assumption of heliocentrism was indeed the actual image of creation. The man had invented a telescope that exposed craters on the moon, that charted the phases of Venus and the four moons of Jupiter, apparently revolving around that planet as Jupiter was said to revolve around the earth. All these discoveries created an atmosphere far different from the old geocentric cosmology, but in no way provided direct evidence of the earth's movement.

Not even the firmest defenders of Galileo's crusade can now claim that he carried the argument. Like Copernicus, he did not set up any experiment by which the heliocentric hypothesis might be tested. The truth he

155

preached was a kind that did not require any integral proof. Galileo knew what Copernicus did, the truth of relativity the latter had recited from Virgil, "We sail out of the harbor, and the land and the cities move away."[57] Proof of either movement of the sun or movement of the earth could not be made by charting the relative motion of either. But Galileo did not provide proof nor did he endeavor to establish an empirical proof of the heliocentric hypothesis. Indeed, it was not until the Eighteenth Century when experimenters began truly to endeavor for proof of the earth's motion rather than taking this as a given. The success or failure of these particular experiments we need not deal with here, but the most famous of these, the Mickelson-Morley experiment of 1887, which sought to measure the rotation of the earth found no evidence of any motion at all. A layman might look at these results and presume the earth was stationary. Whether or not this could be justified need not concern us: Suffice it to say that it constitutes more evidence against Galileo's claims than he provided for them—absolutely none.

But as we said, the supposed revolution of the earth weighted nothing against the upheaval of thought. And Galileo's underlying claim was that a model which worked reasonably well in predicting planetary motion must, by virtue of this fact, have the distinction of truly representing the actual corporeal functioning of the galaxy. The controversy between geocentrism and heliocentrism has often been overstated. Man might live much the same whether the earth moved or the sun. But he could not expect the relation between God, state, and

[57] *De Revolutionibus*, I-8.

himself to endure where a mere model was enough to inaugurate a genuine reordering of the cosmos. The embrace of Galileo's vision of mechanical reality placed the technician as not only the paragon of science and wisdom, but as the explicator and animator of the cosmos, against which all prior learning and wisdom must bow.

This is not to say that Galileo's contestation was based on whim or caprice, that it was a shallow façade for truculence and pride. If his instruments deluded him it was because his metaphysical presuppositions allowed him to. Galileo, like Descartes closely subsequent to him, was a forefront apostle of the creed of Scientism, *that which cannot be measured cannot be known.* To say that Copernicus had measured the universe best or that his heliocentric model was superior to all others, was undeniably wrong. But the earth-centered cosmology that united the spheres could not be borne by a man who thought the universe only truly knowable by instruments, where essences were creations of men's intellects, where the glossy red apple existed only as a kind of mental detritus of the quantifiable. Galileo's grand work did not depend on the heliocentric hypothesis, but it did rely on the dominance of materialism. If the old metaphysics held, the work of Galileo and others would be useful, but if the new nominalism prevailed, then he had ushered in a revolution, one more stupendous than even the Reformation. Protestants, merely negative force as they are, have always been forced to acknowledge the moral leadership of the Church, taking her Scriptures as definitive, keeping the ordering of feasts as she prescribed, and generally binding themselves to the moral system she founded or discovered. The Church was still tacitly acknowledged as the institution best suited to mediate the demands of man, however her declaimed abuses may have estranged her from Protestant favor. It was still with the Church where the Western heart and intellect remained.

Galileo's revolt finally upended this. He declared for himself knowledge and eminence over the workings of the universe based on no apposite evidence beyond technical savviness. He stood as a kind of enlightened shaman, one who felt free to deprecate priest and king to their faces. He was in fact a seditious scoffer whom no competent governor could have endured. After Galileo, acceptable wisdom would come not through the theologians or metaphysicians, nor the religious or the cosmologist; not even precisely through the physicist, for in this matter Galileo was not offering legitimate proof but a mere suggestion fostered by his technological mastery. The makeup of the cosmos would ever after be descried by the mechanist. Afterwards the technician would rule. In no other society but our own has the cosmological and metaphysical order been left in the hands of such an unworthy class.

Model Dependent Realism

The Galileo Affair can scarcely be called a scientific dispute; it did not rise of descend to that level. The Affair was a question about power, and where the seat of wisdom would be lodged. For more than a millennium that seat had resided in the Magisterium of the Church, which attempted to reconcile the claims of revelation, philosophy, and natural science so as to create a grand picture of the universe. Galileo's purpose was to destroy their foundation and build another apart from their ruins.

But it must be restated: Galileo did not prove or even offer proof of the heliocentric system. His great inventions and observations created an atmosphere in which the heliocentric model could appear feasible, but it did nothing to add data in support of the thesis he was set out to prove. Galileo's discoveries unearthed a new richness to the universe, but these marvels were not evidence. As a modern admirer could not help but state, "It was not proof, but it was propaganda."[58]

The great Robert Bellarmine represented the Church in the controversy. He corrected Galileo in matters theological, but also served as a conscience for that great empiricist in the name of science, pointing out that Galileo had failed to provide sufficient evidence to support his hypothesis, and indeed failed to make any showing at all. Modern scientists have been forced to agree. "The judgment of the Church experts was scientifically correct and had the right social intention, viz to protect people from the machinations of specialists. It wanted to protect people from being corrupted by a narrow ideology that might work in restricted domains but was incapable of sustaining a harmonious life. A revision of the judgment might win the Church some friends among scientists but would severely impair its function as preserver of important human and superhuman virtues."[59] The Church had been correct, yet to what corner must one turn to find one who sees Galileo's triumph as anything but the

---

[58] Thomas Kuhn, *The Copernican Revolution*, 224
[59] Paul Feyerabend, *Against Method*, 132-33.

height of intellectual integrity? The mad rush to embrace heliocentrism cannot be understood in a rational scientific sense, only as an emblem of the new metaphysics.

The absurdity of this all is best seen through the passage of time. And four centuries later we confront the person of Stephen Hawking, the greatest or at least best-known of contemporary physicists, the only of the modern era perhaps worthy of placement in the pantheon next to Galileo. The Scientism Galileo founded is brought to its hilarious conclusion in his works, not only tolerating but embracing the incoherence of bogus reification, of adoption of a "model-dependent realism" to explain the universe.

We see in this promotion of Model Dependent Realism the premises implied by Galileo's victory applied forthright. Hawking still adheres to *realism* in the sense that he presumes any model he may propose serves as something like a mirror image of the universe as it actually is. He will not return to the relative humility of the ancients and hold the model as an analytical tool. This would go too far; it would leave open the possibility that something more than the measurable exists and is needful in understanding the makeup of Nature. It would, in other words, allow for the reapproachment of substantial forms and diminish the power Galileo had won for the technician. No, a model still serves as a means to reify the universe. The only change is that now we are allowed to choose which reification we prefer. "If two such physical theories or models accurately predict the same events, one cannot be said to be more real than the other; rather we are free to use whichever model is most convenient."[60] Such is the high judgment of modern science.

What criteria do we use to determine which model is appropriate? Hawkins gives four in all: That the model be elegant, have few arbitrary or adjustable elements, agree with and explains all existing conditions, and make detailed predictions about future observations that might conceivably falsify the model. Leaving aside any question of whether there are complete and sufficient assessments of any model, we note the fact that it is the model, the apparatus of thought itself, that ultimately drives one's choice of universes. It is not even man that determines his cosmos, but the workability of the operative model before him.

So we complete the circuit. The absurdity that Galileo could not assert later scientists have the temerity to define. Hawking has looked back on four centuries of shifting models and proclaimed that so long as the prejudices of scientists are satisfied, the universe can move as our models say it moves. That it is hokum is irrelevant. It is no great departure from the Western cosmology of the past four hundred years, one driven by the musings of experts. Mere empirical science is given a metaphysical significance beyond anything its actual practice can bear. And so we find that scientists are studying what are nothing but self-admitted mental figments, and yet by use of these *res cogitantes* we can both know and in effect remake the cosmos based on their dictates. It is a foolish conceit, yet one adopted everywhere, from the credulous masses to the most sagacious of our shamans. And owing to its exalted place, man is forced to pretend that empiricism is

---

[60] Hawking, *The Grand Design* 7.

interesting, that it is not a task suited for monkeys but has great intrinsic meaning beyond its occasional minute progression: that the task of counting aphids on a leaf could be enlightening. It is a queer, inscrutable system, one of esoteric priests and miserable parishioners. At the top of this hierarchy are the fabulists, the men whose wills close the system of thought under one paradigm and thus set the new cosmos—men like Darwin, Einstein, Hawking. Then with them are the explicators, the disciples of clear minds who best understand the esoteric models their progenitors have provided them and most fully inhabit the new cosmos. They are the men of aptitude but not genius, whose vision is whole but not new, who best proselytize the belief that science has something at all to offer man. And below them were the aphid-counters, those actually engaged in the drudgery of empirical work. This is *normal science*, the doggerel mechanism of modern wisdom.

The Epicurean had the good sense not to be a hopeful creature: If man is only matter, then man is no more than dust. A man like Democritus or Heraclitus possessed a deeper understanding of nature and matter than the modern empiricist, for the Epicurean understood that the material was no great thing: that it decayed, as all things do, and with it so does pleasure, and thus the lone of good beneath the sun.

The modern materialist has not adopted this pessimism, wise though it was. The priests of Scientism abjured the Christian universe but simply could not rid themselves of her universality, however much their own creeds remained agnostic or even hostile to such a notion. They might like Bacon sometimes linger near the edge of honest nihilism, but most often retained the otherwise irrational and unfounded hope that the order perceived in the lab was order everywhere. A notion like Model-Dependent Reality could only be laughable to the ancient atomists. Yet in practice all enlightened minds, enraptured so far by man's new ability to measure and see the universe, gladly accepted the notion that its substance truly changed with a flux of man's learning. He would allow his most precious knowledge about his place in the cosmos transform at the beck and whim of the empiricist. The new materialists born of the Age of Reason could abjure Christ the man, but not Christ the Logos. They could reject a set order to existence, but could not abjure order itself: They simply fell back on the empiricist to provide them with such order.

It is this metaphysical conceit that allows for the rule by ideology. The materialist scientist posited that his models were sufficient to describe all of Nature; the ideologue posits that his models are sufficient to describe and therefore regulate all society. Both undertake a form of cosmogenesis. Neither party's contention can be *proven*, yet where no proof is asked, none need be supplied. This was the true spirit of the Age of Reason, that which could accommodate an atmosphere that was both capacious yet stultifying. It was an unstated metaphysical tenet that allowed such a conceit to prevail, an unwarranted credence in the Logos remaining after Christ had disappeared.

Bacon and Utility

Yet any metaphysical or *religious* conceit of science must be considered against the fact that it is still a low undertaking on its own terms. If we can never really probe to the essences of things, if our knowledge of unities is in fact a mental detritus, how and wherefore should this endeavor continue? Why should man undertake the arduous task of empirical inquiry at all? The Prince of Philosophers again provides rule and meaning. "The real and legitimate goal of the sciences is the endowment of human life with new inventions and riches.["][61] Macaulay, his great defender, fleshes out the point: "The ancient philosophers did not neglect natural science, but they did not cultivate it for the purpose of increasing the power and ameliorating the condition of man... Natural science was made subsidiary to the art of disputation; and it consequently proved altogether barren of useful discoveries." [62] This was hardly true, as anyone conversant with the work of Friar Bacon or Albert the Great must know. But these thinkers still believed, for all their empirical laboring, that the soul of man was of all things terrestrial the worthiest of study and improvement. These men were scientists, but had not fallen into the cult of science, the belief that it could provide sufficient justification for anything. The highest things of creation were still those the philosophers and theologians had identified, not those given on the tickmarks of whatever and sundry machine.

But "to make men perfect was no part of Bacon's plan. His humble aim was to make imperfect men comfortable. The aim of Baconian philosophy was to supply vulgar wants."[63] The man, to his credit, was humbler than those of the Galilean bent, men like

---

[61] *Novum Organum*, I.81

[62] Macaulay, "Francis Bacon" 362

[63] Id at 373

Hawking who claimed the false powers of cosmogenesis. Bacon's science presumes that its proper end is material, and that the heights of human knowledge it accommodates are to be employed towards the creation of wealth. The process of scientific inquiry itself cannot lead us to this conclusion—Bacon's *summum bonum* cannot be derived from his own terms—for under a paradigm that denies essences, it is not clear if anything really can be known on any values derived from reality. Likewise, there is no guarantee that a scientific endeavor that shines most light on a given topic is also that which will best provide for new inventions and riches. No, the new *telos* is appended only because there is nothing else to propel the endeavor of science.

We should appreciate the irony of what has occurred: Man, through the course of the Enlightenment found himself more and more lowered to the level of a purely sensitive creature, dependent on his five senses and their instrumental accoutrements to possess any wisdom at all. The Age of Reason was above all else an abjuration of man's reason, a fatal skepticism towards the light of his intellect and his apprehension of reality. Just as critically science could no longer justify its own practice. The Aristotelian ethos spoke for itself; science was the study of essences, and therefore the purpose of science was this unveiling. But the New Nominalists had abjured essences. Why proceed on this task which now appears to be measurement for measurement's sake? Those who accepted the Cartesian divide could not truthfully claim to study truth per se, or anything real at all. If Bacon's call to use science to pursue material wealth seemed venal and crass, it at least was comprehensible.

And yet the vulgarity of the task has not prevented our hard scientists from acquiring an aspect of religious totemists, our only true and univocally recognized cosmologists of any repute. And yet if we come to them honestly we recognize how tawdry and mediocre these seers really are. Rather than visionaries, they are reactive vessels, reliant more on the social atmosphere of the elites than genuine empirical skill. "We are not able to make cosmological models without some admixture of ideology,"[64] admits Hawking himself. Indeed the *hard scientist* is more dependent on his social scientist counterparts than vice-versa. He who understands the social changes of the Seventeenth and Eighteenth Centuries understands the science of the Nineteenth and Twentieth. He who understands Luther understands Galileo better than the mathematician; he who understands Hobbes has all he needs to know about Darwin, and he who has a grasp on the German idealists has all he needs to know of Einstein. *Scientific breakthroughs* are rarely anything but excesses the intellectual decay of the age has allowed to prosper.

Technical advances may indeed be perpetual, but if wisdom is anything more than a dataset, she must be adjudged in comparison to the quality of our theories. But no supposedly objective fact, no data or datum can lead us to accept one model over another. Our desire to move from one paradigm to another, from the Newtonian to the Einsteinian, from the Freudian to the Behaviorist, from the Classical to the Keynesian,

---

[64] Wolfgang Smith, *Science and Myth*, 197 citing Hawking's *The Large Scale Structure of Space-Time*, Cambridge University Press 1979, 134

depends on something more than the data. No amount of logic can lead a man from one paradigm to another. Whether man is cumulatively wiser by placing himself in the Einsteinian or the Newtonian universe is a matter of opinion. The latter we are told is less complete, yet we are told by the former that the modern universe is stitched together with claims like String Theory and universe-consuming error terms called *dark matter* that can never be detected. Who is fit to judge the arguments against this hokum?

A great benefit of these grand theoretical apparatuses is that they are inscrutable to a vast majority of the population. To merely attempt to engage with the technical components of an abstruse model is to accept its theoretical premises if just for a time, and only for the purpose of discovering the basic identity of whether the model is what it purports to be. And as a man is awed by the tower clock as compared to the wristwatch, the bigger and more complex the model raises more admiration for it, if not for the model's elegance than for the very fact it does not collapse under its own weight. But no model is so elegant to be able to justify an empty theoretical premise. Nor are models alone able to guide us towards true wisdom, towards a truly deeper and more expansive vision of the world. As long as a theory is modifiable it is never truly falsifiable, and more complex appendages can always be added to it to make the theory comport with new data.

All this runs as a way of saying that science, as properly understood and practiced, is always a singularly human thing. Our instruments are not sufficient for anything alone, nor can our models serve to remake the cosmos. In the end, there is no way to evade the fact that the value of a scientific paradigm arises from an act of judgment apart from any determination given within that system. Nor does a chosen paradigm or model represent anything more than a human apparatus, a means whereby we come to better know Nature, but whose very artificiality exposes our limited faculties and Nature's limitless potential for contemplation. Every man has the power to close his eyes to the world, to the datum he has no desire to see. Scientific knowledge is ultimately a matter of free choice. The humanly human can never be extracted from the course of scientific progress. The progress of scientific truth is, in the end, an act of human will.

Treatise on Ideology

It is impossible to rule men without recourse to ideas. Men can be ruled by fear, but even this fear must become rational fear if the tyrant is to benefit from systematic oppression. The terror wrought by a tyrant can only endure so long, but a tyranny girded by ideas can be perpetual. A man does not often fall behind his king or sovereign because he has weighed the costs and benefits of treason. The material realm constrains us, guides what is feasible, provides us sustenance but cannot give us, in that glorious cognate of our language, a *reason* to live. Man can live with material deprivation but not a moral one.

All things carry with them an idea. To know something is to have an idea of it; to say that a thing exists is to say it exists as an idea. And we are ruled by ideas: Property is an idea. Suffrage is an idea. But they are ideas that center on the essence of a real thing. Ideology is not concerned with describing the essence of a thing. Ideology as a rule always looks past the essence of the thing being studied or expounded upon, to some higher aspect hidden in the object seen. The ideologue does not see the essence of any thing nor even acknowledge that one exists, and instead posits that inherent to all things is some higher relation—to class, to race, to democracy—or whatever ideological force he seeks to wield.

There is, of course, nothing abhorrent in the study of ideas. An error has lodged itself in the conservative mind that recourse to ideas is not fit for the governance of the social order. We find John Adams railing against the *Ideocracy* established by the governments of France from 1789 to 1799, and from there abjuring all attempts to put forth a social order based on ideas. "The logos of Plato, the ratio of Manilius, and the mind of Condorcet, all plausible and specious as they are, will be three thousand years longer more delusive than useful. Not one of them takes human nature as it is for his foundation."[65] In his chastisements, he is following the lineage of Burke, whose hostility towards abstractions led him to reject the notion of efficacious natural right. "Strictly speaking, conservatism is not a political system, and certainly not an ideology. In the phrase of H. Stuart Hughes, 'Conservatism is the negation of ideology.' Instead, conservatism is a way of looking at the civil social order." So said Russell Kirk,[66] settling the matter as it exists for the conservative persuasion.

So far as conservative reaction is limited to the actual errors of the ideologues, it is sound. But as it extends to

---

[65] "Debate with Condorcet" in *Portable Conservative Reader*, Ed. Russell Kirk. 622
[66] *The Conservative Mind,* Seventh Revised Edition.

all conceptual rule of ideas, which must necessarily include the Natural Law, we must depart. For the Natural Law is discovered by the application of right reason to practical matters in relation to man. It cannot be divorced from the *ideal*, which is not observable in reality, and from which in practice men have ever fallen asunder. No age can be found where some tyrant has not stomped on natural right, just as no generation since the Fall can vouch of more than a handful of men who abide by justice in all their affairs. And yet we cannot cast aside, like Hobbes, the very notion of the tyrant; we know very well the difference between a Sulla and a Caesar. Likewise, we know that we do wrong when we depart from the law, however clever our specious justifications, and the literature of all peoples attests to this. Our morals are imprinted on us not as a photo-negative vision of reality, but through the rational mediation of what we know should be. We cannot passively receive the tenets of justice from mere observation—we must engage with it as an ideal form, a due north veiled to us by the cloudy sky of reality.

But the ideologues, however much they may have striven to apply right reason, could not accept the true authority of God or Nature. Where Nature is immutable, the good and reasonable reaction to it can be derived without much trouble. But if God is malleable, if Nature can be distorted, then the use of reason and the application of good and evil becomes not reactive but prescriptive, a question not of how man must reasonably respond, but how Nature should be reasonably molded. Such is the endeavor of the ideologue.

All political philosophy before the French Revolution looked at man and asked what he was, and asked therefore how he should be ruled. Plato built up a republic *a priori*, but it was based on class interests, on presumed concrete roles within the society. But the new philosopher could not accept any natural role for man or any preexisting form of social ordering. Rousseau would accept no classes at all within his ideal state. "For the general will to be truly expressed, it is essential that there be no subsidiary groups within the State, and that each citizen voice has his own opinion and nothing but this own opinion."[67] This cannot be confused with mere democracy, of which Rousseau was an implacable enemy. "What makes the will general is not the number of citizens concerned but the common interest by which they are united." The general will indeed is different from the *will of all*, which merely takes account of the interests of many divergent groups.[68]

"How can the blind multitude, which often does not know what it wants because only rarely does it know what is for its own good, undertake, of itself, an enterprise so extensive and so difficult as the formulation of a system of law? Left to themselves, the People always desire the good, but, left to themselves, they do not always know where the good lies The general will is always right, but the judgment guiding it is not always well informed. It must be made to see things as they are, sometimes as they ought to be. It must be shown how to attain the good it seeks, must be protected against the temptations inherent in particular interests. Individuals see the good which they reject: the public desires the good which it does not see. Both, equally, are in need of guidance. The first must be

---

[67] *Social Contract* II-3
[68] Id.

considered to submit their wishes to their reason, the second to learn what it is they want."[69]

We must apply firmer definitions to such airy stuff. The undifferentiated people he speaks of are the mass; the *common will* is a fledgling notion of ideology.

Defining Ideology

The term *ideology* is slippery, used so often and so haphazardly, and yet with such general consistency that we should not question that it is more than a mere cloud of a word, and that it defines a real thing. Ideology is, like liberalism, a term that everyone knows, and whose features are so acknowledged, that one feels that every party who employs it describes the same thing, however poorly he might fare in actually defining it. Like so many concepts of the mind, it exists and we appreciate its existence, yet our inability to define it makes us doubt its reality.

In our own time, having lived so long under the ideologue's rule, it has become a term synonymous with belief. We find that ideology, in the words of an archetypical academic, exists "to describe specific, fundamental beliefs of groups or people." It is "specific group knowledge, beliefs that are taken for granted, commonsense, and shared by different ideological groups, is by definition non-ideological within that community." It is the "axiomatic foundations of the social representations shared by groups." In other words, ideology is synonymous with any creed or belief. By such definition, one could not differentiate the

---

[69] Id. II-6.

172

Communist from the Mohammedan, the ancient from the modern, the sacred from the profane. No, if ideology is only a belief or a creed, it is nothing distinctly meaningful and therefore nothing useful to us.

A brief return to the roots of the term will be helpful to us. *Ideology* was coined by the French liberal Antoine Destutt de Tracy in the midst of the Revolution's clamor, who called it the "science and formation of ideas" and oriented his masterwork, his *Treatise on Political Economy*, around study of this science. Tracy's work is subtle. His project is not a reordering of state and society so much as a display that the existing order, with all its constituent parts—the *ideas* of property, individuality, riches and poverty—can and ought to be considered through the medium of man's sentiments. We see in Tracy an impulse similar to Kant in his reformulation of ethics: the process of taking traditional forms and mediating them not through the logic inherent in the things and actions themselves, but solely with reference to man's use. We cannot presume an immanent logos of things: we can only arrive at their meaning through the mediation of our senses and our resultant will. Appropriate to the mind of his times, Tracy's orientation is around the attainment of classically liberal ends. Success to Tracy is measured against the attainment of liberty, and society is nothing but a succession of exchanges. "Our sole duty is to augment our liberty and its value. The object of society is solely the fulfilment of this duty."[70] It is through this particular lens that all else is to be judged.

Tracy's work is now all but forgotten, yet its lineage shows it to be a recessive gene in the evolving organism

---

[70] *Treatise* xiv

of ideology. For even from this early date we see the trait, soon to be universal, of an ideologue taking a single notional element—here the vaunted liberty—which can be used to judge the value or demerit of elements of society as a whole. As of most everything they accomplished, the concrete tenets held by the Jacobins have faded away, but the perverted logic used to come to them has been retained and fostered later excrescences that choked out all fruit earlier on the vine. Men no longer venerate liberty or hold it of any value in assessing the legitimacy of a state—how much less oppression we would feel if they did! Yet the modern ideologue has retained the reasoning of its progenitor even after casting aside his values.

Such is the very nature of the Marxist left, those most constant and noxious employers of the term. Ideology is, in this pedagogy, all-consuming, a fetish of the bourgeois minds that were Marx and Engels. From the latter we hear that ideology is a *false consciousness*, a kind of veil set over reality and the true motive forces impelling him. "It is not the consciousness of men that determines their being, but on the contrary, their social being that determines their consciences." The economic conditions of society are all that truly matter, the rest of the spheres of human industry—political, juridical, philosophical, theological—are a kind of effluvium, mental vapors arising from the material motor.[71] "As to the realms of ideology which soar still higher in the air, religions, philosophy, etc., these have a prehistoric stock, found already in existence by, and taken over in, the

---

[71] Letter to Franz Mehring (on Historical Materialism)

historic period, of what we today would call bunk."[72] To understand the congruence between the socialist and capitalist projects will help us understand how the dutch-uncle of scientific socialism could agree so well with the Philosopher-King of Dearborn—Engels the materialist theologian, and Ford the practicing saint. Ideology is, to a materialist, an eternal attribute of human understanding, the intellectual vapors that arise from the functioning of the material. And where there is no force but the material to guide man in his beliefs, the intellectual must always reduce to matter. Whether done wittingly or not, it is this all-pervasive understanding of ideology that fosters the modern definition so often employed by the uncritical of every political persuasion, that ideology is synonymous with belief itself.

It is Hannah Arendt's astute observations that we linger on the longest, for it is with Arendt that we find a definition that is distinct and historically meaningful. Ideologies are "isms which to the satisfaction of their adherents can explain everything and every occurrence by deducing it from a single presence... Ideologies pretend to know the mysteries of the whole historical process—the secrets of the past, the intricacies of the present, the uncertainties of the future—because of the logic inherent in their respective ideas." However, the "isms" of ideologies, such as *race* in racism or *God* in deism, never form the subject matter of the ideologies "and the suffix -*logy* never indicates simply a body of 'scientific' statements."[73]

"The *idea* of an ideology is neither the eternal essence grasped by the eyes of the mind nor the regulator of

---

[72] Letter to Joseph Bloch
[73] *Origins of Zionism*, 316

reason—as it was from Plato to Kant—but has become an instrument of explanation." The idea is not merely a mode of thought that shines a light on certain aspects of the historical record, but are used to calculate the very mechanisms of history itself. "As soon as logic as a *movement* of thought—and not as a necessary control of thinking—is applied to an idea, this idea is transformed into a *premise*... The purely negative coercion of logic, the prohibition of contradictions, became 'productive' so that a whole line of thought could be initiated, and forced upon the mind, by drawing conclusions in the manner of mere argumentation. An ideology differs from simple opinion in that it claims to possess either the key to history, or a solution to all the riddles of the universe, or the intimate knowledge of the hidden universal laws which are supposed to rule nature and man."[74]

Here is the heart of the matter: Recognition that the ideologue does not approach the world looking for the essences of things in his purview. All reality and all of history is subjectivized to one aspect, that one underlying idea of a given ideology. The ideologue is not interested in discovering reality as it is, he is only interested in things insofar as they can be related back to the certain underlying theory he has chosen. He has done as the mechanist did with the new science: established an epistemic closure on his understanding of the social world. The ideologue, like the empiricist, looks not at the thing of his study itself—here, the society in front of him—but views it only obliquely, and with reference only to those attributes measurable against his

---

[74] Id. at 159.

chosen ideal. And why should he not do so? Society had no organic structure and its constituent parts no essences. It exists like an amalgam of free-floating plasma, lying in wait for some expert to arrive and reify it.

All this is a way of saying that ideology is the application of Scientism to the social sphere. No definition can be more concise than this nor more accurate. Arendt was too much the liberal to recognize the relation between ideology and the New Science of Galileo and Descartes, to see that the rule of ideology was only the social corollary of the new empiricists' domination of thought. Liberals are often too humane to bear the sight of scientific principles applied to the ways of men, and instead adopt the romanticism of the Burkean conservative, positing that man is, for some reason or another, apart from the jurisdiction of the Blind Watchmaker who governed all else. Yet humane temperament cannot long withstand logical necessity. As Pope extolled,

Nature and nature's laws lay hid in night.
God said "Let Newton be" and all was light.

How could one hold that the work of Galileo, Descartes, and Newton had uncovered the glories of all creation, yet this same light should not be shone on man? The *novum organum* had finally unveiled the *true* nature of reality, so who in his right mind would deny himself the use of it on the social world? How often do we hear such foolish claims as *Galileo invented Science* from men who will nonetheless deny Science's power to the realms which affect men most? The man who will not accept Ideas or Forms still felt in his gut the heresy of formlessness when applied against man; he could cry with romantic ferocity that quite unlike every other charted molecule in the universe, man could not be known, and therefore ought not be touched by the ideologue. It was a cry as humane as it was empty, divorced from the logical world that Galileo and Descartes had created. The social error could not have existed without the metaphysical error, but where the metaphysical error was nowhere acknowledged, the romantic was left with no recourse but to wail for the dignity of his prejudice.

Modern men are presumed to have ideologies, presumed to have beliefs about how the social universe *should be* composed. Once the seeds of ideology have been planted, it is vain and impossible to be *unideological*, as so many feckless conservatives seek to do. A material order systematically disordered under the onus of an ideology can only be brought back to order through concerted and thoughtful counterrevolution. There is no return to Nature once Nature has been transformed, there is only a conscious and intentional manipulation of Nature towards another ideologue's liking. We may think of the Old Regime as a perfect untouched branch, but once axe and chisel have been taken to it, one has no choice but to try to wield these tools to one's own liking. The desire to be *unideological* is absolutely vacuous once a society has been infected by ideology. There is no return to a truly *natural* state as the conservative dreams of it; the Restorationist of 1815 could not simply propose the instauration of the Bourbons, but had to be in principle a monarchist, and act through such principle on the leavened mass of society. The inanity of being *unideological* is all the more apparent following the material transformations of the Third Revolution, which we will see penetrated to every facet of life and the strongest bastions of reaction, contorting all men to rule by idea. We are left with no choice but to be ideological. The alternative is to leave man an amorphous thing or, as is more likely, to let him fall into the hands of whatever ideologue desires more strongly to have him.

Ideology and the French Revolution

The ancient philosophers looked at man and asked how he should best be ruled. They differed immensely in their answers: approaching the problem with different conceptions of man, and sending him on different ways in search of his sundry final ends. Their theories sometimes required man take a subordinate role to the state, while other times his individuality and egoism were placed at the forefront. Yet through all of it was man, in all his complexities, who formed the focal point of study. It was only with the French Revolution that this old conception of social philosophy was entirely overthrown. The battle ever after would be how men were to be utilized towards the remaking of the social order. In the matter of political existence, men were no longer an end in themselves, but a means for arriving at an ideologue's preferred outcome.

But it would be impossible, the remaking of society on the basis of such epistemic closure were the *materiel* for this transformation not at hand. This, again, was the *mass*, the group of people who recognized their communal force and begged to be wielded. The English and Americans had long entertained concepts of a rationalized artificial rule, but in sundry and periodic fashion; they lacked a pliant and enthusiastic *mass* who might serve as the elementary clay of the new state. Yet this was the psychology found amongst the Parisian insurgents, who longed to make themselves fungible to the new standard-bearers. The ancient mob that cried for bread or land was responding to the objective needs of man. The new mass of men called out for *Liberte*, which as a political action point can have no distinct meaning. Liberty is a notional concept, not an absolute demand or a good that can be delivered concretely. Liberty can never be total, and can only have little or no meaning when compared to some alleged state of oppression. To long to be ruled by *Liberte* is an invitation to be conquered, to be led by the man willing to define the term and apply it to the real discrete circumstances before him. The mob takes to the streets and cries for the material or political benefits all men desire, while the masses take to the streets to let others know they will be ruled, they will be swayed. It was these masses in Paris who were moved like armies of meat over the Alps and into Moscow, who had cried for the notion of Liberty, and only in time learned it would take the matter of Bonaparte. They had desired a new reason for being, a new motive force, and they received it.

"It is interesting that the cause of the Third Estate should have been defended more eagerly and forcibly by the ecclesiastical and noble writers than by the non-privileged classes themselves."[75] But this was not surprising at all, and only a man of Abbe Sieyes' credulity could fail to understand. For the poor are always best protected when they are most closely united to the bonds that Nature's God has fettered them with;

---

[75] *What is the Third Estate?* Ch. 4

it is to these they can best turn to for guidance in their affairs, and to the Just Judge for recompense. What feeble identities they own, whether peasant, landowner, guildsman, or father confer accordant rights of status, and provide surest balustrade against the onslaught of money and might, which are never long without powers of suasion. The man who was recognized as peasant was legally protected in his objective peasanthood; bereft of this, it was inevitable that money and might would have their way.

The poor will always be with us, in one shape or another, and an underclass will always exist. It is a truism that the weak will be oppressed, and only Christian benevolence can hope to mollify it. But it is under the liberal regime that the poor are oppressed most insidiously and brutally. Man himself has become the territory to be enclosed. Because the notions used to lord over him seem to derive from his natural rights, he does not at first object. But control over these notions is not in his hands, as was his land, his trade, or his natural family. He is now the potency of an ideological system, waiting to be turned into matter by the political moment. Man now could less and less see himself as he was, as God saw him, but instead he longed to know his place in *History* and the *Economy*, in those great notions that might give his existence within the social order meaning. As the Leviathan had stripped men of their consciences, so now did it appropriate their deepest selfhoods, and contorted them towards the ends of the state. For the liberal conquers not by gaining material resources, land, or the will of Providence, but by creating dependence: he creates the territory of *Liberty*, *Equality*, and *Justice* that he afterwards conquers, first standing suppliant to a common dream, then ensnaring those he has enticed.

The supposed rigor of the Age of Reason was transient, and the next generation abjured the full faith that society should operate on the principles of natural science. Yet the ostensible rationalism which provided motive force for the French Revolution was never the Second Revolution's primary quality. The laughing fits of Voltaire provided a kind of inebriating force, a kind of swig of whiskey before one throws himself into no-man's land, but the battle was over the matter, the ability to remake society and the polity as men liked, to begin at Rousseau's homogenous state.

The post-Revolutionary man no longer recognized an essence to society because he no longer acknowledged an essence of man. No doubt this creature still needed to eat, but the structures of social order would no longer need to be directed towards the creature's material ends. *Human nature* was still recognized, but no longer given rational reflection in the liberal state. The state was now formally irrational with respect to man. It no longer primarily served him. It served, rather, theories of liberty, theories of society, theories of economics, all of which posited that man's highest goods could be achieved through those theories' application. It was presumed by the ideologue that if the secrets he held were fully realized and accomplished that man's welfare would improve, that if *liberty* or *equality* were achieved the rising tide would lift man like a barnacle clinging to the mast. In the end, man is not the focal point of this analysis.

The reader will recall how we described liberal change, as a process of enshrining vice and justifying it on the grounds of socialization. The French Revolution was the prototypical liberal revolution because it abolished the last notions of a natural social order. The new socialized morality it would posit would now be effected simultaneously with the change, not after the fact. And yet the proposed changes which were in fact ideological impositions must always have the nature of vice, for they are abstractions away from the essences of the proper objects to be ruled. To accept an abstraction as the *sine qua non* of a thing is to deform it, to truncate its actual existence and yet to take it as the actual completion of the object itself. So does the ideologue see man by the measures of Freedom, of Productivity, of Class Status: attributes of man but none such that can capture him as a whole. His complex essence denied, the social order would now only meet him on the basis of whatever epistemic closure the ideologue adopted. The essences of society and man were denied as a principle, and nothing but shallow inhumanity could result.

The underlying characteristic of the French Revolution is that the state would no longer meet men as they were: as peasants, nobles, Churchmen, Jews, but as universal *citoyon*. Yet the peasant was still a peasant in fact, as a Jew was still a Jew. This new citizen had abjured his protections at law but could make no honest claim to similitude. In succeeding generations, women would cry for emancipation, for equal rights and treatment: for the law to turn a blind eye to her womanhood and thus, on paper, to be free from it. Yet in all she was still a woman—the only change that would come about was that the social order would no longer be rationally ordered around her womanhood. This womanhood would still be impressed into her by her frailties, by her particular strengths, by her child-bearing and her natural maternity; but in the ordering of society, the bulwarks of law designed to protect her and her nature were vanquished, and termed positively evil. The legal fiction of parity between men and women was gradually turned into a moral one—though only when the material means became such that they might occlude the real. And this, as we shall see, is the story of the Third and Fourth Revolutions, when the revolution in the immaterial productive apparatus of society forged in material fact an equality the Jacobin could only posit as legal fiction. In the meantime, the free atoms of contract were still men with real characteristics, who brought to the level field their innate characteristics, but could no longer find succor because of them. This was the great tragedy of the Jacobin revolt, that they who aped the strength and valor of the Peloponnesians in fact were being subsumed into a technician's universal orrery.

A humane politics must always be focused on the human. It is neither wise, prudent, nor charitable to expect the superhuman from anyone as a basis for being ruled. Yet this is what the liberal state demanded for the new deracinated man, all while calling it virtue. The struggles of the Nineteenth Century arose out of the application of the French Revolution's leveling principles, the babble between those who yearned to subsume men into the mass and those who recognized this as unendurable. Fervor for the old ideals died down, but this did not matter; capital could carry men where their ideals would no longer go.

Benthamism

We before discussed ideologies as a whole, but one deserves attention above all, that which has provided the grist for numberless liberal changes, that which grounds

184

in mathematical rigor the philosophy of materialism, that which most brilliantly homogenizes all existence, which has infected every walk of social conception and made itself implicit in all other ideologies, most of which are merely its subset and ancillary form.

That ideology is Utilitarianism. We recall it was utility that stood as the motive of Bacon's *novum organum*, the *telos* of all the age's advances, and the guiding light for all human progress. Now in the science of social ordering utility would stand in a similarly privileged position, the legitimate end not only of all human knowledge, but the very paradigmatic end of life itself.

Says Bentham: "An action then may be said to be conformable to the principle of utility, or for shortness' sake, to utility (meaning with respect to the community at large) when the tendency it has to augment the happiness of the community is greater than it has to diminish it. A measure of government may be said to be conformable to or dictated by the principle of utility when in like manner the tendency which it has to augment the happiness of the community is greater than any which it has to diminish it. A man may be said to be a partisan of the principle of utility when the approbation or disapprobation he annexes to any action or to any measure is determined by and proportioned to the tendency which he conceives it to have to augment or to diminish the happiness of the community, or in other words, to its conformity or unconformity to the laws or dictates of utility."[76]

The totem of Utility stands as the perfect deracinated and universal measure, applicable to the highest spires of Italy to the mud huts of Somalia. Bentham's brilliant

[76] Bentham, "The Principle of Utility," ix.

tautology applies to each and every human action, for
there is none that man performs that does provide him,
in direct or attenuated form, some kind of utility, just as
no matter exists without *being*, just as no idea can exist
without *form*. Utility can never approach the essence of
thing, and any man who considers a thing, action or
abstinence invaluable knows that utility is a poor proxy.
A man's love for his children and his God give him
utility, but to ascribe such bust. It must think defiling the
beloved. The most personal and numinous desires can
be accommodated by utilitarian calculus, but at some
point the easily quantifiable must contribute a quantum:
altars must start to pay their way. The utility of a
monastery versus a textile factory will always find better
expression in the latter; the utility of chastity will be
found wanting against the utility of cash. For the habit
of mind formed by utilitarian thinking will always revert
to prices. The intangible things, however *utile* they may
be to the heart, scarcely can provide the spreadsheet
figures which could make its existence economical. Yet
almost all can at least tolerate the utilitarian system as a
mental construct, for it is, if nothing else, tolerant.

Let us not confuse this an individualist philosophy. A
particular man's utility, gained from any particular
action, is relevant only insofar that it pertains to a
communal measure. Should we ever suffer the horror of
meeting a strict utilitarian, we would find him indifferent
to a vast array of human suffering. He can indeed
witness the immiseration of a vast swathe of the
population so long as total utility of the community be
increased. The strict logic of utilitarianism is compatible
with most systems of mass-murder, and the esoteric

ideologies of Lenin and Mao always seem to revert to this measure.

The superscience that Tracy envisioned was realized in Bentham's calculus. Utilitarianism is king of all ideologies, that which guided Marx in his fever dreams and provides fallback for every modern tyrant who stumbles across Mao's distinction between a tragedy and a statistic. All the world's history can be fit within this paradigm, all heroism and religion. One might try to take up Bentham's gauntlet of finding a common thread more universal, but most likely without success. So long as we are materialists we will find nothing higher; we can conceive of no hierarchy in fact but what is utile to the whole. Most critically, all of modern economics is but a bloom from Bentham's bulbs. And it is with this reflection that we turn to the Third Revolution, that which turned the materialist philosophies from intellectual blueprints into the squalid edifices of the industrial world.

The Third Revolution of 1917

In the long lifetime that is the history of a people, one can be tempted, or at least forgiven of the temptation to look back with relief on the French Revolution. Its lettered barbarity and the platitudes that have proven impossible to dislodge are still a kind of reprieve to a man looking back over many years, like a time of debauchery that has culminated in a present cirrhosis, but a bacchanal which nonetheless stands as reprieve to the tedium of the age before it: the godless meandering of the Eighteen Century. And for this the French Revolution stands as a relief, if only for the biographies it spurred, the anthems it inspired, the recrudescence of poetic imagination it fostered.

The Bolshevik Revolution is a far viler thing. It is a vulgar cacophony, an embarrassment of maturity and late life, when such extravagancies can no longer be attributed to youth, when the hand is singed again by the flame that had previously scarred it, when mirthless pallor sets over a man who seeks to prove his aged muscles are not yet spent. It too was a reaction to and outgrowth of the terrible century preceding it, but its remedies were hackneyed and obsolete. The socialist cause had already spent its intellectual mettle long before the revolution. By the time its seeds found womb in the mutts and thugs of a schizophrenic Russia, its motive force was spent. The revolution mustered onwards on fumes of earlier victories, Manhattan finance, and easy recourse to mass murder. In practice, it amplified rather

188

than negated the monotony and dehumanization of the industrial system it sought to supplant, and its apparatchiks, whatever their putative ideologies, joined the race of mechanics and quibblers that had already made workers' lives a Hell on earth. However much the Bolsheviks trumpeted scientific socialism and a new age of liberation, their revolution was still a bourgeois thing: it was the same ideology that an honest Girondin would recognize after the process of Natural Selection had eradicated vestigial liberties and advanced *Egalite* to the realm of property. Marx's ideal man was a creature of the Third Estate, not fundamentally different from Robespierre's or Rousseau's, realized in the immutable logic of History. "Human emancipation will only be complete when the real, individualized man has absorbed himself into the abstract citizen."[77] Any liberal democrat might ruminate on the same terms. That a true dictatorship of the proletariat shone only dully in the Old Master's mind is understandable when we take him as the bourgeois he was. Marx adored capitalism, and in his Judaic acerbity chanted its prayers with all the obsession of an heir-apparent watching his benefactor drink himself to death. That communism was inevitable was the one thing that Marx really knew, yet communism was really a negative thing to him rather than a firm setting of the imagination, a void which might be filled with bourgeois trifles: with studying and gardening, as Mahamad had filled his afterlife with virgins.

The Bolshevik cause, that vile thing, that greasy industrial effluvium, was also a bourgeois and a capitalist thing. There is nothing worth knowing about

---

[77] "On the Jewish Question."

Bolshevism, Communism or any form of modern socialism but that it is an outgrowth of capitalism, and finally, when Minerva's Owl has taken flight, recognizable only as a capitalist tumor. And hence to us only capitalism is worth studying. It is the true motive force, both ideological and material, for all true socialism, which is always modern, which is always bourgeois. Communism could solve the political problems created by capitalism, it could remove the disparity between capital and labor, between the owners and the proletariat, and it could perhaps solve some of the problems of distribution of wealth. What it could not solve was the problem of industrial production itself, of the technological treadmill on which the capitalist mode of production relies and which, so long as it exists, sets the standard for socialist economics.

The social order that arose and congealed in the Nineteenth Century could foster little loyalty. "Why should I reverence or obey the man who happens to be richer than I am?"[78] The modern crisis of authority arises out of this question. The men who created the technical conditions for industry, the innovators like Edison, Firestone and Ford, could win the fascination of the public, for it was they that truly propelled the system. As chivalry had pervaded and justified the feudal mode of production, so technical brilliance made legitimate the bastard rule of mere wealth, that lifeblood and prerequisite for a functioning capitalist economy. The new economy required growth, and growth required technical progress, a technical progress the capitalist

---

[78] Belloc, "The Faith and Industrial Capitalism"

could tout as superior to any antecedents and competitors.

But capitalist production presumed a new subjugation. Man's well-being depended wholly on the ability of the capitalist engine to create, and his material conditions in the present depended on technology progress in the future. The gambit was, in terms of material wealth and *utility*, a winning one, but the effect was to conflate forevermore freedom and cash, to confuse the limited powers man had in his natural limitations with the ability to create and purchase his way into the new material circumstances he desired. Man could have seemingly endless wealth and power over Nature, all at the cost of his economic and political freedom.

It is this process which we must study, particularly through the United States of America. The American empire, as it now stands, is the most effective tool for spreading the Revolution, and has been since the Second Industrial Revolution, that is, with the coming of the internal combustion engine. It was the United States' enthusiastic adoption of the industrial form that turned it into a revolutionary nation, and perhaps the revolutionary nation *par excellence*. America was formed as a Protestant nation, or perhaps many Protestant nations, but its relationship to the Second Revolution had always equivocal: A great expanse of land fostered true material independence, and its genuine democracy made the prospects of forming a mass an ambiguous temptation. It was not until the initial industrial revolution and the creation of a large proletariat in the Northeastern states that the forces of mass politics and ideology began to overtake the nation, when the liberal

democracy Tocqueville witnessed and described began
to characterize the nation and conquer the old republic.

Treatise on America

America in her first form was a democracy, though
not a liberal democracy. The continent laying before
them, a sparse population of incredibly savage and
hostile natives looming, thousands of miles separating
them from the seat of sovereignty, some kind of self-rule
was only natural. Even on the eve of the Revolution
there was not a generation of American who had not
faced the tangible specter of Indian attack, of raided
villages, murdered children and ravaged wives. The
continent was a Rome waiting to be formed over a
savage Carthage. Its circumstances created a nation of
hard, industrious men, and a population uniquely
predisposed to popular sovereignty. Whatever virtues or
prospects democracy might possess, they would find
their best showing there.

America's revolt against the crown was perhaps an
unwise one, but it was nowhere near a tumult of
luciferian fury such as took Paris. The war was a dispute
between equal parties, operating on essentially the same
understanding of one another. The Americans owed
money for the defense the crown had supplied them, as
was right and just to ask. They objected on the principles
of 1688, principles which may have been unjust but were
the terms of liberty the English had chosen. Sound
retort could only have found force through a
retrenchment of the principles of monarchy such as
George the Third proposed. But the oligarchs could not

trade their usurpation for Columbia's wilderness, and so
America was lost. If the nation of Israel could be built
on Jacob's fraud, no later American was obliged to long
mull over his own nation's founding. The American
nation did not constitute a movement forward for the
Revolution: it did not impose a new theory of man on
the governed. Its citizens had as good a claim as anyone
to talk of the Tarquins, for they were a bold, brave, and
literate nation worthy of what rewards they could extract
from the new continent. These were men of the
principles of Westphalia, and in their wake of their
conquest remade Sparta, Athens, and Goshen in their
image, bringing with them all the greatness of Europe's
secular heritage, a great majority of the tenets of
Christendom, the excellence of the common law, and
the benefices of the Age of Reason without its
cosmopolitan vagaries.

America's role in the progress of the Revolution
must be approached with this in mind. A study of the
Constitution of 1787 tells us nothing about the actual
progress of liberalism in the county or its progress in the
West. Properly understood, the Constitution was
nothing but a compact between thirteen sovereigns, as
the first Constitution had undeniably been. Truly, if it
was a transformative and indeed ideological document,
then this aspect was hidden in a Hegelian coming-to-
perfection. Only demagogues, usurpers, and fools can
see in the original Constitution, the thing it has become:
a new covenant of human freedom, its penumbras
heralding the advance of unencumbered liberty, its mere
phrases laden with the power to make million bleed and
the nations bow.

The transformation of the Constitution from a mere
piece of legislation between states to an oracle of liberal

virtue can be well discerned in the advance of the First Amendment. An understanding of it provides one with a fairly sure understanding of American government and the progress of liberalism as a whole. In the present day, the clause is held up as the apogee of intellectual liberty and affirmative weapon against any state attempt to forestall moral perversion or instill civic virtue. Yet the First Amendment as written in 1791 gave the states the right to do just this.

No man is competent to speak on America who does not understand this point: The First Amendment, as written and ratified, did not prohibit in any way the imposition of laws relating to religion, established churches, speech or the press, and in fact definitively allowed them. *Congress shall make no law respecting an establishment of religion, or prohibiting the free exercise thereof; or abridging the freedom of speech, or of the press.* By universal understanding, these prohibitions applied only to the Federal Congress, the only body in the Federal Government with the power to make such laws, and the only body in the land that might overrule the sovereign will of any individual state to make blasphemy laws or to shoot seditious journalists. These obstacles quashed, the states were left the indefeasible right to make their own laws as their sovereignty allowed them. Not a single state would have ratified the Amendment if it had stripped the sovereigns of these powers rather than bolstered them, and not a few states in New England would have contemplated immediate secession at the prospect of Virginians traducing their blasphemy laws or imposing capital sentences on the established churches of Massachusetts and Connecticut. The First Amendment established as a principle that state governments had a power to regulate speech and religion, and the states did so.

The new First Amendment, the new rule we observe gestating in the overheated brains of late-Nineteenth Century judges and enshrined by those of the Twentieth, proclaimed the exact opposite. It stated that no government body, either national, state or local, could impede the practice of religion in any form. This inversion was accomplished by the doctrine of *Incorporation*, the notion that the victors of the Civil War, through their Fourteenth Amendment, had moved the seat of natural and civil rights from the state to the Federal Government or, more precisely, to the Federal Courts. No layman can read the Fourteenth Amendment and come away with the faintest notion where this revolutionary doctrine hid among such spare words, and any of the Amendment's authors, who thought they were enshrining the Civil Rights Act of 1866 into the Constitution, would be similarly perplexed. [79] A modern lawyer bound to his profession's logicality rather than its innate servility must conclude that the Fourteenth Amendment's impact was a product of the Court rather than the document itself. The practical effect of this revolution was to deny any entity a say in what constituted appropriate *speech*, *assembly*, and *public orthodoxy* outside the Courts. The incredibly drastic nature of this inversion cannot be overstated: Those amendments which once served as recognition of the sovereign powers of the states and their people were ever after to be wielded as a weapon against them.

---

[79] Raoul Berger's *Government by Judiciary* provides the last word on the matter.

The Constitution as written was not an ideological document. Its text, as strictly and honestly construed, was a mechanism of centralizing power, one that could conquer the new continent and lay prone in America's sway and supremacy the entire New World. But conquest was not necessarily ideological. It did not make a claim about man and attempt to see that claim enforced in policy. It was merely a compact between sovereigns to ensure the collective energy of the American states would be turned outward instead of against one another.

But this is not to say the seeds and sprouts of the Second Revolution cannot be descried in those august founding documents. The Virginia Statute on Religious Freedom, so often errantly touted as a forerunner to the First Amendment, really was an ideological thing. It prescribed as affirmative policy that man was better under a regime of Tolerance than under a regime of orthodoxy. It prescribed that the government be fundamentally atheistic. But the First Amendment was not this. The First Amendment was a guarantee to Massachusetts that the Virginia cabal could not force such ideology on her people, and it could not have passed the state legislatures and could not have been ratified, had it been otherwise. Yet the *First Amendment* in the present form is the document of Puritan nightmare, an ideological cudgel.

Taken altogether, a century's worth of Court holdings appear to us as a transformation as severe, profound, and totalitarian as any Soviet restructuring. Yet the modern American gives it no mind, for few forums exist where the complaint might be heard let alone understood. It is this transformation, unwarranted and unheralded, which exemplifies the Revolution's progress in America. A clear-stated and pragmatic Constitution was transformed into an amorphous palate from which all the Revolution's requirements could be applied to the nation and the world. That this transformation is so rarely acknowledged even by conservatives is proof of total victory by the Revolutionists, and a validation of their tactics which would always be employed in America: A complete and total revolution accomplished by gradual changes unnoticed by the subjects of the nation, sometimes seemingly unnoticed by the men who effected it.

American Liberal Democracy

The transformation from a land of tessellated republics into a long blotch of *liberal democracy* was achieved in the Civil War, the War Between the States. More than even the French Revolution, this conflict encapsulated the unscrupulous use of biopower, of human materiel wielded by generals and human mortar used by politicians to maintain unnatural peace. The North's aggression and ultimate triumph was grounded in the attempt to establish mass democracy and quash any notions of Jeffersonian republicanism that yet endured in the land. It unleashed the unimpeded rule of the new industrial elite, which in its turn provided for the opening of the frontiers, the dismantling of the old states, and the replacement of their people with waves of immigrants. In no other free nation on earth had a proletariat ever been so pliable to the ruling class.

Lincoln's victory was the transformation of the old democracy to new, from government that the ancients would have understood to one Tocqueville saw was presaging something new, something mysterious and oppressive. The conservative intellectual has always decried the effects of Demos: its leveling of manners, the complaisance of popularity, the specter of centrifugal forces unbinding the social order. But the force of liberal democracy is not anarchic but centripetal; it is a gathering inward of diverse forms into a stifling core. Since independence, American democracy has always been a centralizing force. The true wasted potential of the American nation was never the aristocracy she may have lost, but the homogenization of the nations her Constitution brought together.

The Southern cause was opposed to this. The Southerner could tolerate and even love Jeffersonian democracy. He clung strictly to the principles of 1776 and 1787, because to depart from them would mean to lose the sovereignty of the state and the organic order risen within them. The greatest of Southern statesmen, and apart from the Founders the greatest statesman of the old republic, was John C. Calhoun, a man who took the principles of the American revolution and placed them on a concrete footing in the ordering of the state. Calhoun understood that the Jacksonian democracy he combatted was categorically different from Jefferson's, that it was not the self-rule of free men but the employment of the masses by Northern capital against men truly fit to rule. Though never departing from the name of democrat, Calhoun drew sharp distinction between pure democracy, governed by the will of the *simple majority*, and the state governed by the *concurrent majority*. The former was discovered by the suffrage of the mass, while the latter recognized a native

constitution of the state apart from the whims of the
voter, one composed of different class and geographic
interests, formal recognition of which ensured they
would not be steamrolled under the movement of a
raging majority.[80] Calhoun's idea of the state was one of
organic development. His final crusade against the
admission of California to the Union was a recognition
that the new Western states were traducing the old
notions of states as homes of distinct cultures and
peoples cultivated through organic growth of centuries,
and thus worthy of distinct sovereignty, but instead were
becoming mere instruments of the growing Federal
apparatus. The battle for States' Rights, whatever form it
took, was always a contest between the organic state
versus the ideological one.

The South was a slave power, it cannot be denied.
However much accord she found in political notions, it
was her slaves which provided the concrete form of
unity. Yet slavery as a means of production, slavery as a
mechanism of politics, slavery as a basis for culture, all
opposed the institution of liberal democracy and its
attendant creation of the mass. For the kind of servitude
practiced in the South was personal, familial, and
envisioned a kind of regulation and statism that was
abhorrent to the whims of international finance and
child labor marketeers. To the Northern zealot, the
abstract moral evil of slavery was sufficient cause for
war, and no further inquiry need be made into the
motives of the assenting industrial class. That the
Southern cause was intrinsically tied to slavery cannot be

---

[80] See Calhoun's *Discourse* and *Disquisition*, collected in
*Union and Liberty: The Political Philosophy of John C
Calhoun*, edited by Ross M. Lence for the Liberty Fund.

denied; but the Northern aggression it opposed was as just tightly knit to faceless industrialism as the South was to the system she defended. Not since Helen's abduction was a war fought for purely *moral* reasons, and the war between North and South was fought for the conquest of Northern industry, the solidification of the American empire, and the dominance of liberal democracy.[81]

Slavery and the Capitalist Form

A moderate apologia of slavery is necessary here. An unequivocal good never demands a strong defense, only periodic chastisements of the fools who cannot see good for what it is. But in the cosmos most everything is permeated with an amount of evil, and the ability to rate one evil above another is often the only wisdom one can strive for. We must understand slavery to approach any historical matter, for our civilization rose upon the backs of slaves, who built the Colosseum and worked the fields of Gaul and Britain. The institution's gradual eradication came about not through momentous political change but the softening of hearts and strengthening of rights: the enshrinement of Christian liberty in the pagan charnelhouse. Both Christian and pagan morality had tolerated slavery as an institution, but only the Christian could find joy in working towards its eradication. Slavery's reinstitution in the New World was a source of grief to the Christian, even if it was his

---

[81] Edmund Wilson's *Patriotic Gore* and Alexander Stephens's *History* are essential dissident narratives on the war. See also Charles Adams's *When in the Course of Human Events*, 2000.

own hypocrisy which brought it about. And yet once established, it could not be easily removed. The Church acknowledged the legitimacy of slavery just as St. Paul had, and condemned the social revolution that sudden universal emancipation would inevitably herald. In this, she recognized slavery for what it was and always had been: an evil system that could not be eradicated without recourse to greater evil. Proper recourse was to the Christian yoke, under which its cruelties were mollified, and the humanity of slave and master were always recalled.

For our purposes, the most essential fact of slavery is the central alignment of interests. In stark rational and economic terms, the slaveowner and the slave had closely aligned interest in a most basic element of the system: The wellbeing of the slave. A slave who was worked to exhaustion was a slave who could no longer work, and a useless slave presaged a poor slaveowner. As a class, the slaveowners' interests were firmly tied to the welfare of the class below them. Compared to the situation of the capitalist, who could always solve his problem of exhausted or abused labor by dipping into the reserve army of unemployed, the slave was not mere labor power for purchase. The slave's humanity was degraded by his position in the system, but the system nonetheless recognized his humanity in the concrete incentives it provided, as was so apparent in the close domestic relations that formed. A century and a half of propaganda has not been able to squelch all the stories of black domestics, the servant class which provided a moral bulwark for much of the white ruling class.

No human endearment of this sort could attach to a capitalist system, and no great man could strive to defend or advance it for what it is. For to be fervent about capitalism is to be by nature a mediocrity. A real man might lead the water-blooded capitalist class through their periodic crises, but an atmosphere that stifles any true greatness of spirit is no place for a striver, such as Abraham Lincoln was. It is no surprise that the man rose from the hinterlands, away from the smoke-filled hallways of Republican wheeling-and-dealing, divorced from the Calvinist furor of the most fervent abolitionists. These settings could not have suited a man so set on replacing the legacy of the Founders, who in his Carlylean exultations spoke to the man's understanding of his own genius. "Happy day, when, all appetites controlled, all passions subdued, all matters subjected, *mind*, all conquering *mind*, shall live and move the monarch of the world. Glorious consummation! Hail fall of Fury! Reign of Reason, all hail!"[82] Like Napoleon, his only modern comparison, Lincoln could have no successors, for his achievements destroyed the project by which similar greatness might be realized, where ambition could meet its fulfilment in honor and manhood. The next generation were industrialists, men who completed the bastardization of democratic feeling, men that through immigration and emigration unwound the heritage of the native North.

Few men have possessed a genius like Abraham Lincoln's. His literary corpus is in total perhaps the greatest every produced by an American. His political domination was so complete that scarcely a man can contemplate the kind of American who existed as the norm before him. His demeanor threw a veil over his

---

[82] Address to the Springfield Washington Temperance Society, 1842.

ambitions, present from his earliest days of maturity. He even had the genius to die at the right time, giving himself up to the ages as perhaps the most completely realized man who strove merely for the promotion of mammon. It was Lincoln who cries that the blood of the slaves should be on Americans' heads until the last generation, he who wrote into American fabric that the gore and squalor of his war were apt sacrifice to his cause, he that would have victims suffer for their oppressors' sins. He was neither the first or last politician to take up the mantle of jihad when the moment found it favorable, and the adoption of Abolitionism could damn the American nation so long as the power remained with him to damn it. Lincoln centered the theological dispute of the war, divinized the victory of liberal empire, and threw open the depredations the American government would condone or inflict on the people of other nations and its own: that if the oppression of the bondsman's whip could be requited only by the blood of the innocent, it would be right and just altogether. All modern racial terror, everywhere across the globe, spilled forth out of this sentiment.

An empire was settled by Lincoln, and the hinterlands have always paid greater tribute to him than the Founders, those pillars of the temple of liberty that have crumbled away. The great industrial revolution, the unequivocal victory of capital over the proletariat extant and yet to be born, was purchased with destruction of the figments of the ancient American regime. The prospect that history advanced was apparent in that wise and homely face, in a man who had anxiously slain the son the Zeitgeist demanded as sacrifice. Any church that dared condone the wretched institution could remain only facades against the moral cataract of his jihad. "You say your husband is a religious man; tell him when you meet him, that I say I am not much of a judge of religion, but that, in my opinion, the religion that sets men to rebel and fight against their government, because, as they think, that government does not sufficient help *some* men to eat their bread on the sweat of *other* men's faces, is not the sort of religion upon which people can get to heaven on"[83]

Perhaps a million slaves died in the war or its immediate aftermath.[84] This was only natural as a proximate effect of emancipation, for the blights of war always fall upon the most wretched. But mass murder simply could not be avoided. The slaveocracy had to be defeated, lest the war be defined by questions of sovereignty and political freedom which the South could not help but win in perpetuity. Lincoln declared that *We the People* held sacred right over the real and personal self-government practiced in the South. The *mass of people* had usurped the erstwhile sovereignty of the states, and now even the mere forty percent of them who had elected him could claim the right of absolute rule. This was the legal theory of the war, that the popular will must dominate and crush the minority, that the government must rise and dominate the men who had created it—just as the abolitionist must triumph and slay the man he had freed.

---

[83] Reply to a Southern Lady, 1865.

[84] This is the claim made by Jim Downs in his *Sick From Freedom: African-American Illness and Suffering during the Civil War and Reconstruction*. For our part, his count of fatalities seems on the high end of estimates, but even if they were halved they would be grotesque and extraordinary.

This was the great spiritual battle that paved the way for so much material subjugation. The United States adopted mass democracy and the industrial system was divinized with the blood poured of the remnants of the old regime, America's *Ancien Régime*.

Treatise on Capitalism

The First Industrial Revolution took place in the late Eighteenth Century, emergent in England and readily brought to America. The steam engine was its emblem of advance, and lent force to all the transformation that would arise: the mechanization of agriculture, the burgeoning of railroads and steamships. The second industrial revolution arose a generation after Lincoln's crusade. The internal combustion engine provided the force for the new transformation, making possible the individual harnessing and possession of the power unleashed by the first Industrial Revolution. The adoption of the electrical grid system expanded access to the powers of technique further, and within the half-century one who did not possess or have access to motor or employed the gifts of the dynamo could scarcely be considered to reside within the bounds of civilization at all. The third Industrial Revolution, that of computer and electronic technology, would follow, but the second was enough to ensure industrialism was complete, total, and universal in all the civilized world, entrenched in every hearth and field.

The Calvinists could steal Church property and defile the Catholic's sacred halls, and the Jacobin could murder a king and upend all tenets of organic polity. But such destructive frenzies could last only as long as the ideological creeds that fostered them retained their intellectual force. Yet such force, being a departure from Truth and the product of fevered minds, cannot be a perennial one. A normalcy must settle, Thermidor must come, revolutionary gains must be entrenched in the political and moral superstructure or, unnatural as they are, they will be lost in the neap tide. There can be no revolution in the ideological sphere without a material entrenchment, a fact which makes perpetual revolution a phantom to all but the most delusive. An ideological change must be regulated and guided by material reality, for the most fervent Trotskyite still needs food to eat and a place to lay his head. The great mass of men need repose even more: they must find their homes a place of rest, in their lives a particular order unto themselves. Every sane man is a conservative in his concupiscence, in the happy succumbing to the flesh at the tempo of quotidian life. Even anarchists prefer to know what they're going to eat for breakfast next morning. This is why the *conservative* is so instrumental to all revolutionary change, for it is he who tapers ideas to what the material environs will allow, who provides a palliative for the ideological poison let into the body politick which ultimately allows it to sustain itself.

Capitalism is the most effective means by which ideological change is given material form. It is in a sense conservative, as it appeals to man's sensibility, which always strives for bodily contentment. But as a motive force it is most anarchic, the material means of perpetual revolution. Whatever Protestant Ethic he may have adhered to, the uncritical capitalist found himself promoting practical Jacobinism in every sphere of life. Ideology seemed to disappear under lever, gear and

206

smog, though in fact it was only hidden under the aspect of perpetual technological change. "Capitalism is by nature a form or method of economic change and not only never is but never can be stationary. The fundamental impulse that sets and keeps the capitalist engine in motion comes from the new consumers' goods, the new methods of production or transportation, the new markets, the new forms of industrial organization that capitalist enterprise creates."[85] Capitalism considered as a productive apparatus is a means of perpetual advance, and as such is a harbinger and instrument of the Revolution, wherever it establishes itself.

Capitalism is the Enemy of Property

Capitalism is the enemy of property. To understand this fact is to understand the wicked force of the Third Revolution. The capitalist process, as any cognizant man of goodwill can see, has a great many evil attributes and effects. But the root evil of the system is the corrosive effect on the institution of property. From the natural working of the capitalist process arise all the disregard for the rights of property which facilitate the ranting of the socialists. Property is a natural right, the foundation of government, a bedrock for social order, and is intrinsic to any free society. And capitalism is the enemy of this.

How can we make this claim? How do we dare to sully this institution, so often heralded as bringing

---

[85] Schumpeter, *Capitalism, Socialism, and Democracy.* "The Process of Creative Destruction."

rigorous reverence for contract and commerce amongst all civilized men?

We must ask first what we mean by *capitalism*. The answer is not always clear. The modern economist will aver it is little more than the protection of property and reliance on markets; he will indeed see the market economy as a kind of natural occurrence, like the formation of a beehive, and any resulting property division is ancillary to the beck of nature. The property distribution within this system, which to every critic of capitalism is its most distinctive feature, is thus elided in favor of a phony naturalism.[86] A more factually literate approach is necessary to descry capitalism's true features. Thus Belloc: "We mean by capitalism a condition of Society under which the mass of free citizens, or at any rate a determining number of them, are not possessed of the means of production in any useful amount and therefore live upon wages doled out to them by the possessors of land and capital, men who thus exploit a profit the dispossessed, known as the *Proletariat*."[87] It was against this state of things that the Marxists roared, that the reactionaries could raise the banner of paternalism against the new free-for-all.

A sufficient critique might end here. Capitalism's very political form requires the alienation of property from a great mass of people, as well as the diminution of contract. For as Belloc well noted 110 years ago,[88] the relationship of contract which characterized the

---

[86] See e.g., Matt Ridley's *The Origins of Virtue,* and Robert Frank's *The Economic Naturalist*.

[87] *Crisis of Civilization,* 139

[88] *The Servile State*.

interaction between capital and labor in past ages could not help but give way to a relationship of *status*, divided between the holders of capital and the laborers who held none. The state could not forever ignore these material circumstances: it could not continue to treat worker and employer as free-contracting parties where nineteen-twentieths of the population did not have access to the means of production. Liability law was the first to transform: employers would now bear responsibility for injuries suffered by an employee at the hands of another, regardless of whether the employer had committed any malfeasance himself. Minimum wages and compulsory arbitration likewise recognized a separate class of proletarians at law, and disincentivized the laborer from staking any claim to the means of production as any socialist or guildsman might prefer. To the law, the man who sold his labor would be recognized as a laborer: not a free-contracting party but as *servus*.

The proletarian was not quite a slave, but he was still constrained by his status to sell his labor to some member of the capitalist class. While to outwards appearances he might appear as he had before, as a freeman contracting out the use of his labor for a wage, his position within the economic structure was greatly changed. Hidden behind every contract was a new dependency upon the capitalist class, a complete overthrow of the old world of individual workers and proprietors and its replacement by one where the capitalist in fact and in law held superior place. Yet so long as the worker received the rewards his status afforded him, he was considered well off within the system. As an individual he still retained the old vestiges of real citizenship, though as a member of the working class he was nothing but a propertyless servant with no real freedom but to hire himself out to whatever capitalist would have him. The freedom that property bequeathed to its owners, recognized by all from the Gracchi to the monks of the Middle Ages, was relegated to a question of no political importance.

Capitalist and Non-capitalist Production

The relationship between capital and labor is the distinctive outward characteristic of capitalist production. But in fact it is only one facet of a more essential and intrinsic feature of capitalism. This is the practice of commodification.

A commodity is a good produced not for use, but with the intent of bringing the good to market and selling it for a profit. It is a good produced not for its own end, but for the acquisition of profit following sale. The capitalist treats most everything as a commodity, for the capitalist, so far as he is a capitalist, is always in pursuit of profit. And he can only make a profit in one way: By selling a commodity at a price higher than it cost him to bring the commodity to market. This is very simple and perhaps trite statement but deserves precision, for it requires, first and foremost, that whatever thing, potentiality, or idea the capitalist wishes to make profit from be transformable into commodity form. It must consist of some resource he can capture or enclose, some chattel over which he can acquire physical possession, or perhaps a notional thing over which he is afforded legal right, such as intellectual property, which he in turn must be able to alienate in order to sell at market.

The evils wrought by capitalism in relation to labor and capital arises from this distinctive practice: The commodification of labor, or the buying and selling of labor-power on a market. The capitalist does not have any interest in acquiring rights to the laborer himself as he would with a slave, but only desires his labor power for a specific period of time. In this way we see we are dealing with a form of contract, the free buying and selling of a service, though writ on an economy-wide scale. But this ideal system runs hard into human realities. Labor by its nature is not a chattel, not a mere good which can be easily and readily alienated. It is the dour fate of man to be forced to labor if he is to sustain himself on the face of the earth, but man will not stand to have this central facet of his life treated as a mere trinket. In the words of Polyani, "To separate labor from other activities of life and to subject it to the laws of the market was to annihilate all organic forms of existence and to replace them with a different type of organization, an atomistic and individualistic one."[89] Commodifying labor had everywhere, before the Industrial Revolution, been though unendurable on such a scale as the new industrial regime required. Men simply did not possess the constitution to be readily tossed and contorted by the whims of the market. In the pre-industrial era, the guilds served to mitigate against such whiplash among the skilled trades, and peasant-production attested to what extent man would have the fruits of his labor power repossessed rather than have his labor commodified. Even the institution of slavery, maligned as so inhuman and dreadful, mitigated this evil.

---

[89] Karl Polyani, *The Great Transformation*, "Market and Man." 1944.

The slave-trader might sell a slave at the market, but he did not sell that wretched soul as a mere implement. The institution was defended by the paternalist, who if he degraded the slave by low rank, at least did not think of him as a mere tool to be cast about by unregulated supply and demand. Any given slavemaster might be a tyrant, but the market was always and everywhere capricious and occasionally a maniac.

Yet the capitalist mindset is broader than one that simply seeks to commodify labor. The truest capitalist finds commodities everywhere. Just as to the strict utilitarian no object or thing is good *per se*, but only judged so in relation to its ability to provide utility to its user, the capitalist sees no real purpose in anything he produces or exploits but for how much profit it can bring him. The capitalist producer is the supply-side obverse of the utility-maximizing consumer whose behavior drives demand. Both look at a product and care not about its essence, any innate good it possesses in itself, but abstract away from this essence and focus their attention and activity on a single attribute of the commodity: For he consumer, the utility it brings, and for the producer its profit potential.

It is essential to realize the difference—the often very subtle difference—between traditional producers and the capitalist producer. Every man partakes in economic activity to obtain a personal benefit. He produces a good or service such as he is equipped to provide and, given the usefulness of his production, expects benefit to come from this, whether through use as a source of sustenance, or by trade. Any benefit he derives must come to him by virtue of the usefulness of the product he offers, and when he receives remuneration for it, he expects no more and no less than what the product itself demands. But the capitalist producer approaches his task of production a much different way. While he still engages in the task of producing goods or services, his final goal in production is not the product itself, but the profit that might be won from it. So long as he can derive a profit from the product's sale at market, he does not really care about the quality of the product itself. The product is only an instrument of profit, and if the remuneration he receives for it is not greater than the cost of production, the product is for him a failure, no matter the intrinsic worth of the thing bought and sold. This difference, this *subtle* difference, might be seen in the practice of traditional farming versus its industrial counterpart. The traditional farmer was engaged first and foremost in the work of the farmer: planting crops, raising livestock, maintaining his land, and ultimately ensuring that his work yields useful fruits. The traditional farm raises a crop so it can be harvested and eaten; he raises a cow so it can be milked, and afterwards slaughtered. Of course, the farmer prefers a bounteous harvest to a meager one, a large cow to a small; but in the end, if the product of his labor is useful, it is good, because a harvest and a cow are good in themselves. Yet the capitalist farmer behaves much differently. A product that cannot turn a profit is of no use to him. So we see on industrial farms crops left to rot in the fields not because they are defective as crops, but because they cannot be expected to meet a desired yield. So we see that perfectly healthy though small livestock—piglets and chicks and calves—are killed not because they are useless, but they are too small to turn a profit. A traditional farmer might sometimes kill a pig who was hopelessly deformed, or if resources were scarce he might slaughter the runts for the benefit of the brood. But these actions were unpalatable exceptions to the practice of farming, which was to cultivate and to create, and to parse only so far as was necessary. The traditional farmer's end was farming: the concrete task before him, with all the dregs and honor incumbent in it. The capitalist farmer's end is the market, the task before him is mere toil, and the living creatures he cultivates are nothing but means to an end of profit, a scouring for surpluses.

Protect the quality of the product and you will protect both the livelihood of the producer and the welfare of the consumer. All traditional regulation of economic interactions centered around this rule. Such was the task of the ancient guildsman, to first and foremost maintain standards of product quality and to undergird the very principles of the trade itself. From there, free contracting could ensure that a quality product would fetch a fair price, just as quality work would fetch a just wage. The evils of the capitalist system rise from the fact that quality of production is manifestly *not* the central consideration of the capitalist producer, for the capitalist strictly does not care about the product at all, only the profit it will fetch him. Traditional producers were rational in the that their central concern was the quality of their product. The capitalist is not rational in the same sense, for while he may be engaged in a similar production process, his end is not the product itself, but the surplus he seeks through its sale at market. Production, to the capitalist, is merely an instrumentality. As such, the market becomes the regulator of all product quality, not the producer himself. And what is long subjected to the market as its only regulatory force cannot long sustain quality, as we shall see below.

The Transformation of Property Law

To understand our claim that capitalism is the enemy of property, it serves us well to look at the institution of property where it is most clearly defined, in the realm of law. At law, property is a notional concept, a bundle of rights and duties protected by the concrete application of custom and recourse to the courts. How these discrete notions changed along with and in response to the rise of capitalist production is, in fact, enough to prove the shift: a kind of empirical experiment whose practitioners, the Nineteenth Century judges, laid out in admirable detail.

At common law, the right of property was not indefeasible, though it was something close to this. *Sic utere tuo, ut alienum non laedas*: This doctrine entitled man to the quiet enjoyment of his property, its use and disposition, so long as such use did not harm his neighbor in quietly enjoying his own property. Accordingly, the maxim gave one the right to enjoin another's otherwise lawful use of property if it caused injury to his neighbor, for in Blackstone's words it was "incumbent on a neighboring owner to find some other place to do that act, where it would be less offensive." In applying this principle, common law judges would cite the example of the man whose sleep was interrupted by the clomping of hooves coming from the fledgling stable-owner next door: The right of the established homeowner to sleep trumped that of the industrious horseman.

With the rise of industrial technology, this conflict more and more came to a head. The fledgling industrialist could not open a mill and employ it but by the use of water-power, use of which necessarily required the obstruction of a river or stream. Conflicts over water rights were inevitable. Said the common lawyers, *Aqua currit, et debet currere*, and so the course of water could not be legally diverted without the consent of all those who had an interest in it.[90] Similar disputes arose over the burgeoning railroads. Train cars flung sparks with such frequency that fires to adjoining crops and property were a regular occurrence, resulting in such damage that any property owner adjacent to the tracks could have enjoined the railroad under his role as *alienus laedatus*, for there are few greater impediments to quiet enjoyment than having one's goods burned to a crisp. An impassible divide had arisen: The trains could not be run efficiently and cheaply in such a way that would guarantee quiet enjoyment of those nearby. The new technology of the locomotive and its widespread use were quite simply at odds with and could not coexist alongside strict interpretations of common law right. One or the other had to cede, and the courts determined it would be individual right.

Numerous cases could be cited to confirm this transformation. The opinion given by the Supreme Court of Kentucky provides a good summation: "The onward spirit of the age must, to a reasonable extent, have its way. The law is made for the times, and will be

---

[90] Morton Horwitz, *The Transformation of American Law, 1780-1860.* 35 citing *Merritt v. Parker*, 1 Coxe L. Rep. 460, 463 (N.J. 1795).

made or modified by them. The expanded and still expanding genius of the *common law* should adapt it here, as elsewhere, to the improved and improving conditions of our country and our countrymen. And therefore, railroads and locomotive steam-cars—the offspring, as they will also be the parents, of progressive improvement—should not, in themselves, be considered as *nuisances*, although, in ages that are gone, they might have been so held, because they would have been comparatively useless, and therefore more mischievous."[91] The sheer power of the new industrial technology supplied its own justification.

Throughout the antebellum era, common law protections of property fall away. What replaced them was a new conception of property, one not so nearly indefeasible, but in fact closer to a kind of Benthamite analysis, one which weighed the costs incurred by the now-deprived property owners against the benefits of industry. "Once priority and natural use had taken on different operational meanings, the common law had moved into the utilitarian world of economic efficiency. Claims founded on natural use began to recede into a dim preindustrial past and the newer 'balancing test' of efficiency came into sharp focus."[92] The once nearly sacrosanct rights of property were no longer presumed. A property itself must first be weighed on the scales of utility against the value of inchoate industry before determining what kind of protection it was to be afforded. A general rule arose in interacting with the railroads: One could harm another's property so long as

---

[91] *Lexington & Ohio Rail Road v. Applegate*, 8 Dana 289 (Ky. 1839); cited by Horwitz at 75.
[92] Horwitz at 33.

one paid for it. The immutability of property gave way to the proportionality of costs.

This socialized conception of property expanded to other realms of the law. The *Charles River Bridge* case arose out of a contract between Cambridge and a private firm to provide sole transportation across the river. When the city sought to scoot around the monopoly agreement by employing another firm upstream, the original firm brought suit on the claim that the city had effectively voided the contract. Justice Story's dissent on behalf of the firm emphasized the sanctity of contract, the unpredictability of commerce, the variability of profit prospects and the just reward owed to honest oath. In contrast, Justice Taney's majority holding for the city lauded the genius of commerce against the archaism of the honored word. "If this court should establish the principles now contended for, what is to become of the numerous rail roads established on the same line of travel with turnpike companies…? The millions of property which have been invested in rail roads and canals, upon lines of travel which had been before occupied by turnpike corporations, will be put in jeopardy. We shall be thrown back to the improvements of the last century, and obliged to stand still, until the claims of the old turnpike corporations shall be satisfied; and they shall consent to permit these states to avail themselves of the lights of modern science, and to partake of the benefits of those improvements which are now added to the wealth and prosperity, and the convenience and comfort, of every other part of the civilized world."[93] The Constitution was not higher than

---

[93] 36 U.S. (11 Pet.) 420 (1837)

the dictates of commerce, and American law must bow beneath the specter of industry, which otherwise threatened to leave her in the world-historic dust.

While running the risk of becoming a case book, we turn to one last legal development, in the realm of Eminent Domain, which enshrines in black-letter law what otherwise can only be gleaned by the decades' progress. The Fifth Amendment principle that no private property can be taken for public use without just compensation is as fair and reasonable as any standards of reason could desire. But its justice depends wholly on what constitutes *public use*. So we arrive in 2005 and find that *public use* encompasses private shopping malls: So was the holding of *Kelo v. City of New London*,[94] which permitted the destruction of livable houses for the sake of a commercial hub. The Court affirmed that *public use* was interchangeable with social utility, and that a project promising more lucrative returns and greater social engagement could raze a standing property with only personal significance. It did not matter that both the mall magnet and the homeowner were disputing the rights of private property. The mall was simply a kind of private property that deserved to own the moniker of *public use*, while a man in his bed seemed guilty against the mall-walkers and consumers his invidious and greedy usurpation denied. Quiet enjoyment of the individual could not withstand the contemplated thrills of the mass.

This process was necessary, not accidental. The contemplated shopping mall in *Kelo* was absurd, but all shopping malls are absurd. Yet there is still a difference between gawking at a clown and having one's house

---

[94] 545 U.S. 469 (2005).

ransacked by one. What rights could a man desire if not those to sleep, eat, reside, garden, till, grow, and tend to all those peaceful travails that constitute man's life in its most quotidian—towards the idylls of the tree grown, the child raised, the life made whole? Why must these activities be proven *utile*? Why must property be a tool for pursuing wealth rather than a source of satisfaction in itself? Why did property become an instrumentality?

The Misplaced Concreteness of the Market

Assaults on the rights of property were *required* by the nature of industrial technology. To understand why this is so—why the process is not merely the fruits of tendentious and paid-off judges—we do best to refer to theory. For it is by theory that we can most firmly grasp the point we repeat again, that capitalism is the enemy of property, but also that it holds this place because of the process we have observed in our discussion on Scientism. Capitalist production tends towards an abstraction away from the real considerations of production and towards those which vis-à-vis the product are notional concepts, and which in turn assume the motive force of the system of production. In terms of capitalist production, this is done by turning the ends of the production process away from production itself and towards the pursuit of profit: of letting the market determine what was once a personal and rational process.

Of course the market does not produce anything, and cannot tell us a whit about the art of the real production of goods. The market is merely a tool of measurement, providing us with information about prices and quantities and a host of other indicators that are good and useful. But the market is not a real thing. It is not the economy itself, but rather an abstraction away from the actual constituent parts of those who make up the body of the productive apparatus. The market does not discriminate between household or industrial production, it only measures *products* and *producers*. The market does not discriminate between goods which are dire necessities and shallow trifles, it only measures *goods* as they relate to production and utility functions. The market does not discriminate between the rich and poor, it only measures *consumers* so far as they compose total demand. And so the market is not a true representation of the actual wholistic thing called the *economy*, it merely provides us the measurement of certain aspects of economic activity.

The amount of profit a product can derive can be found only with reference to the market. And so the capitalist, by pursuing only profits, makes himself beholden to the epistemic closure provided by the market. The capitalist sees the economy with a kind of blinders on, receptive not to any measure of welfare or quality of goods he produces, but prices, quantities, market share, and the like. And that capitalist producers operate on such a basis is only natural, given their incentives and given their roles within the market system.

The modern economist approaches the economy in much the same way, thought his use of blinders is not so forgivable. For the modern economist has taken the market as a grounds sufficient in itself to the study economic behavior, and with this cast into the netherland all that those aspects of human welfare which cannot be contorted to fit within the market structure. It is this particular epistemic closure which disfigures the science and has divorced a vast majority of economic study from questions of true welfare and from wealth production itself. The faults of the capitalist and the doting economist are in other words the same—both operate with the same set of ideological blinders attached—and the reader must forgive if we weave back and forth in castigating the two.

The use the claim of this approach, it is worthwhile to return to the works of the classical economists. These were men who studied and wrote before the complete hegemony of capitalist production, and could see outside of the structures, both intellectual and material, imposed by the market system. The classical economist began his analysis with the study of value. He recognized two kinds: use value and exchange value, use value being the intrinsic usufruct of a commodity to the individual user, exchange value the amount a commodity can fetch through sale. The use value of an apple, say, is clear, and does not really vary whether it is sold on the market or plucked off one's tree. But an apple's exchange value is dependent on social factors apart from the intrinsic usufruct of the apple, namely the state of social conditions surrounding its sale such as seasonable demand, gluts in the market, and so forth. To the speculator, it is a commodity's exchange value that arouses his excitement, for it is through the market that he hopes to make his killing. But to the poor yokel, the average man, the humble reader living hand to mouth, it is the use value of a commodity that is of primary concern. As such, the classical economist well understood that it is the possession of use values that constitutes a genuine material prosperity, and whose increase presages a true increase in welfare for the vast majority of men. For while increases in exchange values are not in themselves bad, they can be merely indicators supply shortages, irrational demand, or perhaps inflation distinct from any increase in social welfare. In contrast, the man who possesses more use value is genuinely wealthier, *ceteris paribus*, than he who does not.

The true end of economics is placing the market and the productive apparatus of a society in relation to genuine human welfare. But as we noted above, the study of economics has been largely subsumed by the study of markets. This is not so surprising, for unique among scientists, the economist arrives on the scene to find a host of preselected quantities awaiting him: prices, profits, and sales. Yet for all the ease of quantification provided by the market, it still must be taken for what it is: an artificial measurement device, one of an innately social sort, yet nonetheless a human instrument, little different from a ruler or a Geiger counter. The market is above all else a method of quantification achieved through the process of socialization. Every individual buyer and seller comes to it with an idea of the value of the commodity to be bought and sold, and the mass of buyers and sellers together, by free contracting, allow the creation of a market price. This cannot be achieved without an abstraction away from the essential features of the good to be bought and sold, and an abstraction away from the good's use value. In this sense, the market operates as any other tool of measurement: It transforms a real object into an abstraction appropriate to the measurer's realm of study, which necessarily imposes an artificial limitation on that object. A tape measure spanning the globe could tell us in the most precise terms the circumference of our planet, but indeed would only capture one of the pithiest and least interesting aspects of it. Likewise, in the study of Mammon, we hope the exchange values derived by the market mechanism are correlated to the true values of commodities, their use values. But we cannot be precisely sure.

In normal times, the market system works reasonably well. Money prices do, at least in cardinal relations between commodities, reflect their use values. It is in abnormal times when the divide between use value and exchange value grows insufferable, as during supply shortages, when the ability of a wealthy buyer to pay outpaces the measure his money would otherwise have in reflecting the usefulness of a commodity. Under the normal functioning of the market, we presume that consumers will value essential goods appropriately, and the good's unique characteristics will be justly represented in their price. But in times of scarcity, no one can believe that exchange values adequately capture the true worth of goods. The last bottle of water, priced outside the budget of a dying man and bought by the rich miser, may be priced appropriately given the rules of the market, but under no human ethics can this conclusion be borne. In these aberrant cases, the market mechanism acts to obscure the balances of social welfare. Such is the evil of relying too heavily on the market.

The Labor Theory of Value and the Failure of Marxism

The classical economists were not entranced with the market's misplaced concreteness, nor enamored by prices or the whims of subjective and transient wants. The classical economists look to us almost the pre-Galilean physicists: There is much mechanical in their work, but the underpinnings they establish in their methods are decisively *real*, and they are skeptical towards any methodological leap that will set them outside the bounds of basic humanity and common sense. Most fundamentally, they are aware of the limitations of the market, and accordingly of the need for a philosophically and logically sound basis for quantifying economic interactions.

To this end, the classical economists established labor as the lifeblood of their analysis. And why should they not? Intuitively, labor served as an ideal unifying thread relating one commodity to another. It is a universal characteristic, true to the microprocessor as it is to the pog, that some amount of human labor was employed to bring it to market. Says Smith, "The real price of every thing, what every thing really costs to the man who wants to acquire it, is the toil and trouble of acquiring it. Labor alone, therefore, never varying in its own value, is alone the ultimate and real standard by which the value of all commodities can at all times and places be estimated and compared. It is their real price; money is their nominal price only."[95]

The fatal weakness of the theory lies in the fact that not all labor is equal. The doctor, lawyer, and surgeon perform their tasks against the same metric of hours, that same slow drag of time, but the value of that work cannot be easily compared to the hour's toil of the ditchdigger. The essence of the labor performed is starkly different and not readily quantifiable. A new

---

[95] *The Wealth of Nations,* Ch. V.

metric must be employed. This the classicals called *socially necessary labor time*, a metric nominally of *hours* of work, but hours subjected to different quantification based on the qualitatively different nature of a given kind of labor. The doctor's work-hour is ontologically superior to the ditchdigger's, and therefore valued higher so that the amount of socially valuable labor time he expends is greater. This measure is supposedly not the same as a wage, for a wage is found by the operation of the labor market. Socially necessary labor, on the other hand, derives its meaning from something supposedly intrinsic to the good itself. Marx, perhaps the last of the classical economists and certainly the field's *ad absurdum*, describes it thus: "The value of a commodity varies directly as the quantity and inversely as the productiveness, of the labor incorporated in it. A thing can be a use value without having exchange value…If the thing is useless, so is the labor contained in it; the labor does not count as labor, and therefore creates no value."[96] But what *is* the valuable labor? It is "homogenous human labor, expenditure of one uniform labor-power. The total labor-power of society, which is embodied in the sum total of the values of all commodities produced by that society, counts here as one homogenous mass of labor-power. The labor-time socially necessary is that required to produce an article under the normal conditions of production, and with the average degree of skill and intensity prevalent at the time."[97] Socially necessary labor time is only explicable through reference to a society-wide measure. But how

---

[96] *Capital*, Ch. 1 Section 1.
[97] Id.

can we actually derive a measure of this value? The answer is that we cannot. It is only through reference to a market that we can discover if a given about of labor put forth in a commodity *counts as labor* at all. But when the market determines what is valuable labor, labor is not an extrinsic measure or variable exogenous to the social mechanism of the market. What good, then, is labor as a measure? The answer: It is not.

The collapse of the capitalist system predicted by Marx never did and never will occur, and the deficiencies of the Labor Theory of Value tell us why. Few scholars are as myopically obsessed with one theory as Marx was with the Labor Theory of Value. Marx's model of the capitalist economy hinges on the capitalist class's ability to exploit labor, particularly to extract more labor from workers than the amount of labor those workers put into commodities. This is this theory of *exploitation*, which is not a sentiment or a mere relationship between classes, but a measurable difference between the amount of labor a worker puts into a commodity and the amount of remuneration he receives for that labor, which is always bound to be less. It is only through this process of exploitation, of effectively stealing labor from the worker and putting it into the commodities in return for profit, that the capitalist system can function. But with every individual capitalist vying for more and more profit, they will tend to employ labor-saving technology in order to gain a larger share of the market by driving down labor costs. But this victory for the individual capitalist must doom him and his class now forced by market pressure to adopt the new technology. Because all true value comes from labor, the shift towards technology removes the possibility of value-extraction from the system. The final result is a world full of machines that cannot produce real value, since they are themselves only heaps of *dead labor*. Accordingly there is a long term tendency for profits to decline until the capitalist class is rendered feckless, and the system can fall into the hands of the dispossessed working class, ushering in the new age.[98]

Such is Marx's theory. Its failure lies in what is called the "transformation problem" of Marxist economics, one that an honest Marxist must admit dooms the theory and turns all its intricacy and force to twaddle. Fundamentally, the transformation problem arises because Marx attempted to assign an ontological characteristic to what is inherently a relative and socialized quantification, namely socially valuable labor time. But he cannot do this. For *labor* to have meaning within his model, it must have a character whose presence or absence has the power to determine the system, regardless of market-determined variables like wages and profits; it must act as the objective force creating all value, and with its diminution, have the ability to hollow the bones of the capitalist structure. But having adopted socially necessary labor time as the determinative variable—and this he must do, or he is left conflating the work of doctors and ditchdiggers—he has nothing *real* propelling or undergirding the system, no solid base for the actual functioning of the economy and the creation of value.

---

[98] See e.g. Ben Fine and Alfredo Saad-Filho, *Marx's* Capital, Ch. 9.

One might go through a more precise study of the transformation problem, [99] but it is unnecessary. Marx's fundamental flaw, as we could repeat again and again, was that he was a bourgeois enamored with the ideals of the Enlightenment, which are themselves nothing but the practical application of Scientism to social problems. Deluded, he could not distinguish between the notional and real in the subject of his study: He believed he had freed his analysis from the vagaries of subjective measure when indeed he had not. In the end he was no better off than the bourgeois economists he was so fond of deprecating, wholly dependent on the figment of social valuation, an heir to bad philosophy even as the black sheep of the family of economists. With his error rose and fell the true Marxist cause, and the prospects of *Scientific Socialism* as a whole.

The Problem of Economics

The labor theory of value was an attempt to attach a qualitative measure to economic production that stood apart from the market. It was a measure which sought to tie man's actions to the creation of value, not a way to quantify use value per se, but to serve as a proxy for it. Yet it failed. The response of economists was not to seek another qualitative measure which might inform the process of value creation independent of the market mechanism—quite the opposite For the new generation of economists, those called *neoclassical* and who adhered to Alfred Marshall's use of marginal analysis, economics became synonymous with the market mechanism.

---

[99] See Robert Paul Wolff's *Understanding Marx* for the most accessible critique of the transformation problem.

In the neoclassical model, everything was subjectivized. As we have already held, the actual use value of any given good is immeasurable, for value is an ontological characteristic. To get around this, the neoclassical economist abjured any attempt to find objective value whatsoever. He instead turned to the preference orderings of consumers, and from this, their utility functions. These utility functions were inherently subjective, they could not tell us that bread is an intrinsically more valuable commodity than tulips, but could direct our attention to preference orderings which would allow us to draw conclusions that in normal times, this was so. If one could not determine the intrinsic value of a loaf of bread, he could at least determine how many loaves a person would want compared against bundles of tulips or other commodities. The consumer's preference orderings accounted for both necessities and flittering thrills, spanning all commodities from bread to automobiles. To anyone seeking to assign real valuation to these goods, it stands as a completely useless measure.

And very clearly this method cannot operate independently of the market. Preference functions themselves are not cognizable without reference to prices, which are found only through the interaction of supply and demand. Because preference functions only have meaning with references to prices, value in the neoclassical model cannot exist prior to the market. Value is no longer derived from human labor or any other attempt at an ontological characteristic, but is rather created by the actual force of socialization itself: its participation in the market process.

And so the market becomes the indefeasible standard of analysis. The classical economist had once looked at a bubble for tulips and agreed with the man of commonsense that it was a bubble: that the exchange values discovered by the market mechanism were grossly divorced from use values. The neoclassical economist saw no divide between use and exchange values, for he no longer saw use value at all. If the market at times appeared to be irrational, it was because of something exogenous to it. Mathematical rigor was given to the model in the form of a modified utilitarianism on the demand side called the rational actor model, which made at various times assumptions not only of a man's ability to order his preferences, but also more outlandish suggestions such as the individual possession of perfection information about relevant market variables. No economist made a strong claim that these were empirically verifiable, and any man with commonsense and common experience could surely attest that the assumptions were false. But this did not matter. Any whisperings of market failure had to be suppressed, for if the market failed, so did the science. And if the neoclassical economist is anything but a mathematical trifler, then it must be presumed that the market conveys to us signals of real value reflecting true changes in welfare. Absent this, the market is only an empty measure, and the economist himself a useless drudge, damning others to penury on a mechanism he does not understand at all.

The Tendency of Use Values to Fall

Under a market system, and accordingly in neoclassical theory, the use value of a product is of indirect concern to the capitalist producer. It is *only* the consumer who directly cares about a product's quality in and of itself, and it is only through consumer preference functions that any kind of use value enters the neoclassical model. Insofar that the producer has an incentive to achieve a certain level of quality in a product, it arises in him only through his desire to satisfy consumer demand. Accordingly, a producer will not supply a product so shoddy that no one will buy it, not because he cares about the product's shoddiness per se, but because a product that no one purchases can win him no revenue and no profit. In the end, it is only the consumer who immediately cares about quality, entering the producer's decision-making process only through the intermediary of consumer demand.

As we have established, all commodities have a use value, for a useless commodity will never be brought to the market. And the use value of a good is an ontological quality. It cannot be determinatively quantified. Some use derives from immutable biological necessity: the need for caloric intake, the need for shelter, the need for sleep. Other valuations arise from appeal to man's rational soul and not the bare mammalian: objects of entertainment and pleasure. So are there objects that brings man great pleasure but which can never strictly be commodities, such as precious heirlooms and religious relics, and which are only ludicrously comparable to those goods necessary for sustenance.

The price that a commodity fetches at market is an abstraction away from the actual use value of the good. Most certainly it abstracts away from the ontological qualities of the commodity which make it particularly good or bad. Yet also the market moves away from pure utility comparisons, for at market it is not only the utility of a product that matters, but its utility considered against its price. All other things held equal, a rational consumer will always prefer the good product to the bad; but where the good product is greatly dearer than the bad one, the income constraint ultimately determines that bad is purchased rather than the good.

It is through and because of the market and the commodification of goods that the use values of goods in a capitalist society will tend to decline. This is owing to the contrary incentives faced by producers and consumers, for in the market interaction the consumer's goal is always to purchase the best product he can for the price, while it is the producer's to derive a profit, that is, to acquire the most revenue against costs of production. The producer is driven by profit and profit alone, and therefore the quality level of a commodity is maintained solely by consumer demand. This, again, is because the consumer is the only market actor who directly benefits from a better product, while the producer benefits only indirectly by virtue of his better product as one better able to fulfil consumer demand. Should demand bear the acceptance of a shoddier product, the producers will naturally comply and lower the quality. Should consumers accept nothing but higher-quality goods, producers would likewise comply. Hence it is consumers, and consumers alone, who protect the quality of goods.

Yet the capitalist always has an incentive to make his products worse and worse, in fact as bad as his market share will bear. For the capitalist's sole end is to increase profit. He might do so by raising the quality of a product—but this will raise the cost and accordingly eat into the quantity sold. He also might do so by lowering the price of the product and thusly increasing his market share, but this will lower the amount of revenue he receives. Yet the capitalist has another alternative open to him: He can make the product insidiously worse. And indeed, the capitalist always has an incentive to implement *planned obsolescence*, or the intentional diminishment of the use values of commodities for the purpose of promoting sales. The product that does not last is one that needs to be repurchased; and from the producer's side, reproduced and resold with revenue rewon. Consumers of course prefer to purchase products that give them the highest use value for the price, yet the situation they find themselves in as both consumers and wage earners means this preference cannot subsist without outside suasion. A kind of Greshem's Law can be found not only in base coin but shoddy commodities as well. On a macro level, as more and more of these consumers grow dependent on the capitalist process, so accordingly do they become more and more dependent on his wages, whose flow of course depends on continued production. In short, those who depend on shoddiness for their wages are less prone to gripe when shoddiness comes to prevail. And as capitalist production drives out of the market all that is non-capitalist, the consumer simply loses the opportunity, or as against his supplier the *credible threat*, of purchasing goods that are not prone to the forces of planned obsolescence. Where mass production is the norm, mass consumption must be the rule. And while it is consumer demand that keeps up levels of quality in products, that demand itself is precarious and will tend to accept the new shoddier status quo.

On the micro level, individual consumer behavior likewise tends to shoddiness. In general, once a man has succumbed to the worse product he is not likely to go back. He may have a revelation after having tossed his tenth pair of plastic shoes that the old mode of buying and maintaining a product was superior to the new mode of constant waste. He may desire to hire a cobbler to fix up a nicer pair, but find that the old shoes he knew are now extinct from the market. He may find a pair of rubber soles, but stroll into town and discover the cobbler is out of work. In time not even the knowledge of the cobbler's skill will exist in the minds of the living; an absolute recrudescence would be necessary to capture even a figment of the past art. The technical apparatus for maintaining the old form simply will not exist, and the discouraged consumer will plod forth in his plastic soles.

Even in cases where a substantial demand for higher quality may exist, it is unlikely that a producer will be able to exploit it. Mass production is not a fertile ground for marginal improvements in quality, even where there is potential for the market to bear it. Production regimes that requiring vast and diverse inputs are not fertile ground for great innovation, placing their revenue prospects on the hope that consumers will change their behavior enough for an improvement to be worth it. In the realm of commerce as well as culture, fallen standards are rarely raised again. And so cheap product gluts change consumer expectations, draining out higher quality products and establishing new baseline preferences. The consumer may rue that his purchases have become progressively worse, but his inability to find ready substitute precludes effective response. In the end, he is subject to movement of a faceless mass, against which his own individual preferences can play scarcely a part.

What we often hear referred to as *late capitalism* is this: Capitalist production at the point where the market bears the tendency of use values of basic products to fall. We recall that the original promise of capitalism was that in giving up his personal property, specifically his access to the means of production, man would gain more wealth and ultimately more useful property. His fallback means of subsistence would be gone and his dependency on the wider economic structure would grow, but his actual income would so increase that one could not much care: he would be stripped of his fallback, but he would in turn be free from the vicissitudes of nature and poor fate. In the present day, man owns more *stuff*, but it is less real, less useful. Not only has he further removed himself from the means of production, but the progression of shoddier and shoddier products causes him to be more dependent on producers to supply the barrage of junk that now characterizes modern economic life.

This is all a way of repeating that modern capitalist production tends to diminish the use value of commodities. The primary end of traditional production was to make a product with the most usufruct possible given the technical means—this is simply what it meant to have a good product. But the modern economy does not exist to create good products. The end of modern production is profit, through more and more production. And the end of technological advance is not the greater usefulness of commodities, but the opposite: The more a product is useless on its own, the more dependent the consumer is on the producer, and of course, the better-off is the producer. Modern man may be wealthy, but all that wealth is tied to greater and greater dependency on capitalist production. And with the coming of the Third Industrial Revolution, that of digital technology in the Twentieth Century, he is more and more reliant on merely notional things. Standalone chattels themselves are rendered less and less utile and serve only as a kind of conduit to render services: His computer software requires constant registration; his digital books are merely licensed for access. All commodities begin to take the form of a fiat currency, and property itself has transformed from an individually useful thing to a mere social value—a notion.

The Inanity of Socialism

Socialism, the abolition of private property and the residency of the means of production in the hands of the state, arose as a cohesive ideology during the adolescence of the First Industrial Revolution. It was then, and only then, that the ideology could hold any cache. Where the means of production had once lay scattered like wildflowers across the land they were now accumulated in corpulent bouquets before the bourgeoisie, the fields bare. What loyalty should a man have to this scouring, this deracination? If those accumulations fell into the hands of the state, what matter was it to the proletarian? Let this poor wretch, under the principles of Christian charity and 1789 gain a voice over the productive apparatus, one denied to him in his servitude to the capitalists. The violent and filthy slavemaster that was the steam engine demanded Molochean entreaties, and socialism seemed the greatest ally that might stab this beast in the heart.

But socialism could hold no cache outside this context. The internal combustion engine left socialist theories in rightful obscurity, and in practice an embarrassment. That the socialist movement's greatest and last real feat, the Paris Commune, rose at the advent of the Second Industrial Revolution was entirely appropriate. The internal combustion engine would soon democratize transportation, communication, and all other aspects of material life in a way that made the socialist's treatises seem paltry. Meanwhile the electrical grid would socialize man and his habits better than any bomb-hurler could imagine. The airy works of Marx and Bukharin paled against the concrete accomplishments of Edison and Ford.

As we have stated before, because socialism is only a response to capitalist production, it is not, worth a whit of discussion on its own. Capitalism by itself is sufficient to take us to a point of degeneracy. Capitalism has at its core the same defective attributes scattered and arising gradually that socialism possesses in heaps. The problems of socialist production are many and well-reported by contemporary conservative capitalists, the best plaint probably Hayek's in his unanswerable critique of central planning. Of course, central planning can have no meaning outside of the industrial context, outside the complex network of inputs and costs and their rational organization in the market and within the firm.

Industrial production requires complex interactions both
between firms and within them that markets seem the
only feasible solution to coordination problems. The
failure to disseminate information of prices was the
Soviet Union's most egregious and embarrassing defect.

But the problem runs deeper than this. The socialist
was forced to take property seriously according to his
creed; the capitalist, as we have seen, was under no such
obligation. The socialist saw property as his avowed
enemy, which he was obligated to attack, while to the
capitalist it was merely an instrumentality, a nuisance, an
impediment in the perpetual pursuit of profit. By the
time of the Soviet collapse it was the communist alone
who took the institution of property seriously, standing
like the wrathful atheist in a room of careless drunks and
libertines, finding that he is in his hatred the last to give
God His due.

The slave labor of the Soviet Union had still been
able to make clumsy use of the fruits of the second
Industrial Revolution. But it was decimated by the Third
Industrial Revolution, the rise of microchips, electronics,
complex financial instruments and inane consumer
goods. It was not a stagnant growth rate or a diminution
of spirit that killed the Evil Empire, but its failure to
attach itself to the true perpetual revolution, which was
capitalistic and technocratic. A technician in the socialist
system may be driven by the thrill of discovery or the
patriotic desire to benefit his country or the whole of
mankind; but he will always lack the incentive given to
the technician in the capitalist system, that of
unadulterated greed, so capable of oozing into unseen
crevices, enclosing old realms through technical mastery,
creating dependencies no humane person could ever
have envisioned, upending the last era's technical state

and rendering any complaints against the new feckless: the clamoring of old coots. The capitalist mindset, which holds that every opportunity for profit must be exploited, is comfortably dovetailed with the technocratic mindset, which holds that every faculty of man must be enhanced.

A producer always benefits from creating dependencies in consumers, whether through brand addiction, material necessity, or simply not being able to afford any other. The Third Industrial Revolution, that which brought about digital and electronic technology, brought with it a new kind of dependency, and heralded a new era of socialized property. The technical advances achieved by this revolution could not be realized under the old conceptions of property.

Indeed, the great technical feats of the Third Industrial Revolution scarcely resemble traditional chattels at all. Instead, the use values of these goods are socialized, dependent on the existence of preexisting networks and fundamentally useless without the continued intervention of other producers. We take as emblematic the smartphone. A smartphone has a use value, if only for its tiny light, but its intrinsic utility is tied to the social aspect of its use. If a majority of phone users stop using a given software, or usage drops to a level where networking becomes a vain endeavor, the individual phone's use value shrinks to nothing. The smartphone is not a chattel in any traditional sense. Its use value is not intrinsic to the individual phone. It is not so much a thing as an idea, a service whose physical existence is necessary only the way a ticket stub is necessary to prove one is eligible for entry to a show. The formal and final causes of a traditional chattel were the same: the map and address book both held information, and their physical existences were formed by the need to retain this information. The smartphone, in contrast, is completely malleable, and has as its end any human knowledge conceivable. The real physical phone is a façade for the host of functions enclosed within this little hunk of plastic. It is not a singular good; it is more akin to a second consciousness, behold to all other consciousnesses surrounding it.

Three-dimensional printing is perhaps the *reductio ad absurdum* of this. One finds himself paying not for a good, but rather the information how to make a good. One is no longer purchasing physical ownership per se, but only the opportunity to have physical access. All commodity production approaches a kind of rent-seeking, for the producer no longer manufactures at all; he is rather the gatekeeper to the information necessary to produce the good, comparable to the landowner who provides access to land or other resources under his dominion, but who personally produces nothing.

The property arrangements resulting from this technical environment are far more radical than any socialist could have imagined. He had raged against property with demonic fury, yet it fell not from external battering but the hallowing out of the bricks that composed it. "The capitalist process, by substituting a mere parcel of shares for the walls of and the machines in a factory, takes the life out of the idea of property. It loosens the grip that once was so strong—the grip in the sense of the legal right and the actual ability to do as one pleases with one's own; the grip also in the sense that the holder of the title loses the will to fight, economically, physically, politically, for 'his' factory and

his control over it, to die if necessary on its steps."[100]
Schumpeter had witnessed the political aspect of this
transformation long before, though the modern
dilemma is more pronounced than even he identified.
The modern disrespect for the rights of property arises
not as a reaction to socialist agitation or thought, but
from the technical advances of the age. Where will the
young generation learn reverence for property where
their most precious objects are mere subscription
services? This is the atmosphere fostered by industrial
technology, and especially the digital technology of the
present age. It is not merely that the political attitude
towards property has been attacked, but the very nature
of the property itself: Its use values socialized to the
point when it no longer appears to us to be even a
chattel, but more like a rented good, used at the
sufferance of whoever controls it. The socialist,
committed as he was to his old and even traditional
notions of property, could barely recognize what went
on. The Soviet was left in the dust.

Summary of Capitalism

We hope this discussion has not driven the reader
into boredom and despair. One should never pick up a
book and wallow in fear of an unnecessary economic
discussion breaking out. But the adoption of capitalist
production is critical in understanding liberal change. By
nothing more than its natural operation, capitalism
promotes the tendency towards the creation of the mass.

---

[100] Schumpeter, *Capitalism, Socialism, and Democracy.*
"Crumbling Walls" (142)

As both producers and consumers, the individuality of man is slurred, and he is made part of a shapeless clay, ready to be swept up by wave of aggregate demand and turned into automata by the demands of industrial production. We attributed to the men of the Second Revolution the psychological desire to be manipulated as a mass; the capitalist process tends towards this materially. A freeholder's daughter or deracinated peasant shoved into a factory likely had no desire to take on the yoke of the social machine, but eventually arrived at the same faceless fate in the end. As consumer, one could scarcely resist succumbing to modern industrial goods, while as producer one could not long endure against the modern forms of production. The move towards the capitalist form was simply irresistible.

The evil of the system arises from this fact: That the nature of capitalism promotes the abstraction away from real considerations within the productive apparatus. The centrality of profits distorts every aspect of production. This is achieved by a new increased reliance on market forces and an according emphasis on price and profit. Let us recall that the market is itself a kind of measurement tool, one that can directly chart an attribute of a commodity—its exchange value—but not its intrinsic characteristics. In this way it imposes an epistemic closure on the system, both in the rather shallow preoccupations of the new economists but also in the capitalists themselves.

It was the unmooring of the notional from the real that has driven the violent and calamitous history of labor relations, and kept alive the otherwise moribund name of socialism, however inapt it may be. Modern calls for fair wages and consumer protection arise because the contractual relationships at the market can no longer be depended on to assess the real value of the things contracted. Again, this arises from the disparity between the ends of consumers and producers, the consumers who seek an increase in actual welfare and the producers who seek only an increase in profit. For the capitalist, the commodity he produces is not a good in itself, but only an instrumentality, towards greater profits. And the capitalist will pursue his end by whatever means he can, namely by a constant revolution in productive technology. The stability of production processes stood as the underlying regulatory form of the old economic order. The ancient guild sought first and foremost to regulate production; this established, other questions about wages and quantities would follow. The modern labor union justly calls for rights and privileges from the capitalist class, but its ends are towards remuneration, not production. How could it be otherwise? Productive methods are ever in flux, and must be for the capitalist system to find its fulfilment. The workers cannot be given free hand over the process of production because this would negate that central feature of capitalism: The promotion of unimpeded technological change.

Industrialism and Technology

For our purposes, capitalism and industrialism are basically one and the same. Capitalist production has existed everywhere at every time, but its universal dominance could not be imagined without the technological advances industrial technology provided. Capitalism would be indefensible on a society-wide scale if not for technical advance. It was the advances of the

First Industrial Revolution which provided the material cause of taking production out of the home and into the factory, thereby spurring the capitalist revolution,[101] and it is the mad progress of technology which created and maintains the dependencies of the present day, and makes any return to order contemplation of an older order an idle dream.

And it is with the growth of industrial technology that the usurpations of the Revolution look completed; that a genuine reaction seems vain and demented, as madcap as the revolutionist seeking to undo the Fall of Man. And truly the Industrial Revolution was for us a kind of Second Fall. We contemplate technology and we see how the human race must end; we see the forms of our extended selves, the glimpses of our new beings in the transhumanist future, the nightmare we do not have the intellectual mettle to oppose nor the spiritual wisdom to fully recognize. *Techne* is the only god that matters to the modern. It puffs up his Luciferian pride, it withers every threat to the prior ages, and makes wan every glory of the past.

With the industrial revolution we arrive at the lifeblood of the Revolution, why its progress is ineluctable, why our nightmare is not a passing one. The Protestant Revolt ultimately cooled, and no Protestant can claim his creed is an active force wherever the four winds blow. The classical liberal and the Communist must concede the same, for those movements which at times could garner a supermajority of support amongst the masses can barely find an adherent who can enunciate the tenets of his chosen creed, and so

---

[101] Paul Mantoux, *The Industrial Revolution in the Eighteen Century* (1983) 74

numerous and various are the political perversions of the day that scarcely one can ever muster majority support. The number of men who would die for the active principle of *anti-racism* are few, even if those who would passively suffer beneath it are legion. Yet the modern mass will degrade, defile, and debase itself for the continued use of electronic technology. This is where the *Zeitgeist* is hidden, the ferment that the average yokel wears in his heart's core, and the only existential impulses he possesses are in defense of his right to own gadgets and digital knickknacks. He is by his consumption made a loyal footsoldier of the Revolution.

There was never a dictator whose power was more absolute than the inventor of the iphone. Steve Jobs has achieved the spiritual subservience in men once reserved for the greatest of divines, and has conquered territories as only rape and pillage once could. The oligarchy of technicians has the power to control men without needing their actual support in terms of their arms, commitment, and blood. From the masses, acquiescence is enough. The pure human materiel of consumers is the balustrade of legitimacy, and thus the technician who can enrapture and entertain this monstrous thing is the ultimate man of power.

It is acquiescence to technology which constitutes the true *End of History*—the term is meaningless otherwise. In the modern day there are no serious arguments about forms of government, and scarcely even relevant ones. There are only progressions of technology which dictate the form mankind is to take. There will continue to be political strife in places where technical reforms are forced upon the populace, but barring a collapse, there is no chance that these risings will result in a government departing from the technocratic form. As long as the progress of technology is given universal moral and practical support, there is no alternative to the liberal system, for it alone provides the basis for unimpeded technological change. Man's spiritual and practical limitations are set. We have accepted that technology should have free rein over us, and so we offer ourselves to whatever governance such technology sees fit to provide.

What is Technology?

Technology itself is a kind of realized idea, a reformulation of man's native powers, and accordingly a reordering of his role in the social order.

All technology presupposes the enhancement of some desire for power. "All media are extensions of some human faculty—psychic or physical. The wheel is an extension of the foot, the book is an extension of the eye, clothing an extension of the skin, electric circuitry an extension of the central nervous system." [102] New technology always presages a new power. As is the case with any novel force introduced into a system, the effects of the change must extend beyond the newly acquired faculty itself. "Media, by altering the environment, evoke in us unique ratios of sense perceptions. The extension of any one sense alters the way we think and act—the way we perceive the world. When these ratios change men change." And so, "the 'message' of a medium or technology is the change of

---

[102] *Understanding Media*, "The Medium is the Message."

247

scale or pace or pattern that it introduces into human affairs."[103]

We take McLuhan's favorite example of a medium: The lightbulb. Unlike book or film, a lightbulb has no content; it does not strike an onlooker as being a medium for communication at all, and thusly McLuhan wants us to understand it. For a medium's content is more than the actual words-on-page in the case of a book, or the images-on-screen in the case of a film. "A light bulb creates an environment by its mere presence," and the information it conveys—its special attributes inherent as medium-qua-medium—is not *content* in any realizable form, but the alteration it has on the environment.

And yet the book, a medium more easily recognizable as medium, may serve as a more helpful example. To think of a book as nothing but a compendium of words is to be deluded by its content: it ignores the distinctive quality of the book, which is the unique sense-environment it fosters. The book is very delusive, for we are likely to forget that any media for communicating words existed before it, so dominant has that medium been in our society until recent years. Ultimately the book transformed those compendiums of words from mere mental things to objects with physical existence, and in turn revolutionized our mode of retaining social knowledge. It was with the rise of the use of papyrus and the creation of the first rudimentary books that oral traditions first began to wane in the West, and the notion that any man could retain something like the Iliad was seen as absurd; it was with

---

[103] Id.

Guttenberg's printing press that those oral traditions became nearly obsolete, and the notion that a spectator at the Globe might be able to imbibe Hamlet's philosophizing took on the aspect of mystery.

The process is a recognizable one: A medium acts as an extension of man's faculties, and in turn contorts those faculties in novel ways. In the case of the lightbulb, the tyranny of night and the paltry aid of candlelight are overcome, and the eye is allowed to function in any indoor space at any hour of the day. In the case of the book, man's ability for mental retention and oral recitation is weakened by the availability of the long-form written word, though his ability to unabashedly expatiate on himself before the public is improved—hence the creation of the novel and the political pamphleteer. In both cases, a faculty is extended in some external medium, that medium in turn establishes itself in man's psyche, solidifying and heightening that faculty extended, and thus transforms the entire menu of man's faculties.

This way of thinking about technology is atypical, an exercise few feel necessary to conduct. Man is and ever has been a creature who exists beyond himself. His lack of native instinct leaves him no choice but to rely on his reason and his ability to organize social life. His naked skin requires clothing, his lumbering body and terrestrial confinement require social organization: He cannot survive by his natural means alone. Simply to survive he must employ the social knowledge that is technology. Were it otherwise, he would be nothing but a brute and, defective brute that he is, he would soon be dead one.

But the *natural* aspect of technology cannot occlude the fact that technology must have stupendous transformative effects on man in the reordering of his mental and material environs. Through technology, his voice can travel faster than sound, louder than any vocal chords; his body can be moved faster than sound, his intimate thoughts transmitted at the speed of light. His faculties so extended, his native powers given such potency, what can result but the revolution of his material and psychic existence? To travel by foot or *carriage* is now tedious to him, who is used to zipping wherever he can desire to go, to confine his thoughts to letter and post now appears cruel to him who is used to instant expression and response. The words of orators, oath-takers, priests are rendered almost feckless against man's new desire to hear, and the words seem something valuable only if they can be broadcast, as if their hearers somehow grant meaning in their listening rather than the innate values of oaths and prayers. The electronic world becomes more real than reality, an ape of thought more vivid than thought, a medium truly more *personal* in that it engages more with the person. Once immersed in the new technological environment, removing a man from it resembles a kind of amputation. And if Aristotle and the Scholastics were right, and the soul truly is the material form of the body, then removing such faculties from him is a marring of the soul.

Technology is Ideological

All technology has within itself an idea about man. Technology's idea is independent of its inventor, for the relevant idea is that which inheres to the technology itself, not what the inventor desires it to be. The lightbulb holds within it the notion that a man should be able to see in the nighttime as in the day, a notion that remains intrinsic to the invention whether Edison consciously endeavored this or not. The car holds within it the idea that man should be able to zip around at 60 miles-per-hour; it holds in it a theory of man, a plan about how he naturally is not but should be. There is no way to use a given piece of technology without partaking in its normative idea of man, that manner in which man's nature is modified by technology. Technology as such is always ideological, and always expanding man's material capabilities, increasing his power over his environment and his own faculties.

These effects are readily apparent, yet can be difficult to perceive. We generally do not desire to see them, for they are bonds so harsh and so inextricable that they cannot be pleasantly considered. To think about the social fracturing which has occurred under the influence of the automobile is not a pleasant pastime for anyone with a stony will and spirit. Few relish the hours and hours they spend in the automobile; few relish the great distances which now separate man from his family and his work; few relish the sprawl, noise, and squalor of the attendant infrastructure so necessary to support the widespread use of cars. Perhaps the automobile's ample benefits outweigh its cancers, but any specious weighing can be nothing but idle recreation. Man's opinion on the automobile no longer matters; its force has spoken determinatively, and seared itself into all facets of life, so much so that we might just as well contemplate the beauty of man if he did not have a nose, or the pleasantness of water if it was not so very wet.

There is not and never could be any right to live unimpeded by technology. We are all of us born into a certain technological environment: We grow in it, we

come to know it, we know ourselves in and through it.
We inherit this world, not as a natural or eternal right,
but as happenstance, one nevertheless as natural as the
personality of one's father, one's race, or one's climate.
We are all born in a kind of Commonwealth of Fact,
bequeathed to us at birth, dependent on all the past
generation's progress, and most of us simply have no
reason to make note of it.

A new development in of technology always lays bare
the old status quo, the world unadorned by the new
advancement and the old rights that arose from it. It was
Edison of course who ushered in the momentous
freedom to use a lightbulb—any man who could possess
one acquired a kind of entitlement to light that no
generation prior had possessed. But this modern man,
with his new right to light, was soon to find the rights of
the old world fall into desuetude. Ancient man had
possessed a right to darkness. At night, this right could
be discovered: All of the outdoors belonged to shadows,
and the sky to the stars, aurorae, and the Milky Way.
Indoors, flames could dimly light the way, but could not
mask Nature's conspiracy to have men slow the tempo
of life and ready them for sleep. This was no profound
or dear bequeathal, it was simply the night as it had been
since the fourth day of creation. This was the
constitution of the Commonwealth of Fact as it always
had been, existence all men had always found, whose
Constitution was the working of Nature, and whose
statutes were the small advances made by man in
concord with her great gifts and against her intrinsic
cruelty. No man had a say in his place within this
commonwealth, any more than he has a say as to his
race or sex and only an idle speculator could fall back to

abstract rule in contemplating whether his native state was just or unjust. All men know this native state, this Commonwealth of Fact is not ideal, but the nature and habit of every man adjusted him to this state, and he could be happy only so far as this was so.

The technician is always the enemy of this commonwealth, and the industrialist stands against it like the bomb-throwing anarchist. It is he who arrives in this commonwealth and affirms that its citizens' inherited rights and liberties are incomplete, that their stodgy freedoms are unjust, that their constitution should be overthrown and rewritten on new terms. It is the technician who declares that this Commonwealth of Fact is not sufficient, that man is too feeble with regards to a certain technical aptitude, and that a greater man, one not bound by the material constraints of the age, must be born. Man's faculties must be extended; his existence must be transformed: The Commonwealth of Fact must be reconstituted on new terms, as one that recognizes the novel rights new technology has given him.

Man was once constrained by the dictates of the old commonwealth, which were simple enough for any fool to grasp. Under the new world revolutionized by the industrialist, all is different, and the contours of the new laws do not provide man with ready understanding of new impositions or equal access to its novel rights. As Lewis aptly noted, "Each new power won by man is a power over man as well."[104] The greater the technical achievement, the greater the subserviency can be established over man. Such is apparent in even that most benign of modern achievements, the lightbulb. The man

---

[104] *Abolition of Man*, III.

who was once servile to sun, moon, and candleflame must now bow before the man or group which controls the use of the technology. One cannot imagine modern society without lightbulbs. An individual might persist without them in his hovel, but cannot engage in any form of social life, whether professional, political, or religious if he will not place himself below the bulb's glow and drone. His life is greatly transformed and his dependency on the new technology is total. The power of the technician has only been lent to modern man conditional on the continued dominance of technical experts and submission to the infrastructure the technology has demanded. The coming of the electrical grid made man's dependency active, omnipresent, and perpetual. All modern notions of civilized existence depend on access to electricity, and so the constitution of technical society is stripped of any democratic trappings and becomes an oligarchy of dweebs. Social ordering of whatever kind relies on hierarchy, and with this an implied dependency on one another; man is a social being and is used to this and is not himself apart from other men. And yet man has never been so dependent on such a class of moral and intellectual mediocrities for every facet of his life as he is today, ruled totally by technicians.

Man before the Revolution could be fairly sure that his position in this technical society—that is, his relationship to the government, his neighbors, and his work—would remain much the same through the course of his life. Surely he would be wounded by all the horrors of the regular course of life, but at least he could be fairly sure what his life would be like and what world he would leave to his children. But since the rise of

industrial technology, every man undergoes a change as
drastic as the French Revolution in the regular course of
a generation's progress. He cannot, like the man of the
pre-Revolutionary commonwealth, have any assurance
that the role he finds himself in at birth will be remotely
similar to that he leaves to his sons. One's economic
status is upended, his social life is transformed, his
psychic environment is manipulated. The moral forces
of conservatism are useless against unimpeded
technological change, any more than the moral force of
pacifism can shout down an infantry charge.

The Moral Revolutions of Technical Change

Blessed are the poor, for they are naturally restrained.
Nero and Elagabalus could offer limitless romp to their
perversions, could tempt infinity and immortality in their
power. The average man is blessed to be poorer than
they, to be immune from such temptations and
immiserated against such conceits. The poor are
inherently conservative with regards to their own
natures, because those who attempt to live beyond
themselves will starve. *Blessed are the poor*, Our Lord said
in the Gospel of St. Luke, finding no need to addend to
it, *poor in spirit*, for the materially poor are so favored
against the idiocy of allurements and power.

This ancient fact is distorted under the reign of
industrial technology. The poor will always be with us,
but none is so impoverished as to be free of electronic
snare. On its own, this can be nothing but disastrous.
For every new technology distorts a man's soul and
environment, and thus requires a moral realignment—a
determination to control oneself in a way that he simply

did not and could not have needed before. The reckless fool who could do no harm to others on his feet will soon be given access to the automobile; the would-be lecher will soon be given access to oceans of pornography; the slothful worker will soon be given allurements that can refine him into a slob. If used often, these new media must form habits; if their effects are not guarded against, they serve to permanently alter man's mental states. Man must be forever vigilant against sin and vice, but who will fight back against an enemy he does not notice and cannot see? The technological changes he perceives as *natural* can scarcely strike him as needing special recognition at all, any more than breathing the air around him. Vigilance requires first awareness, but who will see the approaching enemy who does not know he was on watch?

A rise in inner power, mental and spiritual, must accompany any technological advance. Against new technology, a moral creature must show a new strength of character, an advancing resolve to gird with firmer mettle whatever physical or psychic faculty the new convenience has provided for. It cannot be otherwise. A technological change creates an artificial capability where before there was physical or psychic lacking. Every new medium is a casting open of the powers of the will for good or evil, one that might be used for mental and moral advantage or detriment, greater good or ultimate damnation. All new technology holds within it a moral quandary: How must I act within the new environment this technology creates? What do I owe to my neighbors given my heightened faculties? What do I owe to my own moral integrity, given these new extensions it provides me?—moral question all directly arising from the natural use of the new technology. The progenitor of a new technology is always indirectly a moralist by virtue of forcing these questions on the world at large.

Technocratic society is always a planned society. Either the technician will rule on the basis of the order laden in the technology he promotes, or some other mediating institution, the government or otherwise, will form a barrier to the technology's full effect. In either case, a conscious decision is made about the makeup of society, either in adopting the technology or spurning it. There is in no sense any kind of spontaneous order or reversion to a regular mode and regulation of life, for technology is always artificial, always exogenous to the system in which it is introduced, always encompassing a new power, always creating a *new man* who must engage in a new ordering of his will and faculties if he wants to retain moral composure. All technology is laden with the power of moral revolution, and if man does not recognize and oppose this change, he is destined to become its victim.

The Zeitgeist and Technology

If there be any advance of *History* as it existed for men like Hegel, Marx, and Kojeve, it lies in the progress of technology. It is the only way that ideas are systematically reified, or that the growth of *freedom*, however we might define it, can be distinguished from happenstance. It is through technology that man acts on the material world and transforms it, establishing and enshrining a new rule of idea.

That Hegel did not focus more of his analysis on technology is owing to his method, which relied on being vapid where it is not incomprehensible. Truly if any underlying theme exists in his writings, it is the rise of the ideal and intellectual over the material; that the unmaking of the real and its replacement by the notional constitutes *freedom*, and that man is greater as a creature when released from the fetters of physicality. Greek philosophy declares *Sophia* to be a universal thing, and the Romans through conquering the earth declare for themselves universal imperium. Luther frees the Christian from the bonds of the incarnation and the sacraments, and grows in enlightenment the more man stakes out independence from God.[105] The French Revolution establishes the principle "that thought ought to govern spiritual reality,"[106] and so constitutes the ideal state—the end of History—achieved by the standard raised by the victor of Jena, declaring complete political freedom and founding the perfectly ideological state.

We will not linger long on the great wad of Hegelian philosophy. Suffice it to say that it could not satisfy Hegel's closest readers or greatest disciples if some kind of progress did not track along with his *geister*, if some kind of freedom had not grown through the ages. And this progress arises only through the advance of technology—technology which by its very nature solidifies the intellectual in the material, which expands the territory of intellectual suasion over Nature. The *Zeitgeist* for Hegel is little more than an attempt to sacralize the progress of technology.

---

[105] *Philosophy of History*. "The German World." Section 3 Ch. 3.
[106] Id.

258

Hegel does not completely elide the effect of technology. On the miracle of gunpowder, he cries in exultation: "Humanity needed it and it made its appearance forthwith. It was one of the chief instruments in freeing the world from the dominion of physical force and placing the various orders of society on a level. One may be led to lament the decay or the depreciation of the practical value of personal valor— the bravest, the noblest may be shot down by a cowardly wretch at a safe distance in an obscure lurking place; but on the other hand gunpowder has made rational, considerate bravery—spiritual valor—the essential to martial success."[107] The Emperor of the French infamously knew the "grammar of gunpowder" as compared to his enemies, but what man of character can bear to contemplate the thought of Hector's brains blown out from a half-mile and calling it considerate bravery? For that matter, what man of Hegel's intelligence could not see depravity of the Marne had already been written in his hero's Peninsular campaign? There is no honor in a sniper, only abnormal skill in wielding the technology that falls into his hands. Who cannot see that all honor is removed from war with his appearance? The course of history is now wholly dependent on armaments, and the nation that can build and maintain the biggest bombs will rule.

All further discussion of hegel is of the most recondite and complex recounting of what is really a facile whig history, an ex post facto narrative pasted on material changes. What else can explain the advances of freedom in the Caesars supplanting the Republic, or why Luther can be preferred to Aquinas or Bellarmine in

[107] Id. Section 2 Ch. 3.

advancing the mind? Hegel did not have the courage to confront what his *spiritual valor* really signified—a technical aptitude, not a moral one. And yet Hegel remains the great metaphysician of liberalism, the greatest advocate of "pure and general freedom." If modern man was more free, it was owing to his technical capacity; even those transformations of the purely intellectual character could not be supported without material progress. It is technology which gives man, if not his consciousness of freedom, then the technical means by which he may practically apply that freedom. A *pure and general* freedom means only an unquestioned progress of that technology, and according rule by its tenets.

The New Artificial Society

What are the fruits of capitalist development and its accompanying technological advance? Industrial infrastructure is the most notable, for it bodes no comparison to the incredible cities of old, which grew on human conditions. Even a planned city like St. Petersburg was not similarly artificial: it grew from the will of one man, his eyes set on political relevancy and modern design, yet the city was still a human city, one which did not depart from what man have always known a city to be through the ages. Likewise were the streets of Washington made geometric by L'Enfant to aid in the massacre of any mob that might infringe on the new Xanadu of republicanism: the city was still in human dimensions however unnatural the temples of democracy upon it might have been erected.

The modern city is not designed for man, but for the automobile. Weighed against human needs, both material and spiritual, the modern city is irrational: needlessly large, needlessly dirty, needlessly ugly. The half-mile a man might be happy to walk is extended to five; the roar of traffic is omnipresent; mirages simmering over oceans of concrete leave visible only blaring lights of advertisements, with the remainder a drone of faceless buildings and landscapes. Ornate and beautiful buildings must be allowed to fall next to the force of the highway, for to erect buildings worthy of admiration would be destructive to the highway's purposes, not to mention to any gawking drivers passing by. Modern man has power to conquer distances, to easily traverse entire continents as no man ever has. Yet he has no power to live well without the automobile, or in fact to live in any way recognized as decent or desirable to any previous age.

The dangerous thing, that lethal weapon of speed, rubber, gas, cannot be without strict regulation. Every time man leaves his house he can expect a semi-regular interaction with the state police. He severely curtails his right to be free from search, his right to be tipsy with a friend at the end of an evening, his right to walk the streets free from fear that the metal beast will turn his body and brains to gruel if he fails to mind his surroundings like hunted prey. The historical and geographic circumstances of his location may have created impediments, but few are so stalwart as to long resist the fate of having a highway smash through. The automobile will eventually conquer his land like an invading army, and he can do little but submit. The *driver* is no longer a citizen. He is, in wielding a large homicidal weapon, selfish, impatient, insolent, fat, discontented, and above all complacent, an indolent slave to passions mechanical powers have heightened and let loose. He is in other words made effeminate, and all society and culture must conform to this transformation. In few and far between instances we see resistance, yet outside insular and piquant communities, the automobile has conquered all.

Is industrial technology a boon or a bane? The thoughtless answer must run towards the definite affirmative and snarl incredulously at anyone positing the contrary. But an eternal law of matter dictates that the sum total of human misery will remain ever the same, and that what benefice is granted in one realm will be stripped from another. Ford believed he had democratized travel, and he did—though within a generation of the Model T social life was very near impossible to those unable to partake in this new rite of citizenship. The medical techniques that lessened infant mortality rates to incidence scarcely worth mentioning is an unequivocally excellent success, a removal of one of the great oppressions and miseries of the human race; yet what medical science gave it took back manyfold, to the point where a quarter of a nation's children can be easily and medicinally eradicated with scarcely any notice. The new technological powers given to the race are a means of subjugation of the individual, for *he* is the terrain to be captured by the ideologue, and ultimately finds himself trapped within the mechanical power open for his employ.

The Soviet Collapse

Why did the Soviet Union collapse? Let us not squawk like materialist fools and claim that a nation that in close succession withstood the terror of Stalin and Hitler was one that could be toppled by two-percent growth in Gross Domestic Product. No, that state which once prided itself on being the most ideological of all nations could only die by spiritual death, and found itself fatally weighed by a creed now moribund. The Soviet Union had taken as immutable antiquated notions of class structure, property, and man—a perverted, wicked, and vulgar idea of man, but one which could not outlast the coming of a viler thing. The Soviet Man was simply not ready for the depravity of capitalist advance and the technical changes of the Third Industrial Revolution, for the acceptance of McDonalds *taste scientists*, the subtle and brilliant arbitrage of Wall Street's new financial architecture, to say nothing of the banal insidiousness of the NGOs that soon plundered his country. The Bolshevik believed he knew what he needed to know about the perversions of capitalism, but his materialism left him no better off than a bourgeois pig in seeing the true state of things.

We repeat again that the rot hidden in the socialist creed rose out of the flaws of the capitalist system. The Soviet sought to move power over property into the hands of the state, but this very process required a firmer and more coherent definition of property than even the Nineteenth Century capitalist was comfortable holding. The fatal irony of the Marxist experiment is that the socialist was forced to retain a reverence for property long after the capitalist countries had all but lost theirs. The socialist never dared to turn property into so instrumental and notional thing as the capitalist yearned to do: he never dared to divorce it wholly from use value. The socialist abhorred the commodification of goods and labor—against it arose all the great and heady cries of the fledgling movement—and meanwhile the capitalist achieved a fuller perversion of property through this very process, enclosing and transforming into commodities goods that the maddest Kalgari could not imagine.

As the first Industrial Revolution gave way to the second and third, the capitalist sought more and more property's overall diminution, its transformation into a notional concept to be better wielded by the powerful—its *true* socialization, not its mere reallocation between proletariat and the owner-state. The capitalist did much better in letting the revolutionary influence of the market economy work its influence: To turn property into more of a notional thing until what was once known as a chattel comes to resemble a rented plot that a manager or software engineer fills with seed. Likewise did the capitalist succeed in creating a race of perverts that the Leninist could only envy: Creatures whose moral, religious, and national ties melted away beside the role of *consumer*. The worse the man, the better the consumer. If men of the capitalist class can be admired for their abstemiousness and personal probity, it can only be responded that an institution that does not guard against degeneracy and depravity must ultimately work in its favor. Material support will eventually lapse into moral, and so did capitalism create a citizenry malleable and amoral, immune from the harkening of duty and prone to the tyrant's sword—or more likely, his marketing campaign.

A great mass now sells its labor with an almost demented fury: The commuter making a second income offering Lyft rides on his way home from work, the grad student selling her chastity on international markets, the bum selling his plasma and internal organs for drug money. This is a moral cataract, arisen from the material change and its inevitable perdurance, the total revolution in man, in a new *homo economicus* who sees himself and his labor as no moral gem to be cherished but a constant resource to be plundered and sold—and the vile concupiscence of the slut becomes the livelihood of the whore.

The socialist formally loathed the mechanism of the Servile State that prevailed under capitalism. In practice, his lust for control and his effeminate longing for petty power was fully satisfied by the managerial structure under the new proletarianism, and his facile humanism was satisfied with reforms entrenching the difference of status between capitalist and worker. What the Western leftist gave up in explicit government power he lent to Human Resources departments. The bullying government need not appear the thug in maintaining the party line when the actual wage-providers could far more naturally threaten workers with starvation to the same effect, bound by *regulation* and market forces. Such was the beauty of petty control, which the Western governments achieved in magnificently efficient manner under the Civil Rights regime, a rule more radical and complete than the Stasi could ever enforce.

Capitalism and Liberal Change

What again is the predominate evil of the capitalist
system? It is the fascination and total reliance on profit
and market value in the place of concern for real
productivity. The traditional methods of production
were directed towards an end fitting to the process used
to achieve it. The textile manufacturer strove to make
textiles; the blacksmith endeavored to shape metals to
his liking; the attorney to provide for his clients at low; and the
doctor strove to live up to the standards of Hippocrates.
In all cases these employments earned due
compensation, enough for subsistence and the quality of
life due to one's standing. But profit was not an end in
itself. *Surplus*, whether thought of in terms of revenue or
as a measure of utilitarian welfare, could not be the
regular fruit of labor, for what was above and beyond
equitable recompense could not be expected absent a
continual exploitation. The shift to capitalist production
was a clear distortion of this. In England, the fledgling
proletariat provided the material means of the new mode
of production; in France those workers liberated from
the guilds by the Constituent Assembly provided a
reserve army of labor; in America the opening of the
Midwest and improvements in transport finally made the
working of New England soil unfeasible, and the
farmgirls of Lowell and Manchester fell into the
factories. The change was made; those who failed to
acclimate were driven out of the market. A new standard
was established, a new order set in motion whose
progress might be slowed, but never halted or undone.

And this demoniacal orgy, this burlesque of self-
abasement, arises out of a simpler process of
exploitation than the socialist conceived. For the

socialist made every attempt to ground his notion of surplus and exploitation in terms of class structure, a construct which was scarcely tenable in the twilight of Marx's life, and laughable today. No, the true exploitation arose from the nature of technological change, that change that capitalist production constantly advanced and relied upon. Continued technical advance ensured that those who had access to the new technology would control society, and those consumers who relied on it would beg to be kept in such dependency.

So we arrive at the present state of things. There is no man and no good that does not demand a technical accoutrement. The sunset is incomplete if not photographed, the life milestone not valid if not caught on video. What is efficient is presumed good, what is newer is presumed better. Those technical changes that find resistance can eventually find an ally in economizing. To say a change is always preferable is to say the existing world is perpetually inferior to the contemplated new, though in what manner the modern malcontent cannot precisely say; *melior est quid est venturus*. And so every man who embraces unquestioned technical change becomes a footsoldier of the Revolution. A vast majority of men are now exposed as enemies of reaction, in their mere acts of consumption creating bulwarks against instauration. This is not to fault them too much: They are the masses, thoughtless and impure. What rules them is not a creed or a man: they are moved by the progress of technology itself. This is the *technocracy*, and the subject to which we now turn.

The Fourth Revolution of 1968

The Modern Indeterminacy

We think things in their sameness, but we love things
as individuals. Poetry is greatest and only truly poetical
when it cannot be translated, when its composition
transcends and completes its form and meter and topic
and comes to be a unity in itself. And so we love men
not so much for their types but for the perfections they
achieve by them. So we love a man not because he is a
man—and what is so perverse as to love *mankind* for its
own sake?—but because of the particularities which
complete him. It is such peculiarity that makes a man,
that makes him unique beyond a mere object of
commerce and conversation. For in a man, as in all
objects under the sun, one's excellency is consummated
in the act of being, in taking what we are *in genera* and
giving it concrete existence: in wedding spirit to matter,
and thereby taking on traits that are not intrinsic to our
essence, but which serve to perfect us.

The perfection of the individual is in his accidents.
We love *Beauty* in all things, but in the individual we love
her distinguishing marks, those marks which perfect the
beauty of one what might mar that of another. And so
do we love a man not as *man* or his virtues in
conception, but for how he lives out his life in their
achievement. All things strive first and foremost to *be*,

and it is only through being that any one of them can become perfect.

It is man's unique place in the cosmos never to be at home with himself, never to be sufficient in his own means, alien not only to others but to himself when he is removed from the social order. The city was organized to satisfy man's soul: to find that ineluctable node where man is most individual in his sociality, where he is most free where most propitiously bound; it is the imposition of a paradox, out of which grows all happiness and the beneficence of civilization. A good man can look to the well-ordered state and be assured he will find some contentment there. The well-ordered state is but a reflection of a just man, a macrocosm of the happy soul. But when the city falls apart and the social structure collapses, he loses these means to his perfection, the means to hone his virtues and discipline his faults, as well as the schools to grow in wisdom and the manners that direct his energies. He is left only with rude means for attaining perfection, of the scattered pages of wisdom and Nature's harsh reprimand of his faults.

The classical state was always a very real place, erected to cultivate the human soul. The modern world is not like this. Man is educated, but where education once presumed a kind of leading and formation, he is now filled like a vacant bowl. The old form saw man as a kind of clay to be molded, demanding an indefinable interplay between societal forms such that all institutions existed towards this complex and endless task. But modern man is no object to be formed, he is one to be created, as if conjuring matter out of nothing; he is not an interaction between craftsman and subject but an empty thing, pliant to all the demands of the new digital world, a creation of vulgar intellects and milquetoast hacks.

Gaze upon the modern landscape: Man's labor no longer provides him an ethic. He no longer needs to wake at dawn to feed his stock, nor his wife to rise before him to tend to fires of hearth and stove. The mix of play and utility and intelligence which characterizes any craft, upon which the hierarchy of work is scaled as the latter grows in influence, is transformed by mechanics into a world where almost all work is a mental endeavor even where it cannot rise to the level of *intellectual*. In the liberal trades easy access to information makes logic superfluous, indeed the enemy of the granular tidal wave of knowledge the mechanics prefer; as such, any artistry or creativity in these trades must disappear. Man's social clubs still provide him amusement where they exist, but where neighborhoods are founded by chance, not by tradition of creed or race, true sociality can scarcely arise. His religion and creeds can remain in the mode of hobbies and idle curiosity, subjects of conversation in the great babbling cataract of discourse, but cannot be hinted as being able to form an independent superstructure of their own.

These are all different aspects of the one impetus, that of practical and actual equality. Equality as a principle is nothing and can be nothing but an annihilating and depersonalizing force. It is nothing and can be nothing but a mechanism for dissolving all forms of genuine diversity in social organization, which alone provides the means of cultivating individuality. In the Twenty-first Century it is for Equality that neighborhoods cannot be formed by the will of its inhabitants, why churches cannot adhere to any rigor of practice or speech, why restaurants and stores cannot freely contract for business, why boys' scouting and sports cannot be limited to boys and men clubs cannot be exclusive to men. It is why schools do not exist to educate, but to integrate the new protected classes, to socialize according to the programs of the wholistic egalitarian creed. Organizations that do not fall in line with this ideology must be reformed or eradicated.

A sculptor has more power over plastic than over wood, but his work becomes less impressive as the relative ease of his toil is met by the lesser awe of the admirer. In his frustration with lathe and chisel the sculptor may dream of abjuring the lot of it, and of the day when he might implant the image in his mind directly into those of his benefactors and patrons. And yet that sculptor would condemn himself in his liberation, for an artist is nothing without a medium, and the moment he loses his medium he ceases to be an artist. We love poetry more than our own dreams, however rich they may seem to the dreamer, in just the way we love sculpture made in stone more than that molded in plastic. It is from a seeming intractability that the greatest art is made. This holds true for sculpture and poetry as much as individual man.

This is what civilization is: The matter out of which man is made, the forms of custom, commerce, pomp and education which make the medium from which the virtuous soul is forged. A greater man can be made from these things, for man is greatest when etched in the most magnificent material, and when the subtleties of his character and genius are most distinct in the surest stone. It is the city which gives man matter from which as man, the artist of the self, becomes great or small.

But the city is now gone. It does not form man, it only inoculates them to participation in the new structure, no longer a city so much as a hive or a vat of plasma. Like the artless sculptor, the act of forming men is taken to be an act of conjuration, not a creation through medium but the implanting of ideas, the channeling of propaganda and the cultivation of a desired psychology. The subject is perfectly free, wholly deracinated, a soul transcending matter or mankind, one disincarnate, waiting for the matter that will form him.

And so we find a baby is birthed at the hospital, weighed, measured, and vaccinated for the benefit of the worldwide immune system. The child grows and is sent to compulsory school, where rudimentary behavioral patterns are enforced though no true morality is impressed in him. Cruel matrons grant him a bare literacy, raising him to value towards most menial tasks and creating the vessel in which the unction of propaganda can be poured. A militarized police force regulates a bare amoral safety, and aids at every moment the destruction of every facet of manly self-rule. His marriage is a figment, not even a contract worthy of enforcement, and his children are ready sacrifice to social workers and psychiatrists, should his wife get a taste for the license the courts and culture will allow. His entertainments are digital, antisocial, beamed into his home, though there is no escape from screens and music in any space: a perpetual ether of radiation denudes the stars of their light. Concrete extends everywhere, to and around every space, sacred and profane. This world can offer him nothing as a hero or a saint: its sages tell him he is nothing but a vat of chemicals, and that to embrace the subhuman and schizophrenic beast in his mind is his

272

highest good. And death looms, and a vague dread still grips him, though he has nothing to fear because life, which is but one great sensation, is merely halted for the gentle darkness awaiting. His body is incinerated lest he be forced to think of being consumed by the animal earth.

The Dissolution of the Political Form

"The Fourth Revolution is characterized by the dissolution of the political form of society, the State, along with the disintegration of reason, the sovereign faculty of the human soul."[108] So Plinio described the still inchoate revolt he saw before him. The characteristics he notes are all related, and spring from the critical event of the era, the rise of the technocracy. It was the technocracy which allowed for the emasculation and destruction of all productive institutions, and with these institutions vanquished, to leave personality untethered from any guides of morals and manners, and to leave man as a kind of free-floating electron until some technician, so often called an *expert*, could poach him for his apparatus.

What are the fruits of this revolution? A bacchanal of creativity burst forth in the electronic din, but how to truly assess media of such immersive powers and with no historical antecedents is no easy task. Suffice it to say that no great books have been written, no great portraits painted, no kind of refined music composed, no stirring architecture can rise to give hallowedness to the world.

[108] Roberto de Mattei, *Plinio Correa de Oliveira: Prophet of the Regin of Mary*. 204.

Great art simply cannot be produced in an environment where all men who are not directly employed in the working of the technocracy are maintained in a kind of gestational vat of barbarism, a servile idiocy meant to leave men in a perpetual larval form. The intellect may aspire to greatness, but the material by which it might be erected is gone. The modern genius is a soul without solace, a crying ether without body or form, with no medium or refuge from the incorporeal demoniac.

We live in an age that is thoroughly unreal. All figments of the past have faded away. All institutions perdure only as commentary on the former institutions from which they take their form, and the empty temples and vacant thrones they inhabit. Though their outward appearances differ, modern institutions are all formally the same. All adhere to the same morality and strive to achieve the same ends. Cities still exist but are technically unnecessary. The family unit still exists, but only for itself; the greater social structure has little functional use for it, and a man not enamored with the notion of wife and children for their own sakes has no reason to pursue them.

Why have a child? In all times since the expulsion from Eden this question was so easily answered that it scarcely need be asked, for the economic benefits of children were clear to individual parents as they were to society at large. The modern parent now sees the personal costs of child-rearing either the same or greater than those of times past, yet benefits which are not so eminently clear. Succor in old age can now be provided by social security and a race of professional nurses, and household chores are now performed by legions of electronic slaves. The child as he stands is a sentimental object, more akin to a pet than the fulfilment of the life's work of man. And with the universality of contraceptive devices, a child's first struggle into life is against his parents' own ideology, which pits the frivols of the age against the continuing existence of his bloodline.

Do we come across a conquered people? A nation of men subjugated by some foe and thus deprived of their mature civilization by wretched barbarians? It would be simple enough to say yes—yet at the same time we find that movement has not stalled, that unraveling of the social form has not resulted in a falling back to the elements. How have new buildings arisen, roads been built, the frittering images of a *culture* sustained, when all traditional motive for creation has disappeared? The structure that propels the continual movement is the technocracy. It guides the modern world not on the basis of any constitution or rational method of rule, but by virtue of its completeness and totality.

The result is a great indeterminacy. The institutions of the past were developed for rational creatures. They existed for the purpose of serving man's ends guided by reason. But with the ration of man denied, the reason for existence of these institutions dies, and all institutions come to form a kind of Potemkin Village for a society lost, or perhaps a façade put in a doll house or the interior of a rat's cage. The forms are still useful as human markers, simulacra of a natural order now extinct. They exist to explain the world in a way man can still understand. In the context of politics, they adopt the vernacular of traditional forms long after these forms have stopped have any effect on the concrete functioning of the system. This meaningless compendium of notions is called neoliberalism, the language of ruling used by those in power. Who possesses this power is no easy task to answer, for sovereignty no longer lies in men, parliaments, or other traditional systems of power, but resides in a cloud hovering over no one office, one place, one people. Sovereignty shifts away from political figures, who no longer matter except as signposts for governance. Real sovereignty instead shifts between institutions: the government, the press, academia, industry, all acting roughly in concert under a latent or explicit promotion of the Revolution, all somehow cohering as if under the weight of one scepter. And yet the tyranny is more pungent and more pervasive than under any autocrat, for the walls of this gulag cannot be seen or struck at, but stand as a spiritual border around every heart. This is the effect of perfectly ideological rule, one in which the powers that be are only loosely tied to the *material*, and so the one prerequisite to rule is the ability to control the myths.

The hollow edifices of the vanquished past would not be necessary if man still had a useful role within the productive apparatus of society. But the man of the Fourth Revolution is divorced from any connection with how his real, material life is conducted. It is the final divorce of the real from the ideal that allows for the unimpeded rule of the ideologue. Man has no role in his own economic production and provides no real contribution to his culture, and he does not and cannot produce anything in the indefinite and larval state in which he is maintained. The entirety of his material existence is regulated and determined by others, he has no stake in reality but in his brute animal existence, and no choice but to submit to rule as it stands. "So we arrive at the era of social engineering in which entrepreneurial talent broadens its province to orchestrate the total human context."[109] This is the technocracy.

Treatise on the Technocracy

The technocracy is the state in which the logic of technology is allowed to determine its own social structure. It is that system where the ongoing progress of technology is undertaken not for the explicit benefit of man, but for the purpose of further extending the faculties provided by a given kind of technology. The technocracy is not the same as a technologically advanced society, which need not place technical advance as the *summum bonum* of social ordering. Its crucial and distinguishing feature is the abstraction away from man's welfare as a motive cause of technical change, and the fact that the logic of technical advance replaces all competing notions of the common good.

We saw the spiritual genesis of this in Galileo, whose tinkering was held sufficient by his acolytes to reorder the cosmos. In 1968, this doctrine reaches its practical completion, the fulfilment of the baseless premise that rampant technological change will necessarily result in a better state. No honest observer can deny that we live in such a state as this—that we accept technological changes as a matter of course. This constitutes not an act of faith, which is always an act of will, nor some kind of *religion*, for a religion is always an examined dogma. No, within the technocracy, "the citizen, confronted by bewildering bigness and complexity, finds it necessary to

---

[109] Theodore Roszak, *The Making of a Counter Culture*, 6

defer on all matters to those who know better. Indeed, it would be a violation of reason to do otherwise, since it is universally agreed that the prime goal of society is to keep the productive apparatus turning over efficiently."[110] Even this understates the case, for under a technocracy, technological advance resolves to is a kind of natural or biological necessity. The good of man is no longer the primary consideration. The technocratic state is one where technology leads itself.

How can technology lead itself? We recall the way technology impresses itself on the world through the logic of its own constitution. The *end* of any piece of technology is not necessarily found in the mind of its inventor, but in the actual concrete effect it has on man's behavior. Because technology is an extension of men's capabilities, its inhering nature, its *logos*, is always reflected in the changes it effects in the faculties of man. The establishment and entrenchment of these changed faculties are the booty of technological advance.

When man orates, he necessarily desires to be heard. What a trivial fact!—for if it were not so, a man would not bother with the task of oratory. The microphone was invented in response to this very elementary fact: it allows man to be heard by hundreds and thousands, its power making the old force of the human voice almost comic in its feebleness. The orator who employs the microphone fulfils his function better than an orator who does not. What orator, committed to his task, would deny the ability to better engage in it? It would be vain to try to analyze the microphone apart from these facts, for the microphone is itself a normative statement

---

[110] Id. at 7.

that man *should* be heard beyond the limits of human vocal chords. The microphone has inherent in itself an idea of man, an approach to him and his capabilities, stating, *Man's vocal chords are not sufficient to his true needs, and therefore he requires amplification.* A man who has a microphone available to him and does not use it is no longer acting as a natural man, no longer acting towards the function he set out to complete. The obstinate orator is no longer directing his actions as a rational orator. He may have some other consideration that succeeds as a countervailing consideration to being heard, but the logic of his oratory is overruled in this. The speaker who turns down use of the microphone is no longer fulfilling his true goal of speech, whose objective purpose is to be heard. To make war against technology is to combat the nature of the act itself, which is better realized through technical apparatuses than to leave the task to natural human faculties or inferior technology. The orator who declines the use of this technology appears either dishonest or a fool, one denying himself the end which a given technology can best accommodate.

Because the use of technology arises out of the objective nature of the acts one wishes to amplify, there is no sense in saying technology is not *superior*. Were technical changes not superior vis-à-vis some human faculty, they would not be employed. Ranked by his powers, the technically-modified man is higher than the man in a less advanced state. Assessing mankind by its capabilities, a technical change must always be adopted if considered against the faculty it advances, and the capability won against mere Nature for the exaltation of mankind. Man has never been without media, he has never existed without extensions of himself, and no honest or sensible person can deny that any task he desires to perform will be better done with technical modification the collective wisdom of the race has discovered. What fool will plow land without a plow? or pound a nail without a hammer? He who abjures technology is making a conscious decision, rejecting the notion that man should live up to the standards mankind has won for itself, that he should bind himself to the happenstance of the arbitrary age.

Just as the perfect racialist sees history through race and as the communist sees history through class struggle, the perfect technician sees man as a bundle of capabilities meant to be expanded. The inventor of the microphone sees him as a voice needing amplification, the creator of the automobile sees him as an ambulant thing treading far too slowly, the smartphone developer sees a creature whose cognitive and sensitive faculties are waiting to be better united with those of the multitude. The technician is as much an ideologue as the racialist, communist or utilitarian. His mind is always ideological, guided towards rule predicated not on man as he confronts him, but man only as a conception against technical perfection. Man is thus subjectivized, measured against the ever-expanding idea of what accoutrements can be laid upon him. The perfect technician, that man who strives to increase man's technical capabilities with no principle but that technological advance should be perpetual, sees man not as he is but for what he should be; he sees man placed in history as a stumbling infant, always incomplete compared to what advanced technology can give him, forever metamorphosing from the creature of one age to the next.

Technological change is not in itself an evil any more than the wisdom that fostered it is an inherent evil. Man has never been without his arts, nor ever so degraded as to be foreclosed from the use of technology to improve his lot. The morality of a technological change must be based on the effects it has in relation to God, Nature, and man himself. But technical change accepted uncritically can only be an evil, and a great evil. It is change which occurs not in relation to man as an end in himself, as an individual and everlasting soul, nor with reference to the entire social body of which he is a constituent part. Just as the act of indiscriminatingly ingesting whatever is in front of him can be nothing but a categorical evil to a man even if a bushel of apples or a marinated roast should fall on his plate, adopting technical change without the mediating consideration of the health of the social order is an evil no matter what positive changes may happen to result.

It is with the technocracy where the forward propulsion of the Revolution becomes sufficient unto itself. When technological advance is pursued as its own end, true government is by technical change, in whatever form this might inhabit.

Rule of Technology

How does technology *rule?* All rule arises from an applied logic, whether through the will of a leader or the practical effect rendered by a functionary. *Will* is always a form of practical expression; even the solemnest and surest law is ultimately given effect only through the actions of an executive, whether king or vassal, and the torpor of the bureaucrat can supplant the noblest desire of the legislature.

The *will* of a given piece of technology is its power to transform man's faculties. It arises out of the practical effect it imparts. Our responses to a given technology are not free. We are bound to react within the dictates of the objective nature of the technology itself. A man may react to an automobile insofar that may conform his behavior to the effect the automobile has on him but he cannot control the fact that the automobile has a particular way of acting on him and extending his faculties to travel. This principle extends beyond the effect on man. And so the creation of the highway is not a choice in a free human sense: it is a natural reaction to the immanent nature of the automobile, which is to transport men at great speeds. Political consequences must arise out of the same process. One might chastise the government for passing laws that cede city streets to cars rather than man, or coercing every driver into purchasing insurance before being afforded the privilege of using his streets—yet what could one say but that these are inevitable, universal reactions to the nature of the beast, which is a deadly weapon when wielded by the average individual man, who scarcely possesses the intellectual abilities to meet the mechanical requirements of vehicular operation? The human mind is what it is; the automobile is what it is; and so such laws follow as a matter of course.

The dictates of technology become all the more unavoidable as dependency on them increases. To disallow further advance is to waste the technology's potential, to deny its objective nature, which is to advance man's faculties. To forestall technical progress is illogical; it runs afoul of the original reason for adopting the new technology. The nation that adopts the automobile but not the highway acts against the initial logic of adopting the original technical change, like a gardener refraining from watering his plants at the moment they begin to sprout.

This is what we mean by *technocracy*. It is the state in which technological advance becomes a sufficient end in itself, a state in which the logic of the technology takes precedence over any consideration of whether its adoption is good for man. All technological progress provides some increase in utility; it would not be produced, sold, or purchased were it not utile. But the technology is only utile with respect to one particular attribute and extension of man's, not man's good as a whole. It is only with respect to singular faculties that it is used and produced, allowed to dominate.

This is technology ruling itself: The advance of a technology's own particular telos in the place where human welfare once stood. Technical progress in this case is not an act of human will, for what remains of human will lies only in man's reaction to the new technology. Man might take or leave the technical advance or its corollary improvements. But in doing so he will behave in a *formally irrational* way with regards to the technology and the faculty that will not be farther advanced.

The rejection of new technology is almost always a personal, individual act. A legislature or regulator may decide to disallow a particular innovation, and such disallowance may be a blessing to the vestiges of human welfare that remains in the state. But against technological advance, the war is overall a losing one, and the victories often pyrrhic. For in the modern state, man is always part of a mass, and a mass is always desirous to be led: longing for an ideology to rule them and to fulfil the intellectual substance of their lives. Technological advance provides this. A minority at first adopts the change; more adopt it; a propaganda campaign intrudes to encourage men to believe that extended faculty simply *must* be extended for true happiness, until adoption is so widespread that abstaining will find the abstinent without the basic social entitlements he possessed prior. Mass man does not really cognize the technical state he inherits. He might at times be able to gather visions of a world outside it: When the beauty of an autumn afternoon rent by leafblowers, maybe he jokes about joining the Mennonites, and at wistful moments in traffic shouts out as if he is half-serious about it. But he dispels these thoughts as ultimately unserious, fables of Old Hobbiton. He might ally himself to an interest group that, through some ulterior consideration to the environment or *historical preservation* strives to stem the forces of change, but these must always be reactive, unencumbered by any positive motive force of its own. Against the technocrats, the spirit of the Luddites must always look like crankery, for it is technology which makes our world new, and technology which makes the man of ideals a reactionary, a constant adversary of the times.

And these are the exceptions. In general, men are content with their technology, as they are content with the sun, the trees, and the air, which when they prickle him he can complain about as fogeys complain of growing old. Technology provides a peaceful way to be led, a harmless and unideological ideology, and as time passes the bases on which opposition might be enunciated fades. Why would a man oppose a technical change that is *better?* What notion of man can establish a standalone principle of opposition? Has not man always been a creature of his arts? Who is worthy to choose the state of man to be retained by technical stasis, and how can this choice be anything other than a matter of taste and bigotry?

The Technical Conclusion

In 1968 we see the technocracy achieve perfection. All technical problems facing society have been solved, at least in principle. The questions of how men should be fed, clothed, and otherwise maintained in their quotidian existences have been answered. The progress of agriculture is sufficient to prove the point. The great political dilemmas that stood preeminent before History's end—Who would own the land? Who would own the means of production? How would labor be hired? What would be grown?—these questions are all answered. Corporations would own the land, and own the means of production; great machines would do most of the work, and where labor was necessary it could be purchased as a commodity from a large international market. The economies of scale to be had over the heavy machinery is nothing compared to those advances over which they had monopoly power: The custom-produced seeds and manufactured fertilizer protected by the tenets of Intellectual Property. The perfection of this system could hardly be surpassed; to attack one balustrade is to topple the whole. Should small farmers organize or a party find a way to socialize the means of production, they would place themselves outside the beneficence of the new technical advances. Planned surpluses obviate the need for bread riots. All historical dilemmas of production are solved.

Where no material contradiction any longer exists, political problems have a tendency to disappear. The question of land distribution and land reform which was once a constant through history has become obsolete. The average man, small farmer, or even mid-level firm cannot compete with the productivity of the industrial farm. *Land*, which in past ages was clearly the foundation of all economic productivity, now has little or no intrinsic meaning against the techniques of production. The chasm between productivity under new techniques and those available to a small proprietor makes the matter of *land* a veritable afterthought. Perhaps the small proprietors will stage a revolution, but their victory can be no heady feat. Their labors will result in less productivity for the greater sweat and toil, and their position will be secure only so long as they can prevent market forces from acting upon them. Any kind of land reform, to have a lasting impact, must run parallel to a political effort to constrain the use of technology.

This is not to say that the technical dominance of the moment is immutable, or that the present makeup of the economy can long remain static. Monopolies disappear when power of exclusion is lost, and conglomerates often crumble once smaller producers are able to find competitive advantages. What has changed is the primary nature of the dispute, which is no longer between haves and have-nots, between the wealthy and the plebs over resources. Further, the new struggle is inherently an intellectual one, one pitted over the products of the mind. As such, it will always tend to be a contest between relative elites. All previous forms of *class struggle* are eviscerated under this battle of the minds.

It is for this reason that almost all examples of blatant *political movements* in the modern world are fake. All the mobs, protests, and the attendant destruction are conducted under the orchestration and allowance of competing elites. They are elite phenomena, concerning elite topics, of how the technocracy should be managed. If there is a debate about scarce resources, it occurs between two elite groups: between corporations and an environmental lobby, between Manhattan banks and their proposed regulators. In the rare case where a genuine grassroots protest arises, especially one adhering to a right-wing cause, it will simply be ignored or outright suppressed so they can have no effect on policy or public opinion. A peaceful protest is only effective if the ruling class at all care about seeing how many people can show up; absent this interest, it is simply a lame social event. A riot is only effective where a group of people possess a credible threat of real violence against the regnant power. There are no credible threats against the militarized police forces, there are only those so-called agitators whose violence is found handy by some faction of the elite. There are no modern bread riots; there is far too much bread, its ingredients cancerous and vile, its consumers elephantine and tumorous in body, demented and suggestible in spirit. The masses have been sated, the indigent have been tamed, and the great struggles of history have been mollified on their way to being eradicated.

The Completion of the Industrial Revolution

It was with the Revolution of 1968 that the Soviet Union's demise was written. Against perfection who will prevail? In concrete terms, that credibility besmirched by the invasion of Hungary was eradicated by the invasion of Czechoslovakia. But more fundamentally, the advances of the age proved that the Communist thug was no longer revolutionary against the progress of the Revolution, and the sclerotic Soviet constitution must now wither under the rising sun. The changes wrought by the electronic technology of the third industrial revolution were far different from those of the prior: they threatened to dull men's intellects and smother his soul in electric cacophony. But they no longer threatened to grind the average proletarian within its gears. The course of industrialization seemed more than complete, its excesses excised, its benefits democratized and seemingly costless.

What the new technology offered was a kind of happy stasis, a completion of domestic life. The mechanized household, dependent as it was on gadgets and the electric grid, had become the baseline for civilization. Later technological iterations could promise to improve efficiency, but would grow on networks already formed, habits and dependencies long ago acquired, on the graves of countless generations' technology already long dead.

The power of this transformation is not felt by those who see man as nothing but a consumption function, by those who recognize nothing in him but his role in the reigning ideology of the day. But the man who arose was something history had never before seen, and Nature had never been able to bear. For this was no longer a man who well knew his role within the productive apparatus. He was the universal bourgeois: he produced ostensibly nothing, and what faculties he had were spent wholly or primarily on the task of earning money and keeping it. The fundamental transformation of the material economy was complete. *Late capitalism* had been definitively reached, and with man's needs so well provided for, his barest concupiscence was now the primary target of market forces. The pressing questions now lay in the field of home entertainment and color television, the work of *taste scientists* applied to poring over the mysteries of the potato chip, and the tinkerer seeking to place a microchip in every household good.

To meddle with the system would usher in financial chaos and raise the specter of mass starvation. If the quality of goods has diminished—as it has, and as we have seen, it must—then this decline still stood tall against the imagined calamities it avoided. The system has consistently resulted in food surpluses, large producers relatively immune from the variances of the market, and a solid base for financial investment. It is a system as labyrinth and gluttonous as any a Soviet commissar could envision, but it is a resilient and often plastic beast, whose wastes and excesses are flung off its flanks to those waiting in obeisance. White markets were still allowed for the consumer who desired produce not depleted of vitamins and drenched with pesticides, who desired goods made of something other than plastic and that had not been formed under the toil of the slave; who longed to give partial refuge to the small anachronistic producer, now so clearly obsolete, but who had been the bedrock of political liberty throughout the Christian era.

To call this rule by corporations would be too simple. The corporate interests' interactions with government, the mass media, and academia show that their influence is not plenary, and is in fact often checked within the system. All movement within the system is presaged on the sway of mass psychology, on the leading of the mass from moment to moment based on how much *progress* the social order can bear. The forces of neoliberalism and the mass media are called upon, the corporate interest *right*, and if the latter sometimes must be diminished by these other powers, it is ultimately made stronger and more versatile by having them as nominal checks, for it forces corporations to invest and in mold these countervailing institutions. A member of the ruling class may decry the level of power held by productive corporations, but the dispute is likely a difference of temperament, not politics. *Left* forces may deprecate the notion of capitalist production, but only in a facile manner. For all modern institutions ultimately seek the rule of the technocracy, the same dismantling of the old order, the same leveling of hierarchies and imposition of equality, and towards this there is no better tool than the technical advance fostered by capitalist production.

A fable is recounted of Michel Foucault entering into a literal deal with the devil, terms of this acid-soaked pact being that the French pervert would guide the political left away from economic issues of class struggle and towards social perversions, the *identity politics* of race, abortion, and the rights of Sodom. Perhaps the diabolic could have thought of a higher Faust to ensnare, for the pact was merely a recognition that the crises wrought by the First and Second Industrial revolutions had been solved by 1968. Why would corporations oppose the moral deformations which made consumers all the more malleable? Why would the leftist seriously oppose the corporations that provided sustenance to his wretched life and no impediment to his perversions? Weak turrets of opposition might rise against the bloodthirsty international form of this process under the name of *anti-imperialism*, but this could stand only insofar as it could be wielded against a socially conservative administration: The transition from the warmongering Bush regime to the warmongering Obama regime shamefully testifies to this fact.

What politics remains when the great questions of political economy have been solved? This is neoliberalism, or the ideological form of liberal progress. It is the sham politics that arise when all real questions of material organization have been solved, and governance is no longer a question of the organization of the productive apparatus but one of mass psychological sway, a form of therapy upon the Leviathan state.

Treatise on Neoliberalism

As with *liberalism*, as with *ideology*, we find in *neoliberalism* at term that is scarcely ever defined, yet used with such accord over so great a span of time and ideological modes that we come to believe we are dealing with a real thing with distinct existence. As with *liberalism* and *ideology* we confront a term applied confidently in description but with infinite trepidation in defining it. A lack of definition is far from a denial of a thing's existence, and in fact our claim may be stronger where the object exists in the mind's eye before reason can trace its contours. Left or right, critics of the system acknowledge the existence of neoliberalism and can provide characteristics of it, along with the dreadful atmosphere it produces: Cheap products, decaying morale, commoditization of everything. Put simply, if a real thing did not underlie it, the term could not endure.

Most definitions of neoliberalism are quite cramped, constrained to a particular political moment in time, and thus neoliberalism serves as a relational term rather than an attempt to ascribe fixed attributes to it. Thus critics place neoliberalism entirely in the context of economics, specifically regarding the conservative reaction to the post-war triumph of Social Democracy.[111] So we find in many critiques of neoliberalism a facile conflation of the term with market economics, and any defense of the free market whatsoever. "One of the best short definitions of neoliberalism is a political doctrine depending upon a strong state to pursue the disenchantment of politics by means of economics."[112] Yet of course, this is nothing different from what the Soviet Union did: An attempt to contort all social relations under the guidance of economic analysis. To come to any deeper understanding we must look more closely at the neoliberal use of market analysis, and what this signifies.

The vile sodomite Foucault, however much he masqueraded as a critic of neoliberalism, was in his work and life tied up with its ends, and made himself a better

---

[111] Philip Mirowski, "Neoliberalism: The Movement that Dare not Speak its Name." *American Affairs*, Spring 2018.
[112] Id. citing Will Davies.

observer than most. He took no umbrage in borrowing from the University of Chicago and Gary Becker in their attempt to turn all facets of social life into a pseudo-market interaction. "Foucault observed that for someone like Gary Becker, crime should be dealt with by acting on economic incentives and not by constructing criminal subjectivities. In the neoliberal view, the criminal is merely someone whose cost-benefit calculus inclines them toward crime."[113] As we will touch upon below, Becker's analysis scarcely had use for the individual subject at all. Man indeed was little but a utility function that would commit or abstain from crime upon weighing its costs and benefits. Such notion of man could not help but appeal to a Freudian pervert of Foucault's caliber, who as with all enlightened opinion of his time viewed man as an agglomeration of neuroses and pleasure centers, and would not deign to see him as a moral agent. Foucault's writing on the carceral state are simply the amoral Chicago School method with a perverse Freudianism sprinkled on top.

Yet from the Right, we see criticism which eschews any mention of the market, instead noting its managerial nature. And so we find from Michael Anton,[114] no free-marketeer himself, that a another name for neoliberalism "might be 'managerial leftist-libertarianism,' for this governing ideology is top-down, bureaucratic, and anti-democratic, committed to social engineering and grievance politics, while undermining virtue and promoting vice. Neoliberalism elevates as a matter of

[113] "How Michel Foucault Got Neoliberalism So Wrong," *Jacobin*, September 6, 2019.
[114] "A Tyranny Perpetual and Universal?" *American Greatness*. August 28, 2020

'principle' the international over the national; it rejects the latter as narrow, particular, cramped, even bigoted, and celebrates the former as cosmopolitan and enlightened. Neoliberalism is (for now) forced to tolerate nations and borders as unfortunate and unhelpful obstacles but it looks forward to a time when such nuisances finally are behind mankind forever." The author here is getting closer to a universal tendency, not merely listing its effects but focusing on its unique and inherent characteristics.

Both liberalism and neoliberalism are phases of the Revolution, and necessarily promote the destruction of hierarchies. But the forces of liberal change are applied to real social structures. What is neoliberal is applied to the *notional*; in historical terms, it is the ethos that develops and is fostered after liberal change has already uprooted the social structures which the liberal sought to rationalize and reform. Those reforms pursued by the liberals were grounded in a wide variety of ideological bases, a smattering of which we have seen, but through all of it liberal changes were *real*, applied to the extant social structure it confronted. Neoliberalism is more generally ideological; it is a belief that the reforms wrought by liberals were good in themselves, a belief in deracinating reform for its own sake. Liberalism is the women's suffrage movement, meant to reorient society and women's role within it; neoliberalism is *Women's Rights*, which has no set end and is of course incoherent. The former had some concept of being oriented towards human wellbeing—at least this was its claim. But "Women's Rights" are an end to themselves, waiting for an active force to arrive and give it concrete meaning.

It is the transition from real ends to notional ends that characterizes neoliberalism. The less real are men's concerns, the easier they are to sway with propaganda alone, and the easier they are to subjugate. The politician who can conquer his subjects with concern for nebulous rights has less reason to fear a revolt over their material degradation.

Neoliberal Economics

We return again, briefly, to the transformation in economics, which tracks well the path of a science moving from real considerations to the notional.

We recall those early economists, those we call *classical* economists and who embody the tenets of economic liberalism, all operated in a conceptual world grounded in reality. We turn our eyes to men like Quesnay, Adam Smith, and David Ricardo, all favoring the breaking down monopolies, of dividing labor, of establishing uniform property rights and promoting capitalist production, all against feudal structures, government monopolies, and other impediments to economic growth. Efficiency and common utility have prominent roles in their analyses, but most prominent to our eyes is their emphasis on the labor, and the labor theory of value. The theoretical reason for choosing labor as the universal measure we explained before: All commodities require labor to be brought to market, and the amount of labor required to bring any given commodity to market seems to be intrinsic to the commodity itself.

Modern economists operate on a much different basis. At the center of modern, called *neoclassical*

economics is the concept of utility, the universal
measure under which all other considerations fall. The
methodology finds its rooting in the work in Bentham,
and came to maturity in the work of Alfred Marshall,
whose supply/demand format is recognizable to anyone
who has taken an Intro to Microeconomics class. Its
method abstracts away from individual consumers and
firms and takes us into the realm of utility- and
production functions. This innovation allowed great
developments in mathematical modeling, for economists
no longer had to deal with individual consumers, firms,
and industries. The goal of study was henceforth not
finding answers to discrete questions based on economic
methodology, but finding a general *equilibrium* at which
efficiency is achieved and the utility of both producers
and consumers is maximized. Equilibrium and utility-
maximization come first; an increase in human welfare
was expected to follow as a secondary effect, but in
terms of the model it was ancillary. The deracinated
quality of the neoclassical model allowed it to be applied
beyond the field of economics, and the utility-
maximizing *rational actor* is now found across the social
sciences.

The shift of economists' central focus from labor
towards utility has been momentous. Those who placed
labor at the center of their analysis strove for an
objective and real measure independent of the unstable
and often deceptive market. They were in favor of
capitalist production, but were so because they saw it as
favoring universally acclaimed ends—individual
prosperity and, of course, the Wealth of Nations.
Neoclassicals, on the other hand, base their models on
premises that need not be proved for the sake of

benefits that never need be shown. The elegance of their models and the lithe fatuity of their reasoning yields such ideal and supposedly *scientific* results that few can be found to challenge the faulty premises. The classical economist saw himself as discovering tendencies of economic life, methodological tools to help study the real economy and apply them to concrete scenarios, while the neoclassical saw before him a world of *equilibria* to be reached, of harmonies to be achieved by free-floating producers and consumers, functions to be integrated, a world of disorder to be brought to perfection through the regimentation of rational greed.

The fatuity of a system that puts a notional belief in utility ahead of human welfare must result in real disaster. The economists who gave their endorsements to the mishmash of arbitrage and fraud before the 2008 financial crisis operated under the most perverse of neoclassical market analysis, imposing conditions like "perfect information" on consumers, because equilibrium in their models could not be achieved otherwise. The idiocy of this was apparent to anyone not bound by ideological blinders. The housing market functioned by turning a very real and very critical object, a house, into an intellectual figment composed of countless financial instruments. Many millions in 2008 found they did not live in a house made of brick and wood, but a complex knotted web of acronyms and legal fictions beyond even the wisest man's full comprehension. We need not dwell too long of this sham system but to say that mainstream economists had nothing at all to say against it, and in fact saw nothing but market-clearing all the way through, replete with efficiency and wealth gains up to the moment it all fell apart. Certainly capital investors received as much *utility* from those houses as the men who lived in them—though of course it was only the homeowners who found themselves sleeping on the curb when the market collapsed.

This is the transformation from liberalism to neoliberalism. Again, both liberal and neoliberal economists promote the same means: the breakdown of monopolies, the encouragement of commerce, the fostering of production ... But the ends of the neoclassical are greatly transformed. Liberal economists wanted an increase in wealth by better technical use of labor. Neoliberal economists abstract away from concrete goods and needs altogether, and opt instead for production functions and utility analysis. That real wealth comes from labor is a truism as old as time; "In the sweat of thy face shalt thou eat bread." Now, real wealth is only a kind of side effect or epiphenomenon of growth, elision of which fact lends to the modern market economy its only legitimacy.

Milton Friedman envisioned a day when individuals would sell advertising space on their t-shirts, when everyone would exploit his marketable potential to the fullest. He envisioned the "gig economy" of today. Young people are expected to maximize all their productive potential—they are after all utility-maximizing machines. The only problem is those machines are humans that still need to eat. The individual person—that creature that still needs food, drink, and shelter to live—is lost as an end in himself, is at best a secondary consideration in the grand theoretical apparatus of the neoclassical market.

Neoliberal Property Rights

The same phenomenon is observable with regards to property rights. The political economy of liberal land ownership has an eternal feature: The redistribution of property from the hands of the Old Regime into the hands of the new rich. At the forefront of the long English revolution, land went from the Church to a wealthy class of private landowners. In France, the old estates went to the bourgeoisie or the State. In America this process was more benign. We find Jefferson attacking the legitimacy of inherited wealth, whose dreams were realized with Lincoln's Homestead Act which distributed meaningful property on the most democratic grounds. Such was in perfect accord with the belief that large landowners tended to waste the productive capabilities of their land, whereas small yeomen in great part exploited them. This theory, whether false or true, need not have weakened the institution of property itself. Indeed, the distribution of property to the bourgeoisie had the effect of vitiating the Old Regime's various forms of corporate property for the sake of increasingly rigorous personal property alone.

And yet the apotheosis of personal property gave way to capitalist production which, we have seen, is the enemy of property. Property becomes a mere instrumentality for economic growth. What was once the abstract effect of property ownership is not its explicit end. No proponent of capitalism can long resist touting its supposed ennoblement of property, yet in practice its legal and practical conception dissolves into a notion of power that can be employed. This was the *instrumentality* of property, the remaking of it into a notional concept, which we have discussed above and need not discuss again.

Political Neoliberalism

Where all questions of political economy have been solved, all political conduct and discourse becomes a battle of figments. All political concepts become mere notions relating to no material consideration or concrete policy, providing a source of tedious gibbering that must fill the mouths of democratic pols, designed to captivate the ears against the technocracy's endless drone.

Let us consider the vaunted notion of *Free Speech*. Approaching the history of the modern First Amendment, the liberalization of speech rights was always—absolutely always—done for selfish ends, towards which greater "freedom of speech" was speciously appended. Hence the Seven Bishops case could be used to unmoor English libel law for the sake of treason against a persecuted king, or the exalted *Aeropagitica*, which can be read only with knowledge it was written by a regicide and heretic who in justice should have been hanged. It is perhaps to their credit that such arguments are specious and instrumentalist. The moral whim they would use to attack a particular enemy within the state was not to be confused with the principle that it should undermine the state as a whole. These seditious men were not so debauched to believe *sedition* could be a principle.

Yet within the modern state this is the notion adopted, that Free Speech ought to redound with all its acidic force and dissolve the bastions of legitimacy the reformer seeks to spurn. Thus the United States are granted the holding of *Brandenberg v. Ohio* that allowed all manner of violent speech so long as it did not rise to direct incitement.[115] The closely subsequent cases surrounding Daniel Ellsberg's release of the Pentagon Papers established precedent even more despicable, establishing a right to seditious speech so long as the parties committing the sedition were recognizably advancing a neoliberal cause. These holdings could scarcely be characterized as *law* in any meaningful sense, for they were not and could not be universal guides for conduct. They served, rather, to grant to mainstream media a more formal role within the new constitution, one that gave scribblers and smut-peddlers an effective veto power over elected officials. The propaganda apparatus is given power that not even elections can overcome.

Free Speech of course is still no affirmative principle. However much obscenity, pornography and anarchism may have sept into the general discourse, the state has never abjured the prestige of establishing public morals through the regulation of speech. Thus any interpretation of the Holocaust that departs from the trial transcripts at Nuremberg must be met with jail time, and all expression of contempt for another race must be met with civil suit and unemployability. Anarchy of speech will be loosed so far as the regime can sustain and employ it, but anarchy weighed against the old forms of order, blasphemies against God, the Church, the family, and all other forms of traditional life. But against the true regnant moral code no ridicule or personal dissent can be tolerated, and any expression contrary to the regime must be more strained and

---

[115] 395 U.S. 444 (1969).

artificial than under any prior system. Where speech is
not only the expression of men's thoughts and wills, but
a legally recognized dissolving agent of morality and
public order, it naturally requires more regulation and
more fervor in enforcement than the past age's
prohibitions, which required only to nip seditious
movements where they sprung and to appease the egos
of tyrants. The new speech codes cannot help but be
totalitarian.

A Lexicon of the Technocracy

It is appropriate in the ideological age that politics
has been synonymous with pamphleteering, and in our
own century synonymous with digital one-upmanship.
The point is not to discuss political ideas, it is merely to
establish and calibrate attitudes towards particular
ideological programs. In the technocratic state, the
political lexicon has become arbitrary, and almost all
political designations have become matters of sentiment.
All politics of the previous ages are bunk.

Democracy was once the rule by the people. Now it is
a sentiment, with *democratic* meaning *good* or *just* with
respects to the liberal project. An electoral candidate
may win a healthy majority of the vote yet still be
undemocratic if he supports immigration enforcement or
opposes racial preferences in hiring. The Allied victory
in World War II made the world safe for *democracy*,
however popular the defeated governments may have
been, however often the Allied forces meddled in the
internal functioning of the enemy governments before
and after their victory.

302

Communism and its related term *Marxism* are not systems oriented towards abolition of private property, nor do they need any reference to the array of socialist thinkers of the past. *Communism* now signifies a forward thrust of the Revolution that has not been thoroughly mediated between the dialectic of *liberal* and *conservative* party programs. *Marxism* holds the same meaning, and *cultural Marxism* when particular emphasis is put on some realm outside of economics, particularly with references to assaults on religion, family structure and human biology. That the Old Master had relatively little to say on these topics is irrelevant. The *Marxist* assault on family life is most popularly the one made by Engels following his partner's death, and is one whose impetuosity and lame speculative anthropology would not likely have found approbation from his partner in crime. Still, this does not deter somewhat serious men from hurling the term. The changes these critics decry might accurately be termed *diabolic* or *Luciferian*, but that would require these words of Christian opprobrium to hold a minimal cache in the *political conversation*. Of course they do not. The constant airing of blasphemies and the steady progress of Tolerance means even the devil gets a hearing in the marketplace of ideas, while *Marxism* can still at times arouse the Burkean's indignant ire. *Communism* is merely a revolutionary change that "shocks the conscience," but has no meaning outside of its passing obscenity.

Fascism, as Orwell defined it in 1946, is something not desirable.[116] No better definition need be posited than this. *Fascism* is never used for any substantive purpose, and those who attempt to use it substantively

---

[116] "Politics and the English Language."

expose themselves as dupes of the regime, as men who wish to oppose the tyrannical nature of the system yet do not have the wit to see out of it, or the perspicacity to find a language apart from that imposed upon them by their oppressors. It is an attempt to repay with a faulty coin what an embezzler has just used on him. *Racism* is functionally the same.

"The whole tendency of modern prose is away from concreteness," said Orwell, though when he wrote this line he made sadly little endeavor to explain why this should be. The great sage and artist could see the Stalinist devil and wage active war against him, yet was largely passive as the concrete political world around him was reaching an equilibrium of formlessness. The Second World War had been fought precisely to make political language useless, for it had been fought over the supremacy of the technocracy.

"It is now clear that Marxism is an expression of the Jewish effort to abolish the importance of personality in all departments of life and to substitute for it the mass of numbers. In politics the parliamentary form of government is its expression. This is what is causing such mischief from the smallest parish council to the power of controlling the Reich."[117] Laughing off his clownish inveighing of the Jews, we recognize that his political concern was the wielding of the mass. Hitler was not a reactionary; the First World War, and indeed his own triumphant rise, rendered any true political reaction against the previous revolutions a feckless dream. Hitler was a man who adored the first three

---

[117] *Mein Kampf*, quoted from *The Making of Society*, Modern Library. 456

304

revolutions, who longed to make himself the Bonaparte
of the industrialized masses. Yet he was a man who
opposed the pure formlessmess of technocratic rule over
the personal, the notional concepts of citizenship and
market economics over the reality of flesh and blood.
The Allies' war against *fascism* and *racism* was not and
could not be about American or English corporatism or
their policy towards minority races, treatment of which
in these empires' hinterlands even Hitler perceived as
overly cruel. The Allies did not fight for or against any
concrete treatment of minority races, but against the
notion that *race* and *nation* should be guiding principles
of the state. This was *democracy*: that the masses should
not be controlled by something historically or
biologically palpable, but that the amorphous sentiments
of freedom that best allowed technocrats to rule should
be fostered. The National Socialists, so far as they
understood Spengler, understood this to be the dispute.
Their loss heralded the victory of the technocracy, the
death of the notion that Caesarism or indeed any kind of
state supremacy over the technical apparatus would be
allowed. Spengler in the end was an optimist, a man who
believed his nebulous *race feeling* could overcome the
threats of money power and technique he clearly
discerned.[118] But he ended his analysis where he ought

---

[118] *Decline of the West*, "The Form-World of Economics
Life: The Machine." Spengler indeed notes that "Faustian
man has become the *slave of his creation*," noting in broad
terms supremacy of the technocracy. He ultimately finds that
the "last conflict is at hand in which Civilization receives its
conclusive form—the conflict *between* money and blood."
Spengler's capacious definition of *race*, which seems to
constitute every facet of a people's culture, is perhaps

to have begun it, and his naïve hope in a renaissance of personal rule could be held where a vague Hegelian heuristic occluded the actual process of decline since 1789, which has always a replacement of the personal by the faceless, of the real by the notional.

Capitalism as we have previously seen has been a slippery term. Following the Second World War it signifies to the forces of conservativism a respect for property rights and free markets, in effect always deferring to the interests of corporate control. From the progressive wing, it suggested government moderation of some aspect of corporate affairs. *Capitalism* in fact took on the practice of commodifying everything, of abstracting away from the concrete forms of goods and leaving in their place a world of instrumentalities. Property is no longer sacrosanct, but an opportunity to derive surplus, utility and economic value from everything rises to the forefront consideration of all good and bad.

Conspiracy Theory is merely a conspiracy observed. It applies in the Fourth Revolution to those who notice that modern politics is nothing but a discourse between elites. Alternatively, in the time of mass media, a *conspiracy theory* is only a conspiracy that goes against the narrative of mass media, those tenets of the enforced culture of neoliberalism which strive to make the productive apparatus cognizable on a human level. The idea that forces within the United States imperial structure would conspire to destroy the World Trade Center is no great affront to a student of history, but

---

mirrored in his use of *blood*. Regardless, there is no doubt that *blood* found itself the loser in the contest.

brings into question the legitimacy of a political consensus posited as total and universal; it threatens to upend the bauble of mainstream discourse used to guide political conduct. A conspiracy theory is most often any attempt to probe beyond the purely notional discourse and attach real practical significance to the behavior of rulers. It is an attempt to engage in political analysis such as would have been presumed valid and necessary at any time before the chatter of neoliberal principles conquered all. The triumph of *conspiracy theory* as a term of condemnation is a flaunting of the regime's real powers, that something so universal as the existence of political conspiracy can be thought of as inimical to the interest of mankind.

We might go on. The number of these terms has grown fantastically since the end of the Second World War. They are not representatives of any real things, not even totems of a particular ideological program, but are sentimental designators, used by politicians and propagandists in much the same way therapists use jargon to describe and regulate the amoral basket cases they manage. These terms are meaningless, husks of a political ordering taken from past ages for mnemonic effect, retained the way digital spaces retain the markers of *pages* and *home*. But they can have no meaning as political prescriptions. They are used only to direct the masses, to render the political system cognizable to the wise and to spur the passions of fools. Whether the message of Conservative or Liberal, Communist or Fascist carries the day provides a temperature for how the political machine should be made to run. But nothing can alter the technocrat's logic. Neoliberal jargon can guide the technocrats in how the modern state should be administered, but its main effect is a loosening of the rigors of thought, of filling the brain with the sawdust ground from the structures of the old world. Even the men seeking to reestablish political order through good and true ends like *public virtue* must be confounded when these meet the actual structure of the technocracy. Rare is it that any language comes close to capturing the nature of the technocratic machinery itself, and therefore as a means of political organizing, it is quite useless.

Neoliberalism vs. Liberalism

The nominal end of liberalism was human advancement, but what is called neoliberalism is much different. The neoliberal creed has already risen above the good of man. The teleology of neoliberalism is not some universal and concrete human end, but rather the movement of the cause itself, a kind of creation of ideas in the swirling mass of institutions destroyed by Revolutionary change. The end of liberalism is some common good; it is something concrete and real. The end of neoliberalism is an idea, a notion. Neoliberalism is the ideology of liberal change.

A failure to adapt to the entirely notional aspect of neoliberal politics leads to some embarrassing political conclusions. Many Christians who decry the old eugenics movement fail to see the primary difference between it and the pro-aborts today. Margaret Sanger, for whatever her faults, was not a nihilist. The eugenics league broke down the natural restraints of sex and biology, but their end was nominally *good*. The elimination of the weak, the feeble, the stupid was not effected for the end of elimination *per se*, but the

308

supposed betterment of the human race as a whole. We can compare this to Planned Parenthood's modern existence, which is primarily and consciously for the ease and convenience of promiscuous women. Even the richest and most powerful will proudly abort and contracept their bloodlines into oblivion. It makes a degree of sense why the Rockefeller family would want to support contraceptive policies for the underclass; other explanations are necessary to explain why so many modern Rockefellers have sterilized themselves. The former is policy; the latter is true zealous madness.

It bears repeating that the technostate can bear this long submersion in unreality because the regnant ideological currents of a society do not have any ties to its productive apparatus. The neoliberal operates by instilling a philosophy of chaos and progress as ends in themselves, and priming the way for whatever new technical advances may come about in the future. In previous centuries it was only the advanced and progressive, the most bourgeois of the bourgeoisie, who could sustain the burdens of moral anarchy. John Stuart Mill could live the life of dissipation he proposed, as could the Bloomsbury Group in their orgies over tea cozies, for the opulence of their high place could sustain moral anarchy. But with the universal wealth created by the Fourth Revolution, all men are entwined with the airy theoretical premises of perversion.

All societies function based on consent to the premises of that society. But these premises, at all times in the past, bore some relation to the real material situation of the nation. In the modern state, he who controls the concept controls the very *common good* itself, one so exceedingly notional that the tyrant eventually only has to satisfy his subject in an intellectual sense to win a place in his heart's core. The same subject will let every material aspect of his life deteriorate and proudly yelp in the defense of the powers causing his degradation, so long as his ideological needs are satisfied—so long, that is, that his false conceptions of man and state are given succor. Man has often found a way to live on a pittance of bread. But to live without an animating creed is unendurable.

Propaganda

One cannot conceive of a true *dictatorship* established on the foundations of neoliberalism. The office of dictator is a set and firm one, enshrined as personal rule and wholly at odds with the plasticity of the technocratic form. The legitimate ruler of the technocracy is he who can wield its power. But even this power is equivocal. The ruler who cannot garner support to burnish and maintain his position in the technocratic matrix fails to adhere to the logic of the regime and the philosophy of its constituent ruling class. A liberal dictator is a contradiction of the technocracy's own terms. The rise of a technocratic Caesar would admit to a failure to achieving the liberal telos, which is mass manipulation through regulation of the entire technocratic apparatus. The modern governor cannot merely propose or promise to deliver results for a given class; he must prove himself acceptable to the organs of the technocratic government. And a leader can do this only by having access to the channels of propaganda, lest he be foreclosed from making overtures altogether. In a modern liberal democracy, one cannot be truly sovereign if he cannot wield the channels of mass media, for he who controls the terms of the lexicon is all-powerful: gaining the ability to mobilize men and to dictate the acceptable limits of political thought.

Propaganda is the organizing principle of neoliberalism. In a political structure driven by the movement of the masses, propaganda is the means by which these people are not only goaded forward, but made to actively embrace the new ideological forms being foisted upon them. It is in this way that propaganda "is the modern instrument by which they can fight for productive ends and help bring order out of chaos,"[119] the process whereby the masses are manipulated and the progress of two centuries of democratic dogma find their completion in the absolute subjugation of popular will to the desires of the elite.

The task of propaganda is always one of integration, of immersing the mental life of the subject in the conceptual apparatus of the propagandist's making. The fulcrum of effective propaganda tilts when the will of the propagandist is adopted as the will of his subject: It is the difference between a seller crying to potential consumers "buy this product!" to making the potential consumer cry out, "Please let me buy that product from you!"[120] It is going from a seller dependent on a buyer to support him to a buyer dependent on a seller to supply him. Likewise it is the propagandist's goal to make the subject think himself the progenitor of the decision he is lured into, to conceive he is poorer without the desired product than richer with it. The end of the propagandist is always to make the masses demand from the

---

[119] Edward Bernays, *Propaganda*. 159
[120] Id. at 56

decisionmaker what the decisionmaker has already decided to do. A seller that does this cannot be called monopolistic or exploitative, just as the government that effectively employs propaganda can no longer be called authoritarian.[121]

The target of propaganda must be the properly socialized man, the mass man, the man who conceives of himself apart from any one interest group or corporate body. He is one who can be appealed to through his supposed individuality, but whose splintered state is most susceptible to the psychological lures of mass movement. The object of propaganda must be free from the bonds of nation, party, and creed, but not so free as to be able to endure his fragmented state, and thus overcome the enticements of mass programing. It is this object who most readily asks to be sold to, to be haggled over, enticed and lured into submission of the propagandists' promises. "Without this previous, implicit consent, without this need for propaganda, propaganda could not spread. There is not just a wicked propagandist at work who sets up means to ensnare the innocent citizen. Rather, there is a citizen who craves propaganda from the bottom of his being and a propagandist who responds to this craving."[122]

The need for propaganda is universally recognized, its legitimacy unquestioned, its source of power uncontested. The man who clamors for *Misinformation Committees* and *Hate Speech* laws is acknowledging the legitimacy of the system. The man who decries levels of campaign spending does so even more, recognizing the

---

[121] Jacques Ellul, *Propaganda*, 132
[122] Id. at 121

populace truly is a mass of leaven to be kneaded and worked upon by admen. Politics in its modern form is little but the question of who is allowed to propagandize the masses. The question of management is all that concerns the technocrat, and modern democracy is an acid test of temperaments, of scrutinizing the population on how it would prefer to approach the inevitable. The process of mass voting—Election Day—is not a reflection of the people's will, but a final determinative test of how the popular will has been managed and controlled. An election is merely a political opinion poll with legally binding force. This is the reason why political polls are *news*, for they coordinate the efforts between media and government. The relevancy of the poll can be conformed to the logic of democracy only in a system where the propagandists choose votes, not one where voters choose candidates. And so when a liberal rises to power that public opinion poll called an *election*, it means the rate of progress should be maintained or accelerated; when a conservative rises to power, the sign is given to slow the rate of progress. Never is it to be considered that the motion of progress ought to be subverted.

Propaganda in times past was largely limited to simple images and the written word, created to sway man, even to deceive him. The modern propagandist uses electronic media: radio, film, television, the internet—each more immersive than the last, and thus better able to establish a place within a man's psyche, to foster the process of integration into the ideological constructs of the propagandist. Premodern propaganda could spread lies and promote unattainable goals, but modern propaganda does not strictly require any content at all. The purpose of propaganda of the old type was to build support for a person, product, or program. Modern propaganda need not promise anything; its primary end is to give its subject the sense that he has a place within a given ideological system. No longer does the politician need to sway voters in order to achieve political support. The voter still acknowledges the principle that the ruler governs with his consent, but now makes the additional demand that any ruler he choose be that one best able to manufacture his consent, to provide him with the best spiritual positioning within the system.

Biopower and the Civil Rights Act

The practical governance of this system required the forcible uniting of all private spheres under the sovereign technocracy, and was completed with the Civil Rights Act. It established as a principle the right of the government to reform any institution that did not sufficiently conform its operation to the dictates of the technocratic form. It intractably united the government and private corporations, and forced under the threat of suit and ruin the adoption of the advancing tenets of arbitrary equality. It vanquished any old form of constitutional or natural order, and with this denied in principle the notion that organic institutions had right to exist independently of government fiat.

On its face, the Civil Rights Act of 1964 was a regulation of commerce, an assertion that associations could not, in providing services, discriminate on the basis of race, sex, or other protected minority classes. This was true for public institutions as well as private, and the restaurant and country club were made to bow much like the public school and hospital. All institutions now became instruments of the government, existing at the pleasure of the Civil Rights regime. Should any member of the government's protected classes find himself either allowed in or excluded from any private institution, the government gained regulatory power over the institution's existence by the very presence of that protected class member. As a rule, it raised men into power and position who had not proven fit to earn or by the rational ends of the organizations they occupied.

In its operation, little more need be said of the Civil Rights Act than that it established *Discrimination* as a moral and legal pest demanding eradication. Discrimination is itself nothing but the act of determining differences between things, and as man can keep in his head no singular idea without being able to cognize its difference from others, the act is synonymous with knowing anything at all. To know and to understand and to even *desire* to understand have become signs of treachery against the new social order, where absolute equality is presumed and enforced, and any form of permissible discrimination is granted only by government largess. Any movement away from discrimination is a departing from rationality itself, whether institutional or individual, a crusade against the regulation of one's organization or mental processes.

Considered only in the realm of commerce, the Civil Rights Act represents best the blending of government and industrial power. Any vestiges of the private nature of contract were destroyed. The government could now in theory control every form of commerce and any organizational structure that did not view men as homogenous, as both consumers and citizens. And by and large, the corporate class did not object to this. If certain producers lost productivity by accepting enforced equality, they could make it up by standing above the rest of the commercial fray, those sad businesses that could not endure the irrational regimen and the capsizing of order. The mass producer found perfect reflection in the new consumer, the homogenous creature notable only for how much money he could spend.

The Civil Rights Act was the mass democratization of the productive apparatus of a society. While its effects were most notorious in the economic sphere, they sept into all institutions: those not oriented towards the creation of goods but the creation of culture and thereby the creation of men. Every institution was bound to promote the same ends and operate under a common ethos directed by the will of the government. There can be no *absurdity* in the application of the Act. So far as the government possessed the right to pulverize discrimination, it lay wholly with the government to decide what kind of discrimination it chose to uproot and which to allow. Its power was plenary, and its only limiting principle was the sensibilities of bureaucrats and the courts. That it allows men in women's bathrooms is an asset, not a defect according to its logic. The purpose of the Act was to weaken institutions, to eradicate the organic growth of those institutions, and to contort those subjects who benefited by the Act into greater dependency upon the government. The welfare of the favored minority groups cannot be the purpose of the Act; rather it serves as specious means of achieving equality through degradation rather than fostering achievement. Every beneficiary of unjust promotion and inclusion becomes an effective apparatchik of the government, and remains such for as long as he desires to retain his artificial place. Race and sex exist as powerful attributes of man. To announce this is such is not a moral claim about any individual member of the Act's privileged minority classes, who must be judged as all men are on their own merits. Yet nothing can change that all minority classes rewarded by the Act become collaborators, effective shock troops of the Government against the remnants of civil society. Every individual minority was offered the opportunity for unearned benefit, meritless importance, costless recompense, and frail human dignity cannot long last against the beck and call of obsequious power and capacious reward.

The perversity of the Civil Rights regime lies in its ability to corrupt even what is unequivocally good and honest in social relations, defiling any inhering goodness through the means of social engineering. The positive goods of, say, interracial marriages and adoption are tainted when used for the purpose of dissolving the social order, standing simultaneously as emblems of true charity and as the strengthening of regime power over domestic normalcy. These topics cannot help but elicit pain in all who honestly and in goodwill speak of them, who so often unite attempts to counteract true malice and bigotry down to their heart's core. And yet no genuine virtue or benefice can arise from acts that solidify the authority of an unjust regime. As the succoring and soothing of the worker is a good in itself, yet stained when used as pretext for Communist subversion, so do acts of charity become tainted when lowered into ideological affect. And yet the use of protected classes as *materiel* within the system is nothing shocking. It is only the way the Revolution operates: To turn men into biopower within the reformed system, to use their own natural powers as a balustrade of the artificial order. When humans become the raw matter used by the oligarchs, men of goodwill can scarcely help but promote the regime that promises to help them. By such means man's own innate virtue become a weapon against him.

The Jacobins had proclaimed political equality as the basis of the republic, operating on the implicit assumption that order could be forged in the polity without the need for such distinctions. The Civil Rights reformers declared as a premise actual material equality between men, operating on the implied assumption that the productive apparatus would be able to survive the onslaught of fiat equality. And so a man would participate in ruling who had not proven himself worthy to rule, and favored sects would heal, advocate, and labor in fields where they had shown a lesser talent to do so. The institutions those favored sects now occupied could only be weakened as a result, for achieving those ends for which they had been formed was no longer the ultimate guide to their success, but rather how well they could integrate themselves to the dictates of the new regime. To greater or less extent institutions all became formally irrational, their legitimacy dependent not on their original reason for existence, but their ability to adopt the new artificial norms. This would have presaged disaster in past ages. Yet the perfection of the technocratic form kept the productive process going. Managers knew the needs of consumers; mechanics kept the machines running, and the workers running them could be swapped about as easily as the cogs themselves. Some institutions held out longer than others, but all must eventually collapse on the asymptote of equality.

Truly the only constraint on this decline is how much material denigration the system can bear.

The Civil Rights revolution has been total, and so all-consuming that no past revolution can really compare. The Catholic cause endured long after Westphalia, and serious monarchists could be found through the Nineteenth Century, and nostalgia for their former dignity remained a staple in romance and the hearts of even the dourest republican. But no civilized man broaches return to the pre-Civil Rights regime. Those cranks who freely deprecate the Protestant, liberal, and capitalist revolutions will not but cower under the specter of *racism*, which is in the present not hating a race but choosing rather to disregard it as a basis for moral action. A morality which stakes its claims in the good of the mass must always be ambivalent if not actively harmful to the individual. The proof of this is in those supposed beneficiaries of the change: the women doped and debauched in supplication to the corporate economy, and the thousands of blacks slain in rage in the streets, lodged in ordered idiocy and barbarity, whose good fortune lies only in not being one of the tens of millions murdered by their mothers in the womb. Men in the Brezhnev regime had learned of the gulags and deprecated those men who built them, but in our own slave state the oppression and violence are all-pervasive, and thus seen as *natural*, or simply not seen at all. The gulag is everywhere, the apparatchiks are about half the population, and the very process of enforcing the law ensures that criminality will be heaped on the innocent.

The Perfect Criminal State

As we have often said, the striking feature of any revolution is not the party line believers or behavior of the most perverse, but how a revolutionary change makes itself sustainable, how those true believers' perversions are enshrined in normal society. The explosion of perversions, called the *sexual revolution* of the 1960s is not in itself all that interesting but for the fact it was sustainable. The debauchery of the Swiss anabaptists or the French infidels, the irregularity of the free-love communities of the American West or the aberrations of Parisian expatriates, cannot prepare us for the sustained malignity of universal prophylactics and no-fault divorce. In all other times, the sexual anarchy unleashed in the 1960s would have collapsed in tumultuous fashion. The social order could not have endured the breakdown of the two-parent home but that the necessity of female domestic labor was obviated by household machinery, and the rearing of children could not have conceivably be left to the depredations of a broken home but that the government had fully usurped the education of children to universal acclaim. The economic benefit of children had once meant they were necessary for the household economy and as salve in old age, but the modern nature of work no longer required extra hands, and government welfare removed any need for help in senescence. The merely human misery of loneliness, isolation, of the silent scream of dying bloodlines could be diverted by television and pornography, service animals and serotonin-repressors. The new Sex Regime cannot be described by reference to a new *Weltuangshuung,* to a realized development of freedom. It was the regime of Birth Control which provided the essential variable and allowed the perversion to be sustained. Sundry other "revolutions" of the 1960s can only be understood in like manner, as the technological revolutions they were. Not even the burgeoning depravity of the time can be recognized as *novel*. Only the technical means that propped up the system were new under the sun, raising to the heights of moral turpitude those crimes once supportable only in the dankest rooms and most depraved minds.

In similar movement, the wave of violence unleashed in the 1960s should not shock us by its severity, but in the way it has been sustained. As compared to the tranquility of life prior to it, such violence was little less than apocalyptic, and the full thrust of its barbarity is not wholly palpable to the people inoculated to quotidian bloodshed, and never again able to appreciate order unscarred. A generation of obfuscation has made pedantic the terrorism of the era, a topic of memory as remote as the murder of Caesar or the Battle of Waterloo. The lower swell achieved in the Clinton Administration was a supposed victory of love over hatred, of pacifism over bloodshed, of the long-last acceptance of the new and higher moral ordering. Yet the violence never in fact subsided. It was transformed, like a sweltering wax, still slithering into every urban area in the nation. This constitutes perhaps the most jarring material effect of the Fourth Revolution, the acquiescence and surrender of the Western city to a constant reign of rape, theft, and murder noticeable to anyone who wishes to see it, though often imperceptible even to those who have been ravaged, mugged and burgled.

A plague must at some point resolve itself in a kind of order, for at some level of mortality it can no longer transmit and sustain itself. Violence arisen from merely human passions, from the invidious rebellion of the underclass and the moral sickness encouraging such barbarism, likewise could not have endured were it not for the role the government played in sustaining it. This is the system of *criminal justice*. It is a system grown out of one that existed to punish crimes, but now ensures that crimes continue. This grand feat of tyranny is achieved not through recourse to Hessian guard or jackbooted secret police. In the legal realm it is fostered by the tenets of deterrence, which as we will see is only the application of utilitarianism to the commission of crimes. It is given practical application through the medium of a police state. The result is that the regular course of criminal violence committed by putative civilian forces are now a tool of government terror and social control, where irruptions like blasts of steam are controlled by affirmative policy. The resulting oppression is greater and more sophisticated than the world has ever seen.

The Transformation in Criminal Law

We repeat here the difficult of describing the contours of the Fourth Revolution, those institutions so near to us, those which yet wear the garb of old moral systems and extinct institutions the revolutionists in their anarchic fury have slain. To see the criminal justice system as a means of crime prevention is to mistake its primary significance, which is that it exists to permit and control crime, not eradicate it. In our present system violence has been maintained for decades, all in the most civilized of places, and beneath the façade of civilized life.

This occurs through the police state. We note that we do not mean *police state* in a pejorative sense. A police state is one where the functions of enforcing the law belong exclusively to the government. As a corollary result of this delegation, special privileges are carved out for this group, enforcers both in the form of positive rights conferred and the removal of liabilities with regards to its duties performed. Though the law still nominally applies equally to all, though all men are still conceived as equal under the theory of the state, the new privileges effectively create a new class of citizen, one whose specialization naturally lends them to having exclusive or near-exclusive right of enforcing the law.

It was not always so. At common law, an able-bodied man had a positive obligation to stop felonies committed in his presence and to apprehend the perpetrator.[123] This was no kind of anarchy or recourse to vigilantism, but the application of the Law of Nature, of which civil law was merely an outgrowth. Judges had a special role in discerning this law, constables a special role in effecting it; but ultimately the law was a public thing, a *res publica* unto itself, apart from any delegated or specialized roles. It was thus knowable by everyone and enforceable by all men, who partook of its many benefits and thus were bound to take upon themselves its obligations.

Because the civil law grew out of the Law of Nature, all criminal laws were subject to the Natural Law's most basic tenet: That bad acts must be punished, and evil repaid with evil. The purpose of criminal justice under

---

[123] Blackstone's *Commentaries* IV-21.

this system was to determine the amount of punishment that must be rendered in order to atone for the moral evil committed. It was this question, the matter of Retribution, that formed the central aspect of all study of the criminal law, the *res* around which the law's tasks are oriented. The retributive system of criminal justice is in other worlds a crime-centered system, one whose very basis lies in finding the moral harm of a crime and applying *lex talionis* in appropriate measure. So have operated all true systems of justice.

The law, of course, did not rut itself in moral philosophy, but demanded practical application. As such, it was concerned only with the acts committed by men. The actual evil that constituted the moral harm of the crime was termed the *actus reus*. This was a recognized bad act, one to be weighed against the moral order and thus gives a corrollary measure of the harm done by the act and what recompense need be paid. But man could not be indicted for mere harm. Such required proof that the harm came about through some act or omission on a man's part, evidence, in other words, that the harm came about from a volitional act. This was the *mens rea* of the perpetrator, the mental state which united man's actions with the morally culpable act. No man could be punished until it had been proven that both these elements were satisfied, that some moral harm had been done and that this harm came about by some volitation act or omission on the part of the perpetrator.

All modern liberty has its roots in this system, one that acknowledges an objective makeup of the universe laden with moral notions, yet which only involves man so far as his highest faculty is concerned, his freedom of choice. This crime-centered justice system comported

324

well with the ideals of the Christian commonwealth, for it approached man as a rational creature confronting an ordered cosmos. As such, the criminal law was a source of instruction. "As it is not benevolent to give a man help at the expense of some greater benefit he might receive, so it is not innocent to spare a man at the risk of his falling into graver sin. To be innocent, we must not only do harm to no man, but also restrain him from sin or punish his sin, so that either the man himself who is punished may profit by his experience, or others be warned by his example."[124]

The law taught man the makeup of the moral hierarchy and impressed in him the importance of that highest faculty, his ability to choose between good and evil. This was the material operation of the Retributive system, that which placed at its center the nature of the moral evil of a crime itself. Men as rational creatures could not resist being *deterred* from committing a crime he saw or knew would be punished under the system, both from reconfirmed knowledge that the act was indeed evil and from laudable fear in contemplating its punishment.

This is deterrence as properly understood. It is not an end in itself, and never could be within real system of justice. Deterrence has no final cause oriented towards the rational good, but is merely a reciprocal effect of punishment. In truth, any act can be deterred, malicious, beneficial, or neutral, and therefore can form no basis for action by itself. For deterrence to have any place in the criminal justice system, it must attach to some moral opprobrium. To hold the contrary is to establish a right to punish actions that are morally neutral or even

---

[124] St. Augustine, *City of God*, XIX, 16.

morally good, and which is to eviscerate the very name of justice and render impossible any true commonwealth. That a recognized moral harm must be attached to the deterred action is proven by imagining the converse: That as a principle the state has a right to punish a man who has committed an act the state considers virtuous. The vilest tyrant could not frame his specious rule on such terms. As such, all competent men have recognized that retribution must be at the heart of all systems of justice. Deterrence can only ever be an ancillary effect, never an end in itself.

And yet in the present day, deterrence is recognized not only as a distinct end of criminal justice wholly apart from retribution, but in practice is recognized as the only legitimate end of criminal justice. Retribution, when it is mentioned, is mentioned in shame. It is never taken as the central guide for all matters of criminal justice. Instead, it is used only as an artificial cap on what punishments can be contemplated for a given crime, [125] or to tie retribution up with some instrumentalist standards such as the difficulty of finding testimony and the cost of prosecution. [126] In practice, it always means that courts will strike down sentences which do not demonstrate their potential for indirect deterrence. Any

---

[125] *Kennedy v. Louisiana*, 554 U.S. 407 (2008).

[126] See Id.. also *Gregg v. Georgia*, 428 U. S. 153 (1976); "In considering whether retribution is served, among other factors we have looked to whether capital punishment "has the potential ... to allow the community as a whole, including the surviving family and friends of the victim, to affirm its own judgment that the culpability of the prisoner is so serious that the ultimate penalty must be sought and imposed." *Panetti v. Quarterman*, 551 U.S. 930 (2007).

attempt to punish moral evil or even assert its existence is called a recourse to stone-age cruelty and bloodlust. The supremely moral character of criminal justice, so obvious under the crime-centered approach, is occluded, as is the corollary end of moral instruction. In criminal law, deterrence is everything and all.

The Preeminence of Deterrence

The modern primacy of deterrence is owing to the long reach of Caesar Beccaria. It is he who first began the disorientation of criminal law away from basic justice, who divorced deterrence as a secondary effect of retributive punishment and made it an end in itself. His project was recognizably of the Age of Reason. What was the rational use of harsh punishments—of flogging the whore, hanging the fraudster, drawing and quartering the traitor? Were these not the enshrinements of the cruelty and caprices of feudal princes, the residue of centuries of Christian tyranny running askew from the pure streams of universal ideals? In apt fashion, he composes for himself a restored State of Nature, one in which the relationship between a ruler and his subjects is not distorted by Christian morals, but is recognized as existing only to benefit the members of a republic. As such, the prevention of crimes is the only matter worthy of consideration. How much punishment is necessary to ensure that the republic will not be subjected to the depredations of crime?—no further question need be asked but this. Punishment is thus not directed towards the satisfaction of the *actus reus* of the crime, but only such that can instill enough fear as to prevent the crime's commission. The central question of criminal justice is no longer the measure of punishment owing to the moral opprobrium of the crime, but how the harm done to the republic by crime can be prevented. The health of the republic has supplanted the nature of *actus reus* is at the center of the analysis.

And why should it not be so? Were the citizens of true republics not deserving of such?—where the republic was truly a creature of popular will, and civil accord a true measure of the common good? Beccaria's deterrence regime was very clearly tied inextricably to his republican idealism. Deterrence, which considered only social costs of crime, could only ever serve the true common good if the civil order itself was truly representative of this common good—that is, if the republic truly was a reflection of the people's indefeasible will. To hold this requires an idealism and faith stronger than Rousseau's. Yet the conceit was hidden by common humanity, a desire to lessen the suffering of one's fellow man, however much the social order may suffer as a result. No judge has ever imposed a punishment without looking at the unique character of the perpetrator; few statesmen have been so high-minded as to inflict the sword on abstruse good and evil rather than public clamor. The premises of the deterrence regime were illogical, but sentimentalism carried man where logic stalled.

The theories of Beccaria transformed into a more sophisticated utilitarian analysis with Jeremy Bentham, who so often confronts us as the fulcrum between the airy idealism of reform and the drab imposition of politick necessity. And in the Utilitarian scheme, crime is a cost first and foremost; if crime is indeed a moral wrong, its wrongness must inhere in the *cost* of crime. As such, policing should be pursued to the point where the expected costs of crime do not surpass the expected benefits of law enforcement. It is only at this point that socially optimal levels of crime prevention can be achieved, for where excess punishment is meted out, society is bearing the costs of enforcing the law that exceed the costs of crime, making society poorer off as a result. This method reaches its most perfect form in the work of the modern economists, who propose that crime rates are nothing but a reflection of social preferences for crime and enforcement, or that happy equilibrium between the costs of crime and the costs of law enforcement. [127] The conclusion cannot be avoided: We are as a *society* happy with a certain level of crime, and therefore a certain amount of crime should be allowed by policy.

We see here that the fundamental nature of crime has changed. The old system proposed that an evil must be punished for its own sake. It came under the ambit of the criminal law by the very fact that it ran afoul of some aspect of the Natural Law and deserved by its own inherent nature to be punished. Now such notion was gone. Crime was simply a costly thing, and if any opprobrium attached, it was only owing to the harm done to the state, by virtue of the fact that it had been harmed in a costly manner. Claiming a relationship between moral wrongness and social harm is not always inapposite, though any hope of making them synonymous can be nothing but Robespierrean delusion. And yet this premise is necessary in order to give

---

[127] See, e.g., George J. Stigler, *The Optimum Enforcement of Laws*, 78 Journal of Political Economy 526 (1970).

deterrence any sensible place within a true justice system, one that does confuse right and wrong with the mere will of the state. Yet where the costs of crime can be minimized, or where they simply do not rise to the level where policymakers have to greatly care about it, we come to find there is no reason to support the suppression of wrongdoing. Rather, on both the individual and society-wide scale, crime is a phenomenon to be economized and bargained over. Punishment of evil must become a secondary concern, if it is a concern at all. If we liken society to an earthly omnipotent god—a fiction few economists could oppose—we see that crime has transformed from being a remnant of that god's passive will, or the will that permits free creatures to err, to a product of the Leviathan's active will, one that acknowledges a power to control crime and even perhaps stomp it out yet chooses not to do so.

How does this conception of crime compare to reality? Where crime is merely costly, the entire system of criminal justice is clearly nothing but a matter of economizing, an implicit accord between government and criminals about how much evil will be allowed. It cannot be surprising on the individual scale that a vast majority of criminal cases are resolved by use of the plea bargain, which is nothing but an actual enforceable contract.[128] The contract operates this way: The state agrees to give a criminal defendant a lesser sentence in return for not taking the case to trial, while the defendant benefits in receiving a lesser sentence than that which he is likely to receive should he be tried.

---

[128] *Puckett v. United States*, 556 U.S. 129, 131 (2009).

Almost all American criminal cases resolve this way. Almost all criminals know that they will not be punished to the full extent permitted by the law or even what he could reasonably expect were not such bargains the norm. This being the case, the average criminal or would-be criminal does not really fear the law; he knows in practice what the economists advocated in theory: that he is a part of a system of crime management based on utility analysis, not criminal justice; he has nothing to *fear* besides the costs that may be imposed upon him, no more than an ambitious entrepreneur might chart the expected value of his next coup on the market. He is given no more moral instruction than the man trolling for prices. The vast ocean of statutory offenses and conjured rights end up serving only as a kind of *liquidity* for both parties, defendant and state, to be used towards reaching a deal, not substantive balustrades of natural justice. It achieves what utilitarian theory has always sought to achieve, to regulate crime with the greatest possible efficiency at the lowest possible cost.

Under this system, it is only by chance can a criminal or would-be criminal come to know the wrongness of his actions. Under a regime that systematically under-punishes criminals in order to gain plea agreements, retribution is abstracted away and deterrence, a secondary and corollary effect of punishment, becomes an end in itself. The attitude is heightened by the modern nature of the laws enforced, which are not even in nominal form the derivations of the Law of Nature, but only the work of legislatures, enacting their own rules as the supposed proxies of the people. Altogether, the system is transformed from one in which the government acted as the agent of an objective law that preceded and transcended it, to one where the law and the will of the government were synonymous. The government no longer played a particular role in a system of justice, but constituted justice itself, and possessed a monopoly on everything to do with the law: its creation, its interpretation, and its execution. It is to this last aspect that we turn.

The Universal Police State

That *community policing* is a product of the Revolution is clear from any fair reading of its history. Robert Peel's first army of community police was notoriously for the control and suppression of the industrial proletariat, a necessary corollary of the Reform Acts, whose purpose was to wield that deracinated populace and place them in the name of *democracy*. Such a system could not endure against the rule of common law, under which every man similarly protected and every man was similarly bound, as men with true liberty ever must be. The ancient liberties could not hold against the great masses formed by the new party system, the pathetic depredations of the proletariat, and the inordinate power of the newly rich. Since the early Nineteenth Century, the community police force has become part and parcel with urban existence. The positive duties imposed by law were very nearly eradicated, and by the Twenty-First Century even citizen's arrest laws became so antiquated that they could be eradicated with scarcely a complaint.[129] In practice and by explicit law, the police had a monopoly on law enforcement.

---

[129] Greenhorn. "Ahmaud Arbery: Super-Citizen." *The American Sun*. December 6, 2021.

The advance of the Fourth Revolution requires not only that a police state exist, but that the police be omnipresent. *De minimis non curat lex* had been an adage of common law absolving men of the harrying of magistrates over trifles, but even trifles require force where law enforcement not only constitutes the makeup of the law but the very moral ordering itself. This was all the more true under a regime that posited the complete material equality between races. For if the races truly were equal in all material ways, where could *discrimination* arise but with the positive desire of an invidious social order? And so a dragnet method of law enforcement was adopted: All laws would be enforced with equal vigor, lest any discretion by police be confused with wicked discrimination.[130]

The orgy of crime that raged through the 1960s, 70s, and 80s occurred in cities whose police forces were most sophisticated in the arts of data collection and crime research, more dedicated than ever before to the task of *law enforcement* versus maintaining the peace, more willing than ever to snuff out minor offenses—yet at the same time unwilling or unable to curb the huge increase in rapes, murders, and thefts that made decent city life impossible. Had the beat cop who prevented crimes in 1960 simply lost his gumption and resolve by 1970? Of course not. But to stop the real crime would have taken concerted efforts to target specific serious crimes and criminals, a notion contrary to the dragnet method, eschewal of which threatened the requisite tenet of

---

[130] On this transformation from "watchman" style to the "legalistic" style of police, see James Q. Wilson's *Varieties of Police Behavior*, 1978; see also Radley Balko's *Rise of the Warrior Cop*, 2013.

equality. The equilibrium of the system was achieved in the acceptance of a high level of serious crime and the stamping out of any grassroots attempts to combat this orgy of criminality. The regular man suffered not only under the rising levels of crime but the threat of having his day-to-day existence destroyed by the police if caught using too much force against the thug he encountered on his front stoop or foyer. The new dragnet approach saw only *lawbreakers* in its accumulated statistics, and took full advantage of the fact that the foolish homeowner was more likely to self-incriminate to a police he still saw as his allies and protectors. This is the story of the last half-century of policing, the population movement quaintly termed "white flight" but in fact a form of racial terror and ethnic cleansing enabled by the indiscriminating state.[131] This was the explicitly bloody aspect of the Fourth Revolution, a violent scourging of the cities so complete it can scarcely be mentioned.

Where no individual has the clear right to enforce the law, and where no mediating institutions can perdure to form moral notions and give them effect, the modes of utilitarianism look all the more convincing not only in logic but in fact. The conclusion can scarcely be avoided: crime rates become a function of government policy. If strict utilitarian analysis seems facile, historical experience makes it impossible to wholly deny: that where the police state punishes crime, crime rates go

---

[131] Scott Cummings's *Left Behind in Rosedale*, 1998, provides a sociological study of this phenomenon otherwise underexamined in serious letters. See also Harold Saltzman, *Race war in high school; the ten-year destruction of Franklin K. Lane High School in Brooklyn.* 1972.

down, and where it does not, crime rates go up. And in a system where the government controls all education, all law-making and law-enforcement, the concept of *private violence* vis-à-vis state power exists only in an equivocal form. Nearly all violence is state violence under our present regime, as the actions of a dog on a leash are always answerable to its owner, as all the body's acts must be referred to the will. In both concrete practice and the government's own theory of punishment, the prevalence of crime is a matter of social policy.

Even the matrix of the Soviet police, so insidious and so all-encompassing, could not compare to the modern Western police state. Stalinist forces would torture the respectable classes by letting loose felons and murderers, but such shock tactics were tied to early revolutionary pugnacity—they were not systematized such as the grand scheme of crime management that the advanced Western nations have fostered. In a land of omnipresent crime, the average citizen does not even notice the infinite number of petty laws or the bubbly truculence of the soldiers enforcing them. Every nation in the West is a police state. All power over civil affairs lies with the government, and all crime committed in these states is committed at the sufferance of that government.

In this system of crime management, there is little room for treatment of man as a rational creature, and modern man has no real moral sense tethered to any dictate but subservience. He acts not with learned knowledge or in righteous fear of the natural order, but in response to the limits imposed by a government, one that wields the forces of criminality for its liking. The law now formally exists to sustain a certain level of vice.

Moral Degeneracy

What is called moral degeneracy might just the same be called the atomization of the moral individual. Destroy those institutions that form his morality, and man's degeneracy must quickly follow. Only in rare cases can man's moral sense be completely eradicated, but to effectively neuter the moral creature, it is sufficient to remove the native impulse from any adequate fulfilment. There is no modern institution that exists to form man towards anything but Equality. His schools do not teach, his churches to not form the soul, his justice system cannot instill a sense of justice. Any moral sense he has must be oriented towards the only causes that exist in the present day: those promoting equality and against racism, sexism, and discrimination in any form. His taxes, tithes, and charitable giving goes to causes he cannot understand, operating on terms so profoundly notional that no real assessment can be made as to whether it aids men or harms them. Whether his employment betters the world he can scarcely know; he is one cog in a vast machine. He takes comfort in role in the mass, his faceless significance when he is hooting for a sports team or organizing behind a candidate who promises hope and change, or who babbles the cadences of the old order. The man of the past could give himself to his work, to his community, to his homestead and possess a certain assurance that in the regular course of life he would be given social and personal meaning for the role he played. But his work, his community, his homestead are all gone, and in their place is a technical apparatus he can be immersed into but which he can have no meaningful place within. His world is one that does not cultivate his soul but consumes it. Nothing of man's individuality can avail him. The intellectual life is stultifying, all of it mechanical quibbling about the management of the empty lives of men, calling back to worlds of meaning now vacant, which can be dreamt of only as men of the past dreamt of future utopias and longed-for worlds to come.

Vatican II

Of all matters we have approached in this work, those relating to the Fourth Revolution seem most cursory. While the topographies of the Protestant Revolt, the Age of Reason, the Industrial Revolution are all generally and popularly understood, and subject to criticism from friend and foe, the makeup of the Fourth Revolution can be difficult to see, let alone cognize and define. For we are in an age which cannot define itself, however long our *seers* may adhere to terms like *postmodern* and *hyperreality*—meaningless terms, all of them, meant to stir up a sensation but unable to capture the situation with any kind of historical perspective. Few cultural critics are opposed to the regime or feel even discomfort with it, for such critics are necessarily members of the elite, and have risen by using the means of faceless and demoralizing society to their benefits. They criticize their place only as a kind of aristocratic benefice or perhaps a therapeutic introspection, but no real contrary voice can arise to establish even a Socratic dialogue in pursuit of definition.

There is no opposition to the Fourth Revolution. For against the Fourth Revolution there is no Catholic Church—that force that served as a positive foe or mollifying force against every tumult before. We are not here engaged with a program of delineation or narrative history, and we have elided much that might be said about the horrors of 1968: the mass genocide of the unborn, the breakdown of all international law under the American war machine, the invasion of the West by Third World replacements. Yet the most crucial occurrence of the age is the war horn that did not blow, the prayer for reprieve that could not be answered because it was never made. The institution that should have fought did not. What was a spiritual war was won without battle, and the complete and absolute rout might in fact fool one that there was no aggression at all.

This was owing to the Second Vatican Council, a declaration of the Church's armistice with the world, a retreat from the war her Founder declared must be perpetual, and the avowed non-intervention in all the violence and horror of the new age. Where was the Incarnation? The Unity of God and Man? While man the social animal was being fractured and reassembled by the all-powerful superstructure, within the Church a revolution was being undertaken as brutal as the ages have ever seen, a smashing of altars, a decimation of her citizens, the instauration of an alien force in all realms. The Church was the last major institution unreformed by liberal ideas, the last that attempted to gird itself with firm definitions and right reason, which abjured the abstractions of ideological rule and strove for the understanding of essences. Yet after 1968 the Church would not wage war under the banner of Truth. Unlike the great stalwart of Trent against Luther, the revivified Curia against the Jacobins, the promise of *Rerum Novarum* against the depredations of Industrialism, the Bride of Christ offered no salve. Where the world

338

needed bread, the Council could not even give him a stone, but only a sea of words.

The Council was nothing and everything. Its superintending pontiff proposed a reconciliation with the world, an "opening of the windows" of the churches. It now rushed forward and met all four revolutions with rapt anticipation. The innovations of Luther and Crammer it now recognized as correct, going so far as to apotheosize the former in the Vatican and use his songs in its Liturgy. Human nature was now subject to Hegelian progress, and modern man was "on the road to a more thorough development of his personality, and to a growing discovery and vindication of his own rights." [132] The Council Fathers seemed to accept the principle of Toleration the Church had so long despised, giving equal standing to all heresy, blasphemy, and idolatry.[133] The less incendiary of documents read not as derivations from divine law but as the policy papers of an ideologue. They confront the modern social order and propose how it should be constituted not through the hearts and deeds of Christian men, but in how the modern state ought to be reconfitted by the government.

And in the end, the Church accepted the age's fracturing of the soul, the compartmentalization of man, and the role of the Faith was henceforth to serve: not as a means of total moral and material transformation, but as an accoutrement to his life ordered by the technocracy. It accepted a world no longer led by priests

---

[132] "Modern man is on the road to a more thorough development of his personality, and to a growing discovery and vindication of his own rights." *Gaudium et Spes,* ¶41.
[133] *Dignitatis Humanae,* ¶ 15

and bishops, but by politicians and celebrities; not theologians but sociologists, not confessors but psychiatrists, scientists and other technicians who had honed into starker relief the facets of man's life which stood like a row of storefronts to be stopped at for the bundles of goods necessary for the day-to-day. To the new and enlightened churchman, the pursuit of spiritual ends was merely one errand, another bushel to be purchased and brought back home.

Better men have done a better job than the present author could ever do in criticizing the Council. Our purpose is not to analyze the documents, their 100 thousand words of verbose auto-destruction. To analyze the content of these documents is perhaps not a task without merit, but it does most simply to marvel at the gargantuan bulk of them, and their utter emptiness. We have noted that the Church through her Magisterium did not put forth policy prescriptions but rather theories of God, theories which in their logical applications or in their terms averred truths which must be used to orient man's role in life. The new Council Fathers for the first time posited an explicit theory of man, the *human person.* "Hence the focal point of our total presentation will be man himself, whole and entire, body and soul, heart and conscience, mind and will."[134] An individual might blanch away from such a proud and absurd statement. Neither Sirach nor Solomon could ever claim to know man "whole and entire;" only an entire council, puffed up by *periti,* could tamp down scruples and put forth such a statement in print. The Council documents make a martyr of all who must read them. How compelling is

---

[134] *Gaudium et Spes* ¶ 3.

Hegel in all his delusive grandeur; how stimulating is Lincoln in his striving for power—yet how tawdry and dull are these blowhards in justifying their immolation of the Church.

In all, the Council changed the faith from something hard and vigorous to a colossus with the makeup of a sponge. The rigor of thought and stolidity of spirit apparent even to her worst foes now resolved into indolence under the guise of appealing to the heart. It was done without recourse to direct heresy or thoroughgoing dogma. Where would the sharp divide of schism occur in an environment of men unwilling to define any truths at all? Even Archbishop Lefebvre's dissent could not be given the moniker of schism where none of his adversaries had the courage to explicate the point of contest or the intellectual mettle to define their own beliefs. The Church suddenly found itself without a shred of intellectual or moral courage, and clearly no longer existed as she had for two millennia as the only truly radical force in the world. For true radicalism is intellectual; it is of the rational soul, that which can assert boldly *yes, yes* and *no, no*, which can stake out the difference between being and nothingness, the infinite expanse between zero and epsilon. The will of the flesh, in contrast, is towards torpor, the giving way to feelings, guesses, probabilities, the hope that quiddity can be found on a Bayesian curve. The flesh desires that all can be known through the senses, that the world is as it appears, that material reality, tangible, visible, audible, is all that exists. All tendencies to nominalism begins here, in the vain hope that our mere senses alone can be synonymous with Truth, that we can capture it by the sensitive appetites, by mere living rather than a grappling with the world and those truths hidden behinds its veil such as poets have glimpsed and the saints have known. The Revolutionist claims to be radical but is always a man of the flesh. He cannot abide by the Truth, and so for all his bluster, must eventually give way to bathos or oppression. His Puritanism will slide away in Unitarian dross, his Jacobinism to the clutches of Bonapartes, his Trotskyite pipedreams into Stalin's gulag. Only the Catholic Church has ever sustained a radical and unswerving character through the ages, achieved through rigid adherence to Truth. When she tossed this rigidity aside, her spiritual fruits appropriately withered and her adherents slid into apostasy.

What astonishes one about the Council is the bathos—that in the mountains of expert opinion it essentially said nothing. It defined no dogma, made no new deductions about theology and raised no new matter a Catholic must firmly assent to. Out of the first ecumenical council at Nicaea, a Christian became required to assent to the Son's consubstantiality with the Father, as definitively and surely as if he had denied the rudimentary tenets of the Apostles' Creed or perhaps the Laws of Nature themselves. In like manner, after the First Vatican Council a Catholic could no longer deny the doctrine papal infallibility without excommunication. Such conciliar assertions have always been spare and parsimonious, delimiting orthodoxy not by positive proclamations but by negative limitations, *anathemas*, or clear and concise statements of moral and eternal law. They settled large disputes, but as all laws must, raised disputes contiguous to the first: matters of definitions and breadth. But inside those negative boundaries, man was totally free—free as man had been in Eden where only negative edict bound his liberty. The man who damned himself by refusing dogma did so on his own terms, as a free and rational creature worthy of Heaven, even when choosing to embrace Hell. Even the damned were treated with more dignity and more humanity than the modern barbarizing mind can comprehend.

But in the whole of the Council's 100 thousand words there is no dogmatic assertion, no discovered truth or clarification. There were statements within them which no Catholic could in good faith abhor: Quotes from the Bible, past assertions of dogma, drab common sense. But in the strictest sense, there was nothing in the documents to assent to or deny. Nothing novel in the documents appealed to reason. A sensibility could be discerned in them, an attitude detected, a general spirit of liberalism—a confusion of law and mercy, of nature and grace. The documents did not appeal to man's intellect, to his rational soul and right reason, but to sentiment, and any questions of assent could only be whether he found pleasing the attitude the Fathers had created or not. If this could be called assent, it was assent to something that belonged below the level of reason, as if one were to assent to the atmosphere of a novel or the cadence of a symphony. It demanded in effect that a Catholic declaim that the changes wrought by the Fathers were *good*.

And this was manifestly not so. After the Council, established dogmas were rejected in practice by bishops and faithful everywhere across the world. Monasteries and convents fell to the Black Death of feminism and effeminacy. All Christian zeal was turned towards the destruction of high altars and communion rails, and erecting a new structure in plaster and plastic. The noble *Humanae Vitae*, which affirmed the unity of man's sensual nature with his rational soul, was abjured by the

West's bishops and faithful to no consequence. The revolution in the Church was complete, and merely to affirm orthodoxy by 1968 would have been to invite schism—and anyway would have ended the project of Vatican II, of vanquishing the Western mind and asphyxiating its spirit.

Technological Revolution and the Incarnation

The Church had never been a political institution in its purest sense, but since freedom is nothing but living according to Truth, so long as the Church guarded the doctrines of Truth, so as well did she protect the freedom of man. But the churchmen of the Council no longer had the will to fight for truth. They had ceded its access to the *periti* who alone could unite the timeless dogmas of the faith to the tenets of neoliberal order. Catholics could no longer be wielded for any political cause, and became a nugatory intellectual and cultural force. The idiocy of Eastern religions, with their promise of future annihilation, came to set the tenor of all *religious experience*. The West stopped being even a vestigially Catholic thing.

Yet in its 100 thousand words, the Vatican Council's revolution was still unwritten, for it barely mentioned the greatest laurel won: the adoption of the microphone as a central feature of its ritual. The Church had always rejected the use of such technology in her central function, for the mass was a personal affair, between the priest acting *in persona Christi*, and the adorer, ready to attach his mind, spirit and body to those of Christ. The catholicity of the sacrifice shone through these humble practices, for whether uttered in the most luminous cathedral or the dark cauldrons of the earth, the sacrifice was the same, needful of only the barest materials and an anointed man able to conjure the presence of Christ. Parts of the act could be sung, others whispered, and the most crucial part was always said in low voice, heard definitively only by God: *Hoc est enim corpus meum.* There was nothing more a faithful attendant could do but direct his attention to the altar, to give whatever was in heart to the God physically present before him.

The microphone changed this act. It conquered silence, creating a new environment where the actual hearing of the mass became its objective measure of participation. All other external action of the mass would now rank below the radio play being conducted before him. Where sonic fidelity was constantly presumed, the legitimacy of the mass might now be questioned where static entered between performer and audience. The Novus Ordo mass still proposes that Christ is made present through its prayers, and that the same rudiments alone are necessary to command this coming, just as it was with the old mass. But in practice, every lay and churchman sees this confection as done through the medium of electronic technology. The glories of high altars and stained glass, the various chants, the incense and unction, all must pale in comparison to telenovela delivered to man in his seat— why shouldn't his surroundings be sheetrock and plastic against this auditory overload? Few public masses are said today without a microphone. The pope himself, holding forth the Son of God, must lower himself to the little black nub sitting beside chalice and patten on the table before him.

To pray is the highest faculty of man, to unite his will to the Creator's and his intellect to Truth. But one cannot really pray along to a loudspeaker. To succeed amidst an electronic din must be by accident. The central act of worship in the mass is no longer clearly one of prayer. The man whose thoughts are captured by the ruckus of an audio system is merely a passive spectator responding to outrageous stimulus, not a man actually attempting to converse with God. The beck of the audio system may fulfil a duty of the faith, but one cannot offer oneself, engage in contemplation, or be subsumed in spiritual ecstasy beneath a wall of sound. The Novus Ordo mass is a service for TV watchers, for passive receptacles, and what was once a praying army is transformed into a mass: the men in the pews are no longer individuals offering their hearts to God, but atoms of the uniform sound, whose acts of devotion become synonymous with an act of passive acquiescence of each man's inner voice to the whole.

Those who defend the Council, who can look past the wanton destruction of the era and strive to unite it to orthodoxy, do no more than the Council fathers did. Dogma was never truly at issue. What the Council changed was how dogma would be transmitted to man, and how man should relate to God. The Council fathers were not revolutionaries; those men who were not traitorous were men of good will. But their claims that the mass had to be made "participatory" was facile, if not duplicitous, the vapors of liberal democratic dogma. These men did not misplace their faith in God. What faltered was their understanding and reverence for man, in the faith that he could in his personal prayers raise his heart to Heaven and stand competent for the tutelage of his own soul. No, the Council fathers had no explicit desire to eschew the old Faith, but took it upon

346

themselves to heartily embrace the new man. The
Council fathers retained the old faith but took up the
new man: he who was not the rational being a little less
than the angels, but the skincell of the Leviathan, that
who could not move but for the superstructure moving
him. The Council approached Church dogma as a mere
ideology, and treated the souls of her faithful
accordingly.

The Incarnation was thereby traduced, though not as
the heretics had done, by attacking the nature of God,
but by belittling and defiling the true nature of man.
That flesh that Christ had deigned to bear, those senses
that Christ had hallowed, those faculties that He held fit
to hold the Godhead could not be trusted on their own
volition to tend to right worship: They needed the aid of
electric current before grace could be achieved. The
Council Fathers accepted the fracturing of the Fourth
Revolution, the dismantling of man's rational soul, the
acceptance of man as a compartmentalized creature,
whose cultural life could be distinct from his religious,
and that all the various ends of man could be served
properly in their respective spheres by that technocratic
apparatus and its many mansions. The new Catholic
man, that one envisioned by the Council, was a man
who acted for the Catholic cause, who participated in
Catholic ritual, who would go before God on the last
day and recite the Catholic creed, yet who was not a
creature whose nature was renewed and reformed by
Christ, but one who wore it like a party badge.

The attacks on dogma that arose everywhere in the
decades to come sprung not from the fathers' explicit
statements but from their implicit acceptance of this low
conception of man. The tenets of liberal Christianity
were adopted not so much an abuse of the creed as a

slurring of sentiment—the conceit of every humanitarian, that loosening the reins of acceptable conduct is an act of mercy rather than denigration. Heterodoxy in this time enters the body of Christ through sloth more than turpitude, indolence rather than pride. One cannot read the Vatican II documents without envisioning a college of men wracked by acedia, the noonday devil, torpid from the millennia's struggles and too tired to continue the fight. The result is a tragic thing, and honest observers are aware of this, yet can scarcely form an argument against it, so slippery are the received terms of discussion, so weak-minded are those seeking to impress the contrary.

That possession which one will not defend is only nominally one's own, and a Church that did not defend her ethics soon found she had none at all. Where she might have acted, she did not. The revealed preferences of the churchmen were clear. To raise hue and cry against the new regime of child-murder would have been to halt the Church's revolution, and this could not be done. Only by blood of innocents could the sacrifice of the altars be completed. When a generation of clerics had reached the age of repose, they found they were nothing but gang of child-molesters and their enablers. The Church had no power even unto herself to lacerate these men's unctioned hands and to blow out their brains, as the popes of the past ages would have done and as these criminals so justly deserved. Yet in fact the resulting rule by parish councils, social workers and plaintiffs' attorneys could serve the purposes of a *more thorough development of man's personality* where man's personality was a product of the technocracy, and the Church's creeds were only means of tepid consolation as he navigated his life within it. And so concluded the bloody reform, wrought by a retreating host crying songs of victory and new life, an acknowledgement that so long as the reforms held the Revolution would face no further enemy.

Conclusion

If civilization is the imposition of order through the city, the perfection of man's reason through the cultivation of his social desires—if such a thing exists, ours surely collapsed in 1968. This is a shocking thing, for Western materialism this year reached its peak; man could produce and over-produce everything in such brazen heaps that they could afford to send man to what Galileo had recognized as nothing but a floating rock in space. Reason had raised and exulted everything and all—and how quickly it collapsed.

In thought, language, art, morals we see manifest decline, and the decay of a vocabulary to even broach the subject. The self-criticism of the 1950s and 60s and the anxiety about economic growth, education, and equality as found in *The Lonely Crowd* and *The Affluent Society* is fascinating to behold in retrospect. These men see the collapse better in the wavering turret than we can in surveying the rubble on the ground. "The whole of the West no longer possesses the instincts out of which institutions grow, out of which a *future* grows," Nietzsche had proclaimed, much earlier.[135] He was entirely correct, but could not anticipate on what tawdry bases the *future* would be judged, or how thoroughly and

---

[135] *Twilight of the Idols* 39

effectively later observers would lose the ability to discern what a functioning institution looks like.

No, what astonishes the rational mind and seems to tempt a Jealous God is that the collapse occurred and the machinery did not stop. We still maintain nominal growth. The capital of the festering cities flows into the corpulent suburbs, and an unhinged monetary system allows the *sentiment* of nominal growth to stand in for increasing welfare. No great improvements of domestic life arise or can very well be conceived. Technical improvements are all of existing products; use values tend to fall, and every speck of secular commercial growth finds a decline in quality. *Something* is still advancing, though it is not mankind, not his sciences or spirit, not his art or his literature. Man's intellectual, psychic, and spiritual selves all decline, and yet there is no wholesale collapse.

A question haunts one's mind: Who could desire to rule over these people? Who would tame the princes of Europe to rule over these monsters of flesh and bile?— the hollow men, the last men? The force of ambition is not foreign to anyone conversant with history, even perhaps his own heart: the desire of personal glory, to rule over his fellow men, to gain distinction from his people. But what is it worth to be glorified by these people, these obese clots of apprehension, these spiritually dead things? What could drive a man to subjugate such servile populations and peoples? Wealth was once an attraction to great men, for it proxied prestige and power. Now wealth cannot guarantee anything. The rich man's underlings, like soldiers of fortune, know they might as well be managed by any technician. What could a Bonaparte desire of the suburbs? The roads are beholden to the will of the automobile, the design of the houses to video equipment, the schools are beholden to the gurus at the Department of Education. The very nature of corporate governance dictates that the suburbs' commerce is wholly driven by statistics, the buildings beholden to air conditioning units and surrounded by oceans of concrete. Man cannot force his will on such an environment or grant it even the most rudimentary beauty that the most dismal prairie town once had. No greater evidence than the suburbs is necessary to prove that man is already living in a post-human society. Who could be glorified by such a conquest? As an object to be won, the modern world can appeal only to the most mediocre of taste, the most base of ambition. What is eminently worth so little cannot bring to the field any man capable of conquering it.

The men who strive to rule are the least personally ambitious; they are the least personal, the minutest persons—those lichen-like souls who hang on the coattails of some unseen sovereign and judge themselves by their servility to it. It has always been this way with revolutionists. What was Robespierre after all truly but a specter? Or a man like Franklin Roosevelt, who conquered and dismantled four Old World empires, but who in his personal capacity was a stage prop? His memorial in Washington has no basilisk or monument, but is a roaming display of technocratic footsoldiers and the lumpenproletariat his party wielded. His personal statue finds him crippled and blanketed, himself a kind of slow-moving machine, lugubrious and bathetic. It is that iron mass before us, the unparalleled victor of the Second World War, showing us its spoils: the faceless masses he led. The man had none of Lincoln's literary genius, yet his political skill and intuition set him like an effigy above the promised land, overlooking an empire unparalleled in history.

In the solitude of old age a man is owed the ability to look out at the world, at the commerce and conduct in which he can no longer partake, but to see the blooming of the seeds he has planted, to hope that the future he will not see can retain the solaces he has been given and remove some of the pains he has suffered. The men who heard of VJ Day through tin speakers and feted themselves on the final defeat of totalitarian and dictator, found themselves swept through the next century on a war economy, on the mechanical terraforming of their towns under a ceaseless propaganda. The Holocaust their pacificism supposedly enabled was reenacted on their grandchildren in the womb, the dekulakization and ethnic cleansing they were spared from the dictators was bequeathed by streetgangs promoted and engorged by their government. Their children could muster enough affection for life to indulge in it piecemeal, while the next generation of children—those they did not contracept—could be treated like commodities, honorable pets groomed by the state, succored by the corporate system, the pace of his day-to-day life kept by the ticks of Hollywood songsters and the Manhattan adman. The child is of their brood, the universal flock now of the adman's phenotype, its biological parents happily cuckolded—for the new electronic lineage is, after all, one they too adore. The entire world is composed of men and women who are functional children, unable to partake in the productive economy but in a superfluous way, impotent to provide tutelage to their young or to lend them any hope for the future, any firm prospect why the technocrats should continue to find them useful, or why the next generation should not be annihilated from the face of the earth.

The Revolution of 2020

Remnants of the cataclysm now fall away, but the damage remains visible like the highwater mark of a deluge: written in the slouching gaits of the young men in the streets, on the dumbly afraid half-concealed countenances of old women in the supermarkets, the laid-off men blown apart by fentanyl atop a pile of rent-due slips. And then there are the beneficiaries: The new generation of billionaires reaping the rewards of noxious monopoly power, the professionals pulling salaries without leaving the sofa, the prudes and freaks who are always with us turned into the heroic emblems of the regime, earning their adrenaline drips with every social interaction they squelch. At the heart of it is the final destruction of any organic social mores at the hands of world-building expertise. The Western world awoke to find the simple act of shaking hands had acquired aristocratic significance, a fleshly and vivacious remnant of an old regime now brought to disuse by universal lamination.

Every television station squawked of the advancing Blight, every newspaper heralded the approach of Atrocity, all digital babble was made to conform to the narrative of approaching Scourge—and thus the assault by the government seemed almost easy, a kind of monumental drama that with a nod and a smile could be forgiven when it lapsed into deadly force. With the lockdowns, all remnants of civil culture collapsed. The church doors locked, Easter masses fell into the catacombs, the Son of God in His coming found witnesses only through television screens for the remnant who cared. Municipal government stalled, schools stopped functioning, playgrounds were taped up like a murder scene, free travel ceased, courtrooms lapsed into desuetude, trials halted, jails were freed of criminals. All employment that could be done on a computer was done on a computer, and there it remained. Protest was so rare as to be practically nonexistent.

The tepid sterility of early spring, of gray grass and trees unblooming, continued into an unthawing summer. The lockdowns diminished in force, but all governments retained for themselves emergency powers. These included the power to nullify contracts, cancel debts, absolve rent payment; to close all public and private buildings and to wield implicit power over the workforce of entire states. Months passed and no systematic evidence could be adduced of any great threat in the virus. Yet a universal death counter kept ticking on all the news channels, and the oppression it presaged was thought to be unendurable by every respectable man. Experimental research was conducted, and a treatment marketers called a *vaccine* modified the genes of its recipients. It was mandated by most governments and it failed, and killed or maimed numbers of men we still do not know. This failure could be hinted at in the propaganda channels only after eighty percent compliance. If certain cranks called for justice, the cries fell on ears of a mass that could not comprehend them. Justice for whom? Justice against what? What prior right could not be justly traduced in apocalyptic struggle?

The air man breathed was now a threat to him; his face was ludicrously posited as a risk, his lips and nose a source of contamination, his whole body serving as a kind of pore leaking fetid gasses unto the entire race— and the average man accepted these tales about himself. He accepted that he was in his normal biological functioning a threat to mankind. And so he consented to have his commerce squelched, his religion suppressed, to hide all aspects of his life behind a veneer of plastic, to cleanse his altars, to exorcise his friends, to recognize all the sweet things in life were subordinate to the good of mankind.

Every deformation was nominally related to stop the spread of the Coronavirus, but to linger on the nominal reason for revolution is to occlude the real tendency and power of the movement. It is to linger on the state of Bavarian indulgences on the eve of the First Revolution, or to concern oneself with Czarist industrial policy on the eve of the Third. As we have repeated time and again through this essay, a revolution is not interesting for its forward thrust, but for the reactions it makes impossible, the returns it makes untraversable.

And what the Fifth Revolution establishes is a new and paramount right that must ever after determine the constitution of the polity: The right to General Socialized Health. This kind of General Health is not what it at first might seem—it is not the health of the constituent individuals composing the public, nor is it directly or necessarily related to mass biological welfare at all. General Socialized Health is at all times a notional concept, and like all notional concepts it can have no concrete existence outside of some higher power giving it material effect. It is another form of socialized morality, the idea that individual wellbeing cannot be evaluated or conceptualized outside the existence of mass population. In 2020 we see this process extend even into the realm of human biology. With it, a new claim arises that *mankind* has an affirmative right, at least in principle, to be free from disease. This right must trounce all others; it must even trump those aspects of the individual biological human that will not be conformed to the demands of General Socialized Health. Every constituent body may be made feebler in this pursuit of this new sanitation, but this will always be justified by the claim that its final result—the last day in which mankind has eradicated the harmful effects of viral disease—will strengthen the race as a whole.

We see with the Fifth Revolution another abstraction away from the human individual, this time not only as a spiritual or political or economic or a social entity, but his basic biological attributes. With the Fifth Revolution we find that man's personal mental and physical health are ready sacrifices to the demands of the superstructure. The spiritual, intellectual, and social war against him has taken a new battlefield, that of the biological.

The Rights of the Virus

All true rights are inherent in and arise from the nature of things. The rights of property ownership vary from chattels to real estate based on the intrinsic differences of the forms of property and the different purposes they must serve when man puts such property to use. As we have often said before, all true study of rights must begin with the study of reality: with investigation into the nature of the object over which rights might be asserted and the nature of man in his relation to it. Our rights and liberties are first and primarily written in the vastness of creation. The enunciated rights we find in statutebooks and constitutions are paltry against the pantheon of unwritten rights and privileges that form the fundament of civilized existence. Yet how often is man oblivious to reality—and how often is he willfully ignorant of himself! And so our rights are often hidden to us: they are occluded beneath the veil of the quotidian.

Man can scarcely recognize the fulness of his liberties, which are so wide and varied as the expanse of creation. With the advent of the lockdowns, one became aware of the gloriousness of the banal, of all the wondrous rights he never appreciated that he had: The right to face-to-face interactions, the right to walk the streets in times of peace, the right to access staffed and operational public services: Those rights so deeply etched into our lives that they were scarcely noticeable as rights until access to them was denied. They were not rights gained through bloodshed or battle, and were too numerous to be codified. But they were true rights and real, arising from the basic course of life and perduring as long as such a course was kept. "If civil society be made for the advantage of man, then all the advantages for which it is made become his right,"[136] Burke proclaimed. So exist the vast majority of man's civil rights, those he did not recognize until they were gone.

It is in the nature of things that our rights are founded. The logic of any social need, such as buying and selling, such as voting, such as being tried by one's

---

[136] *Reflections*.

peers, such as praising God, all required a place to conduct them. Man knew these tasks had a great importance, and their immanent logic required their own places to conduct them. Our cities give testimony to the logic and necessity of our lives, along with the freedoms they bear. The auditoriums give surer life to speech and democracy, the courthouse to open confrontation and rational justice more than any paper constitution. Our modern trial rights grew out of practice, not theory. Justice Holmes was almost correct in locating the life of the law; it is found not in theory, but in logic through experience. So was the entire edifice of our civilization. The emptied streets provide the bitterest testimony available to ways and ideals corrupted or erased, tasks man cannot be bothered with, shrines to gods now obscure. The liberties universally touted as the heights of man's intellectual and moral development could hardly have developed outside of the temples of their practice; the mind's eye could not have seen what the sense did not experience.

Yet even the temples have fallen into obloquy. The auditoriums ceded place to the television screen, the streetcornermen fell away to the freeway, the market square to the conglomerate. Against these monuments of a dying regime the new rights of the Fifth Revolution established alongside *Liberty, Equality and Fraternity* and *For each according to his ability, to each according to his needs* the theoretical right of mankind to be free from the effects of disease. This right in 2020 was placed near the pinnacle of the hierarchy of rights and proclaimed to the stones of the old temples that they should not stand. Like the trumpets of Jericho they were made to fall by Emergency Orders and an all-pervasive regime of fear.

But the fact that cannot be overstated: That Coronavirus was never an aberrant threat, and even less of one thirty months after these Orders went into effect. Yet after months and years of efforts scarcely any republic under the sun could muster resources adequate to meet the Virus's demands on normal republican premises. Such admission of incompetence would have, in times past, spoken to the illegitimacy of governments, and a people jealous of their rights would have no qualms crying out that such regimes must be dissolved. Yet nothing could be done where conjured threat was catastrophe, and a servile mass sees nothing in the temples of being that fell. And so in the war on Coronavirus, all governments must remain revolutionary until the peace.

The riposte of those claiming normalcy, *This is just what governments do*, is inadequate to encompass the situation. It is true that governments will usurp power to the very limits that they can, but the salient question is how those limits will be set. None of the new usurpations could exist were it not for the new right that has granted these powers: The implicit right to be free from even middling disease. Without this underlying belief, held by a huge and influential segment of the population, none of the lockdowns, layoffs, vaccine mandates or personal surveillance could have been broached. Again: nothing about the Coronavirus of 2019 made it unique to any other seasonal virus, attendant as they all are to a litany of horrors: Hundreds of thousands of fatalities, *super spreader* events, wretched symptoms targeting the vulnerable and old. One could take his pick to obsess over any one of these—and certainly the flu is a horrible evil, as all diseases are. But only with the

Coronavirus was this neuroticism allowed to break through—was the right of mankind to be free from these depredations recognized as a universal right, one to be pursued and let all other rights be damned. It is as if one generation of Minnesotans woke up and discovered the horrors of winters—deadly cold, icy roads, and short days—and decided to terraform a new climate to avenge this *injustice*. Such would be absurd but for the fact that this is exactly what the Western world did in response to a virus.

There is no way to argue with this, not once the propaganda blitz has been unleashed. The man who says we should live with diseases and the one who says we should uncompromisingly defeat them argue for two competing metaphysical systems, the former adhering to the traditional ordering of man in relation to Nature, suffering, and death, and the other aching in adolescent discontent against the sorry state of fallen reality, and holding in his heart at least a figment of an impression that they might one day be dissolved. There is no empirical way to disabuse this suicidal metaphysics. The countless generations who had no clue about Germ Theory were much wiser than we.

The technical means to the right

The only adequate response to Coronavirus was unconditional surrender: So we heard, so every reasonable man believed, such was the unassailable chorus. *Stop the Spread*—this mantra abounded from every television set, newspaper and website, one that against an airborne disease was formally impossible. But it did not matter—no more than extraordinarily high survival rate of those who had contracted the virus, no more than the lack of adequate studies to assess real harm. It was irrational, and partook of irrationality for its own sake. Mass media had for years and decades prior tested disease for revolutionary potential: A Swine Flu in the 1970s, the Bird Flu and other various *pandemics* in waves through the early Twenty-first Century. Mass media could roil, but events could not coalesce in order to take advantage of revolutionary potential. The press could not overthrow what every previous generation understood: That man can mitigate the harm of Nature but cannot eradicate it. But the technical environs of 2020 allowed a new kind of mania, one that proposed that no one in his workaday life ought to be made susceptible to sickness.

The Revolution of 2020 is the inflection point in the transformation of society into a digital thing. We saw how social life was upended with the Fourth Revolution, and every institution was either defanged or dismantled under the yoke of government fiat. The Fourth Revolution was a remaking of the souls of our institutions. The Fifth Revolution takes aim at their matter. It seeks to move every remnant of the social world online, and to homogenize the existence of the social order under sundry pieces of software. With it, the Fourth Revolution is completed in hilarious fashion, with lockdowns ensuring that institutions would not only be homogenous with regard to their formal ends, but that they need not retain a physical existence at all. The draconian lockdowns could not have been endured had physical reality itself not already proven itself supplemental to the activities of commerce and government. The process of revolution is complete; the long-enervated balustrades of the old regime were finally toppled, and no hope of reclaiming the old ways exists apart from the destructive force of reaction.

The Coronavirus could not have been a *pandemic* if the smartphone had not allowed it to be. The Coronavirus was such a temperate blight that none but moderners could have allowed it to control them. It was only those who longed to have their lives subjectivized by the new regime and its new morality, who longed for a new world they could not see but waited below the façade of the old, struggling to be born out of the lives they led, in the facile existences they had forged, in the dependencies they had subjected themselves to, in the conveniences they had become tranquilized by—it was they who made themselves prey for a mostly harmless pathogen, and most fervently welcomed the severing of the old calendar and Year Zero.

What agency did the rational individual have against this assault? Perhaps he looked back after years of insanity and contemplated how he might have saved his brothers from a death of despair, his children from developmental retardation, or the ire of God whose people trembled at all but Him. But who had incentive to? What man was made of solid enough stuff to even feel the repercussion of the blow? Man had already involved himself so well with the digital world that he could no longer extract himself. He was more uninhibited than ever from any bounds of manhood or dignity, scarcely able to follow his rational self when he heard his conscience's call. To stand against the whirlwind was to be destroyed, alienated from all remaining social events and despised by one's neighbor. Even his churches would not recognize martyrdom he took upon himself. Allegiance to the new regime was shown by one's acceptance of the new inversion, by covering one's face, by altering one's genes, by ostracizing all who did not accept such terms. Events still occur in the real world, but they are bound by the regulation of the new order, all to emphasize that the purely human aspects of sociality are supplemental to the new reality.

In all the hierarchy of creation, there is no distinction as great as that between zero and one. A miserable trinket or a whitewashed country church may rank low in the order of beauty, but in the hierarchy of being they have eminent pride of place in the fact that they *are*, that they have waged a war against nonexistence and won, and in fact make themselves glorious, partaking of that high attribute of God. Between zero and one the gap is infinite. The prior revolutions that leveled pontiff and layman, king and pleb, cannot compare to the leveling we now undertake: the eradication of differences not in kind but of the starkest contrast of them all, between being and nonbeing.

In the modern world our tasks no longer demand physical existence. Even where physical existence is granted as necessary, it is accomplished by plastic junk and gormless shacks. Why should it be otherwise, where purpose of place can be fulfilled in the otherwise homogenous environs of the internet? The civilizational logic that drove the creation of these places still stands: We still need to buy and sell, we still need to legislate, we still need to worship God. But these interior demands no longer need incarnation in real places and things. The digital suffices to capture the function. The courthouse is not necessary for trials, the statehouses are not necessary for government. Your market or church are no better than your armchair.

Witness what has occurred: Millions arrived at the end of the lockdowns and found themselves completely dependent on computer software. Real world interactions were exposed as the supplement to the digital ones. That this transformation was accompanied by the simultaneous torching of American cities in the coordinated color revolutions could not have been more appropriate. The average American had long ago been terrorized from his cities under a campaign of racist violence, which would have been unendurable if not for the fact that cities were no longer essential. Said McLuhan at the time: "The circuited city of the future will not be the huge hunk of concentrated real estate created by the railway…What remains of the configuration of 'cities' will be very much like the World's Fair—places in which to show off new technology, not places of work or residence."[137] More can be added to this: The modern city exists as a radical training camp and cesspool of minority ballot-stuffers. The suburbs, where the decent urbanites fled, are now irrelevant and could be replaced but for inertia and bias against small towns. The digital world is the material world, and the happenstance of where one physically exists is owing more to happenstance and prejudice, not because presence is strictly necessary in a given place.

The hip degenerates who remain in the cities already live the most unlifelike kind of lives. They work service jobs—baristas, daycare providers, NGO staffers—and their relationship to the economy is notional. They produce nothing of value, and they consume the work

---

[137] *The Medium is the Massage*.

of Oriental slaves seemingly forged from one homogenous piece of plastic, each plank interchangeable with any other. The lockdowns seemed a pressure test, an exercise in showing how many men's work was inessential: that the average citizen was the spender of money, not the producer of goods, and that the consumerist economy could survive with walking utility functions with $1,200 in their pockets.

It was no surprise that the dross who most loved the concerted torchings were the same who loved facemasks, partly out of political camaraderie, even more because they both move the zeitgeist away from the material world of real interpersonal encounters that form what we think of as History. And the more sophisticated one is, the more likely he despises that History, not only in its concrete form but in the logical and spiritual roots from which is developed. The facemask is assent to the future, a denial of selfhood as the price of destroying the past.

Hence that disturbing fact that young people are more willing to don the masks than the old. Perhaps this speaks to a sad lack of healthy rebellion in this generation, for where every generation finds itself as the recipients and victims of revolutionary upheaval a rebellion of the youth, however chimerical, represents a movement towards the real. The young have more to lose, it seemed, from the lockdowns: Fresh kisses, active friendships, the great temerity of adolescence, standing before such a feeble world and believing it can be tamed. Yet these young men and women were most likely to wear the masks—and why should this be otherwise? They have already lived the bulk of their lives through the internet, their thoughts quickly or instantly made open to the forces of universal derision or empty praise. Their habits are dulled by constant stimuli, and their most intense experiences are very often not attached to a place nor the attendant sense of touch and taste and smell and dimensional sight, but are only a particular moment of time on their phones. Their selfhood is only in part encompassed in their faces or in their persons, for their strongest sociality is already found behind a veil of pixels and the ever-clinging air of falsehood. Their lives when they are most fruitful and honest are lived behind digital avatars. To the young, sociality already means ceding the self. The facemask only solidifies this fact.

Once the lockdowns began it did not matter had all Emergency Orders disappeared, or if Truth and Justice Commissions had been empaneled to try the thieves and conmen who immiserated so many and whose culpable negligence murdered so many more. None of this would matter. If all the evils of Coronavirus response disappeared overnight they still could be restarted next month to a similar flailing panic and another acquiescence. The physical world can be upended for one quotidian disease and it can upended for another. We may see more in-person interactions in future years, but nothing will change the fact that we have passed the point of inflection, where in-person interactions are seen as an exception and not the rule to basic social existence.

What we lose is literally indescribable. No one can write poetry about digital meeting places. Art is the interplay of human spirit and Nature. But where Nature is eradicated, and digital forms take from her only the barest remnants of logic and simulacra of place, no art can endure. The man of genius is given only transient and bare media to impose himself upon. But this must pale in comparison to the loss of the quotidian. What did it mean for a guilty defendant to see one's sentencing judge face-to-face? What did it mean for your local congressman to shake your hand? What did the smell of incense mean in your churches, or the presence of a beautiful woman sitting on a parkbench? We cannot assign values to these sensations any more than we can create one out of zero.

The world is governed by ideas, but made rich by things; it is ruled by the stark nature of our necessities but made joyous by the individual forms these take. In a happy society, idea and thing support one another, creating a bulwark of our virtues and aspirations. Amidst remnants of our Christian and republican order, we find the old temples and halls vacant and vacuous, hollowed out of the ideals that impelled their creation, standing as a mocking show of how a good society might appear. The new world is one of plastic and intellectualism, infinite fungibility and omnipotent ideology. The very existence of stone and mortar is a kind of affront to it, an obstinate counter to the absolute freedom man posits for himself, he who through his electronics can dictate the structures of his life, whose intellectual life is bound by no books or libraries but in the infinite reaches of the internet, whose social life is bound by no parish or neighborhood but the entirety of squawking cartoon facades across the planet. What we lose is a connection between the tactile and the spiritual, of quiddity and matter. What we lose is a kind of hypostasis taken for granted by all previous generations, an incarnation all men before us appreciated, however rarely they may have put it into words: The belief that reality itself is a kind of sacrament.

Revolution over the Biological Human

The full romp of the Fifth Revolution is found in the reordering of the biological world, of the subservience of actual individual health to the new totem of the public good, a General Socialized Health. This exists, recall, not as the collective health of a society's constituent members but as a thoroughly notional concept whose bellwether *health* is attached to some other metric—in 2020 the complete eradication of the Coronavirus, regardless of what actual effects it had on the health of individuals in the population. With this new standard established, there is no longer any logical reason why protection of the whole should not be accomplished by the harm or liquidation of a part. To repeat: General Socialized Health is a *notional concept*. It possesses no necessary unity to the physical and mental health of the public, but exists to serve some ulterior ends. It is an ideological concept as we have defined it, one that abstracts away from its actual subject and places its end in something apart from this.

This is not to ignore the moral quandaries which give the Fifth Revolution its practical force. Should not the weakest among us, the elderly and *immuno-compromised* be safe from the depredations of disease? The reaction to Coronavirus is inexplicable unless this question is answered in the affirmative. Where man has the moral right to food and water, the government has an accordant duty in justice to pursue this end, and those governments that cannot meet these ends lose their legitimacy. With the Coronavirus and its lockdowns, liberal man now recognizes a moral right to be free from disease, and as such government and society have a duty to ensure this right is respected. Accordingly the government has a positive obligation to pursue projects which combat disease, however much the old rights and entitlements may suffer.

All revolutions since 1789 have called for the torture and eradication of a sizable minority of people in the name of notional good. The Revolution of 2020 is no different, though its specific form sees the denigration of actual biological health. The roots of this can be found in the course of universal vaccination undertaken through the Twentieth Century. Universal vaccination always posited that the immunity status of the population mattered more than the wounded few (or many), that the progress of the biological species warranted the etiolation or severing of some of the leviathan's limbs. With this, the field of medicine becomes torn between the Hippocratic Oath and the notion of Social Justice, between real doctors and scientists for whom individual health is only the residue of epidemiological success.

Whether they are conscious of it or not, for most medical practitioners the health of individual body and mind is not a paramount concern. The injuries and disorders that naturally arise from the practice of sodomy should rouse the condemnation of any doctor similarly attuned to the banes of alcohol or nicotine; yet all proper care is dissolved under the greater concern for *gay rights*. The rise of *gender dysphoria* and the genital mutilation it fosters could not be held by any sane practitioner were it not for the ideological structures of sexual relations. The notional concepts of sexual identity have been made to trump the unequivocal demands and clear and inarguable reality of individual biology. Witness the concept of *neurodiversity*, which is nothing but a nomenclature for the sanity of mental illness. The ability to cultivate mental illness is a great boon to the men who peddle pharmaceuticals and the government bureaucrat always lusting for a more servile mass to control. It is only the all-powerful nature of the technocratic state that props up the atomized chaos.

The story we have seen with each four preceding revolutions is here repeated: The individual is squelched for the sake of the masses, and a socialized and notional figment is given precedence is given precedence over the real. The population-wide hope that the disease could be suppressed or eradicated, tenuous as it seemed in theory and impossible in fact, was nonetheless accepted as a justification for individual debasement. The experimental gene therapy given to a billion people would be inconceivable were the masses not already primed to bend his individual welfare to the notional good of the whole.

Mass extermination is not yet practiced, though its legitimacy grows more feasible with each victory of the notional over the real. The storm of biological loathing may simmer down merely by inertia, but nothing can quash the fire that has been lit. Where man's relation to material reality loses its practical importance, it is not long before material reality must vanish as a consideration of government. And at that point there is no human calamity that cannot be sanctioned. The extermination camps and bloodshed to come will not be excrescences of the revolutionary project, the sad side-effects of midwifing a revolutionary child to maturity, but extermination for its own sake, wholly in line with the ethos of the new regime, a cause intrinsic to the revolutionary ends. The modern revolutionist will not rue with the Committee of Public Safety the razing of Lyons, or the Leninist statesmen the gulag archipelago stretching across the workers' republic; he will smile upon the defective biological cells' amputation the way a transexual will relish the lopping off of his virility, proudly averring it to be a good in itself, a positive principle of policy.

Despair must overtake the man who sees the world and cannot see beyond it, who has read these pages and treasures nothing but the material. There is no escape from our present course of annihilation, not without a complete reformation of those who walk it. For we, the human race, are not our own.

We repeat and clarify what we said in the beginning: Liberalism is the process of enshrining a system of socialized morality. This always involves the diminution of the moral significance of the individual. So we see with the Protestant Revolution that the faculties of free will are vitiated, and the power of the individual soul is diminished among the vast mass of the elect; so with the French Revolution the individual's role within the state is diminished for the abstraction notion of the citizen; and with the Third Revolution, the means a man's material wellbeing, namely his utilization of property, is diminished following the transformations of property throughout the industrial revolution. So we see with the Fifth Revolution, with man's individual health becoming something to be sacrificed to the socialized and notional versions of societal health.

Liberalism is the process of enshrining socialized morality. We use the term *morality* intentionally, for even when concrete changes are made in the social order, such as when the rights of property or status are diminished, the set of man's material constraints are altered, and so must his moral faculties by modified to the new state of things. The change of man's moral perceptions is the most important aspect of the Revolution. For with every liberal transformation effected, man's role as an moral individual is diminished within the social order, his individual resolve is thereby weakened, eventually losing his ability to regulate himself as a singular moral individual. In effect, larger society becomes the only individual that matters, and man becomes the skincell forced to find himself within this system.

Of course, there have always been tyrannies, and always been systems that treat man as an instrumentality to power. The distinguishing modern dilemma is the moral conception man develops of himself. A tyrant may treat a subject like a datum in a universal spreadsheet, but this does not necessitate any very drastic effect so long as man does not adopt the same disposition for himself: Regardless of the makeup of the state, his moral situation is the same. It is the moral change given effect through the social order that creates the true change in liberalism. For where man cognizes his moral position only in dependence to the social order, he can possess no definitive conception of individual morality. And he who does not recognize any individual morality soon finds he has no individual moral rights to claim, no individuality apart from the state.

As we have said before, true rights inhere to the objective reality of things while liberal rights pertain to the makeup of the superstructure. The ultimate and definitive change brought on by the Revolution is the moral change, the self-abjuration committed by man, the relinquishment of his individual claims of right and the coming of liberal rights, which only have meaning in a social context. For man is at his highest a moral being: He who is able to cognize and choose the course of life. It is this attribute which makes man distinct from herd animals, his nature and soul that can damn or save him. Such conceptions were first attacked with the Protestant Revolution, the first great socialization of man, and one conducted against his highest attribute, which is the tutelage of his own soul. This was the first great disorientation of self, and in time the Protestant ruling powers and the subject man no longer saw himself as a unique individual cognizable apart from the social order. So it was further with the Second Revolution, when man's position and his accordant rights within the state were erased with the Declaration of Rights of Man. So it continued with the Third Revolution, when the rights of property, which are the basis for civil government, were etiolated, and his position in the social order made dependent on the will of the industrialist.

Such are the revolutionary transformations that have long preceded us. The cruelest excesses of the Fourth and Fifth Revolutions are still the matter of harrumphing by modern conservatives, seemingly the plots of a new breed of pervert, a new specter of evil that has taken the globe. Yet all the transformations described arise out of the same motive force, which is the socialization of moral notions and the diminution of man as a moral being. Man's moral rights arise out of his material circumstances. And while the progenitors of the Revolution did not have the material means to greatly alter man's physical circumstances—it was not until the rise of industrialism and almighty government that the Revolutionist gained supremacy over material production—the mechanisms of material suasion could never had arisen or been maintained had not the moral transformations of the first and second revolutions already occurred, if the general view of man had not been so diminished. It follows that to counteract the effects of the Revolution, even in its latest forms, one must engage oneself with the project of realizing and remaking man's moral character as it existed before the process of perversion began.

We must repeat that the wicked course of the Revolution is above all else a Christian heresy. It is not the construct of a man or a conspiracy of men, however many have served as individual conduits for the Revolution through these five centuries. It is a heresy, a perversion of God in His form, of Logos and the animation of our world through His Spirit. No human force could puff itself up so greatly as to conceive and bear the Revolution, just as no lie can exist without the Truth, or any rank anarchist can fathom his disorder without reference to an ordered creation that guides his marring hand. For no defiler can conceive of his own evil without first witness of the benefice of creation before him. All evil is a perversion, and the Revolution is nothing but a perversion of the Everlasting and Immanent. From this fact arises its full malicious power It is why no policy prescription can solve the problem, and no one man exists who might rise to suppress its evils. Any attempt at political solution can only operate on the human mass that exists, while any true Renaissance, any lasting recrudescence, must strive to repopulate the world with men apart from this faceless mass.

There is no *past* to return to. The prospect of falling back to an *unideological* mindset, even of returning to Nature or Natural Law, are necessarily in vain. Even the remotest of our globe's own lands has been terraformed by the Revolution, captive to noxious waves in the air and scavenger lights in the sky. The foundations of the old world are dust; a return to them is impossible. The past exists as an Atlantan example of virtue that might be striven for, but it is no continent that can be returned to. Those who strive to live on the old tenets of Nature are basing their lives on a mere idea; their desires are as artificial as any base cosmopolitan's. They cannot live in reaction to the actual state of nature that confronts them—were they to do this they would be liberals. And so the reactionary is forced to play the ideologue just as much as the liberal, to accept that if he is to live as he thinks is right he must resolve to make a world just as artificial as the liberal of past ages had conjured. What the reactionary wants is a return to a former state of being, one that was once very real, one that was experienced by the vast majority of men who have ever lived. But his idea of this past must be merely notional, because unlike those men who could live the reactionary ideal with ease and without thought, the modern reactionary is set with the task of pursuing and outwardly effecting his concept of the good if he wishes to see it realized. He must be a Jacobin for the Old

Regime, a Luther for the Universal Church. He must, after it all, be absolutely modern.

Behold the man: The modern child is not a creature of his parents. He is a nexus of impulses and desires, a potency, like an electron neither mass nor wave until realized by the powers that reify him: those retaining authority within the system and their propaganda channels. The modern young person is a monster. His tongue is a passive antenna, the vacuous receiver of sound and vision, resetting his mind and environs to the month's propaganda stream. His views are carnal, his would-be virtues are technical. He is biased by no ill will towards evil and no serious conception of the good. He has been debauched and his pathetic existence cannot be understood with reference to character or morals, only to influence, like an exposed petri dish percolating with the scum of experiment. Who can look at this creature and see a distinct human soul? Who can come upon him and descry something known and beloved by God?—he who is so obviously but a means of wretched evil? We cannot love this man but through the eyes of Faith, to see the hidden value in those who are intrinsically our adversaries, who in their small-mindedness and bigotry are our tormentors.

How to combat this beast of banality? There is no *return* to Nature, because man is not *natural* and never has been, nor ever could be. He is a creature who by definition transforms Nature, who contorts Nature in order to extend his own faculties. Man is not man without art, if he is not contorting Nature to his will. No conception of man can endure that does not encompass his transformation of and transformation by Nature, for no man exists who does not avail himself of technology, in either advanced or rudimentary form. Our question is not what false Eden we might wish to return to, but what technical state we prefer to find man in. A call to go *back to the land*, commendable though it may be, is nothing versus the question of what tools he will take with him.

To answer this is no easy task. The man who gains technical mastery over nature is more excellent than he who does not, at least with respect to the faculty his technology advances. The man who can drive is greater than a pedestrian in his capacity for movement, and the man with the rototiller is more excellent than the man with the plow with respect to his task. Backwardness in technology is always the rejection of some perfection, a power of man abjured. Even in conception, the question of what kind of technical form we may wish to adopt will control what kind of individual man we desire to see before us: Whether he be gifted a particular ability or left to his own devices, whether his perfections be heightened by human art or dependent only on the gifts of God. A smorgasbord of technology before us, which do we adopt and which do we spurn? No ready answer can be found to this.

We can only offer an orientation towards which this question should be approached. And this orientation must be towards man's most distinctive attribute: his moral individuality. That which cultivates his individuality is good, that which suppresses it is bad. We do not mean this as some kind of naïve Zarathustrianism, a misanthropic rising of the ubermenschen over the herd-animals who are the human race; nor do we mean the atomism of economists or the person-less finding of self proposed by utilitarian freaks. All men are created as rational souls, with personhood and individuality unfathomable. Yet they accept this great gift of selfhood only reluctantly against the temptation of the herd and of the flesh. It is the cultivation of the individual that must be sought above all, for it is and always has been the end of the Revolution to attack man's individuality.

How can this be achieved is too complex a question to even be approached here. Suffice it to say it must be done through cultivation of individual virtue, virtue as it exists between man and God and without the mediation of bastard sociality such as the Revolution imposes. Church and state exist for the cultivation of the virtues of those who compose them, and cannot have legitimacy otherwise.

Man must learn to love himself as the context he exists, as a rational and infinite soul, for the recognition of one's soul is the ultimate individualism. Those means that accommodate this are good, and those which do not are evil. Modern man must rekindle a just and human pride in his own being and will. The creature we see before us, so slothful and decrepit of spirit, is proud only in his flesh. He betrays himself day by day in his venal wagering, that the orgiastic pleasures of experience, if brought to such a peak, can tranquilize and subjugate the pangs of conscience and the protest of free will, withering under its degradation, and finally sliding easily into mediocre damnation.

The uncritical acceptance of technology is the Revolution in its purest form. Technology can be used to foster man's individuality and his greatness, but this requires concerted limitations on its use. For to accept the unregulated force of technology is to deny the primacy and existence of selfhood altogether. He who controls the technical ordering of society is the true sovereign, and the increasingly pernicious nature of digital technology means he is more and more the ruler over men's sovereign souls as well. The broken husk of the creature strewn across the globe at our present date is not competent to create a vision of himself, to rise to any state above subjugation. Yet whatever reformation may come about must rise on the antecedent right of man being given dictatorship over his arts and not his arts total ᴏᴡɴᴇᴅꞮⁱⁱ ⁱⁱⁱ Ɪ ʰⁱⁱⁱ

There is no hope of future progress without the recultivation of the individual. There is no Caesar who might rise to redeem our wretched system, for the masses as they exist cannot foster great men, and any man worthy of the title could have no great ambition to rule over such creatures. There is no fodder for greatness amongst these herd animals, these beasts of caprice who have no ability to rule themselves, these natural slaves who adore their slavery. Man himself must interiorly change before any exterior improvements can be had. Whether political change in any meaningful sense can arise from this only of tertiary importance.

What kind of progress is possible against the all-pervading golem that in five centuries has found no answer? To combat it is, in very real terms, humanly impossible. It requires a return to God, not as an amorphous force of benevolence or even the creator and protector of the moral order, as the mere social conservative and the modern civil religionist can abide, but as God as He is, God Incarnate, the Word made flesh. For the evil of the present age stands against not only against the nature of Christ as God, but of Christ as man. The Incarnation, the uniting of God and man, was the positive means of our salvation. But the raising up to this exalted state also meant that no slight could be done against the nature of God without a wounding of the race as a whole.

No ideological program can change this. There is no Caesar, no Hitler, no Overman who might rise to enforce a new individuality. Not even Christian teaching can provide a catalyst. However many fools exist who confuse Christianity with an ideology, worship cannot be confused with reeducation any more than enforcing the moral law through a police state can instill virtue or true prayer could be funneled onto screens and recited by automata. Christian teaching is insufficient; only Christ is sufficient. The acceptance of Him must embrace both His divinity and his humanity, the unity of which completes all Godhead and Manhood. More than this, we must respond to His preeminence appropriately. To simply *know* the attributes of God is a task for frivolers and academics, and the class of milquetoast intellectuals who have contorted the masses since the Second Revolution. No, the only right response to God is to adore Him. It is this fundamental response to value which must guide all else. Just as anything in existence must be loved to be fully participated in, just as any greatness, even material greatness, can arise only through love: that any family can be fostered, that any city can be founded, that any civilization can be reformed.

To properly adore God is to truly love oneself. It is the only way to fully acknowledge one's individuality, to take in one's own hands his moral behavior and to recognize the destiny of his own soul. It is to recognize that he controls his own fate, that he can grow in strength or defile himself unto eternal perdition. No kind of individualism is possible without this stark confrontation with reality: the nexus between man's eternal state and his own free will, his ability to struggle in the warfare or life for his own salvation.

Our society cannot be remade until men are once again recognized as small bastions of the eternal, as warriors in life and soldiers in the slaying of death. This is the proper role for man, the only one that recognizes him for what he truly is rather than the course the mediocre fates of the age conjure for him. No good government is possible if it does not acknowledge that his spirit is no free-floating, immaterial thing, but bound in most intimate marriage to material reality through his own flesh. Man is not a notion, and his soul is not a figment waiting for reification. Man is a spirit incarnate, dust ennobled by life in God. He is a creature good though not sufficient unto himself, with a selfhood malleable to the happenstance of the age he finds himself in but ultimately made by and only comprehensible to God. As man is indescribably a thing of his own volition and the social order he finds himself born into, so his very being is mediated between the absolute freedom of his thoughts and the body that constrains him.

Any reader dissatisfied by the lack of social or political solution does not understand the problem. Anyone dissatisfied to find that orthodoxy is the cure has not properly grasped that heresy is the cause. These are simply the terms of the war; to battle on any other terms is to lose in part or in full. Any man not prepared to martyr himself to the Revolution is not fit to fight it. Whether man's soul is given to God in martial sacrifice or as tribute in peace, his soul must be offered before the Revolution, the antichrist of antichrists, can be starved. This can only be effected on a large scale by approaching where He is most apparent, tangible to finite sense yet still adorable in infinite contemplation: In the Eucharist, where Truth and eternity cannot be deformed, where Being begins and ends, whose reception cannot be simpler but whose heights cannot be surpassed. It is only here that selfhood can be protected, in the Incarnate Christ where humanity finds the end of the Creature and the wholeness of the Creator, against which the demon of the Revolution will fall and the Immaculate Heart will triumph.